THE
MANAGER'S
ADVISOR

Fairleigh Dickinson University Library
Teaneck, New Jersey

THE MANAGER'S ADVISOR

Revised Edition

DAVID M. BROWNSTONE

IRENE M. FRANCK

with
Rosemary Guiley

amacom

AMERICAN MANAGEMENT ASSOCIATION

Library of Congress Cataloging-in-Publication Data

Brownstone, David M.
   The manager's advisor.

   Includes index.
   1. Executives—Handbooks, manuals, etc. 2. Management
—Handbooks, manuals, etc. I. Franck, Irene M.
II. Guiley, Rosemary. III. Title.
HD38.2.B75   1987   658.4   87-47712
ISBN 0-8144-7682-1

Printing number

10 9 8 7 6 5 4 3 2 1

PREFACE

Managers today need a book that will help them successfully pursue their careers in what for many are personally difficult times. For without paying greatly increased attention to astute career development, lifelong professional self-development, and careful medium- and long-term personal planning, many more managers will find themselves trapped in exceedingly adverse circumstances as this period unfolds.

Our intent in writing this book has been to focus on such personal and practical career matters as building a career, moving up, changing jobs effectively, and constructing a program of lifelong professional self-development. We have also focused on such very practical skills as time management, effective communication, people handling, political maneuvering, and handling the storm of paper, meetings, and telephone calls that threatens to overcome all working managers.

Please note that this book is an abridgment, with modest updating, of our previous work, also called *The Manager's Advisor.*

Our thanks to Rosemary Guiley, whose thinking contributed substantially to the development of Chapters 6, 7, and 8; to Bruce Trachtenberg, whose thinking contributed substantially to the development of Chapter 5; and to Robert A. Kaplan, our publisher at AMACOM Books.

David M. Brownstone
Irene M. Franck
Chappaqua, New York

CONTENTS

CHAPTER 1

CONTEXTS

Managers today are increasingly concerned with personal and practical matters. As the world in which we pursue our lives and careers grows ever more complex, and as the pace of change accelerates, we find ourselves focusing more and more on practical skills, career matters, and lifelong professional development.

Modern managers pay great attention to such career development matters as getting properly started, moving up, managing time and work, changing jobs, networking, negotiating salaries, and pursuing professional growth. They also quite properly spend a great deal of time developing personal skills—among them effective reading, writing, and speaking; working with computer-generated and other number-oriented materials; and handling interpersonal relations.

This book will take up these kinds of matters—and a good deal more. It is intended to function as a guide to lifelong professional development in a world that has indeed changed a great deal in the last few decades and will change even more rapidly in the years ahead.

Managers are pragmatists. There are, first of all, organizations to run, on a day-to-day basis, and most of a career is spent in doing just that, no matter how involved one becomes in longer-range activities.

That is a great strength. People who by temperament and training are capable of routinely solving difficult problems on a case-by-case basis, and who sharpen their skills in the process of doing so, become flexible, pragmatic professionals over the years. They are able to successfully take on a wide range of tasks in what may be a succession of substantially different organizations during the course of their careers.

Personally, however, that very strength can be a source of great weakness—and never more so than in a period of great and fundamental change, when some of the major lifetime career and financial assumptions of tens of millions of Americans are proving to be little more than illusions.

The truth is that no matter how good you are at your work, failure to do astute, all-around, lifetime career planning, which takes into account the vastly changed environment of our times, can enormously damage your future and do a great disservice to yourself and your loved ones. And failure to continuously develop and redevelop your management skills and understandings can do equal damage, leaving you far, far behind in a business and professional world characterized by an accelerating rate of change.

To put it bluntly and sharply, the world in which the vast majority of American managers envisioned themselves spending their working lives uninterruptedly growing profitable companies—and in which those managers saw themselves being rewarded by high pay during their working years and substantial pensions after their well-deserved retirement at the age of 65—that world *never existed*. It was an illusion, a set of misestimates. The American economy was not an inexhaustible cornucopia of golden consuming dollars. Developing countries do not always develop just because we lend them dollars out of our public funds and private banking system, and they are not necessarily the customers we had hoped they would be in the next generation. Fuel and raw materials, in other hands than ours, may cost ten times what they cost when we controlled them.

Our current major economic reality is a business cycle that seems to have stalled down toward the lower end of the cycle. Essentially, it no longer cycles; it is that combination of stagnation and inflation that Gunnar Myrdal called stagflation, in which our economy veers up and down in a fairly narrow range, mainly as affected by government intervention but always around a stagnant center. It matters little which group of politicians holds the reins; none has solved the basic problem of stagnation, which is a worldwide problem and one which is hardly likely to be solved without sustained and massive international cooperation between industrial and developing nations, complete with major new institutions operating for a considerable period of time.

In short, we had best not hold our breaths waiting for the economy to right itself, or for this or that political group in power to "solve the problem." The United States is no longer as rich as it seemed to be, nor for that matter as rich as it really was in the decades following World War II. There are hard new economic, political, and social realities to be faced by all of us as we move into the latter part of the twentieth century, realities that force us to reexamine and revise many of the assumptions we have carried throughout our lives.

One such assumption, and it is a major assumption indeed, is that our working careers will be followed by retirement, meaning a cessation of gainful economic activity. Alas, for most of us it won't happen that way. We won't be able to afford it.

That is a matter of continued inflation, which erodes all savings and investments, and of the facts of life—long life, that is. For many of us will live a very long time indeed by any previous standard. And the implications of long life for career planning are tremendous.

The pace of change has nowhere been more apparent than in the life sciences and medicine. In recent decades, new discoveries, techniques, and tools have combined to dramatically lengthen life spans, and between now and the end of the century, that pace of change can only accelerate. This seems a great boon to mankind—but perhaps for many it will be a great curse, as they live out long lives as impoverished de facto wards of a state that cannot support them at any more than a bare subsistence level, if that. Many will find that the pension plan that looked so ample in 1980 will be miniscule only 20 years later, in the year 2000, because it paid fixed dollar amounts rather than being in any significant way indexed to the inflation rate; and that savings and investments have eroded as prices have risen, while government pension payments have not kept up with the pace of inflation. It will not necessarily go that way; technological developments in such areas as solar and other alternative energy sources, robotics, and bioengineering may open up major new possibilities for economic growth even before the end of this century. But it would be imprudent to urge anything less than extreme caution as to the economic side of life in this period.

ASSUMPTIONS

That leads us to our first stated assumption, which, like our other assumptions, underlies much of the thinking in this book, and therefore should be stated clearly and explicitly.

It is that we will live long and that most of us will find it necessary to engage in some kind of gainful economic activity far beyond our retirement from careers in management, often using the skills and relationships developed during our management careers to produce income in our later years.

Our second assumption, stemming largely from the changed American and world economic contexts of our time, is that if there ever was a time when you could look to your company to take care of you if you held up your part of the bargain, that time is gone. No company, or government, or nonprofit organization, or other institution—no one can be expected to take care of you and those you love but yourself.

To put it a little differently, individual interests are, in the long run, separable from organizational interests, even though to do our jobs well we must identify with the interests of our organizations. In fact, our interests are at all times ours alone, and should neither be merged with nor subsumed to the interests of our organizations.

That has always been so, but it is more obvious and considerably more important to recognize clearly that fact in a time of trouble and accelerating change. As never before, it can happen that you do your job exceedingly well for years only to find out overnight that your company has been acquired, and that you are redundant and out of work, or that the parts you have so successfully made and sold for decades have suddenly become obsolete, or that foreign competition has undercut your company's market position, or . . . you can fill in the blank.

Our third main assumption has to do with planning itself, and it is true for all seasons. It is simply that those who plan their careers carefully and well, year in and year out, all their lives, have a tremendous advantage over those who do not. As it is with companies and nations, so it is with individuals. The company that plans inadequately is far more vulnerable than the well-run company. An individual who lives and works essentially from day to day creates problems that need not be, misses opportunities that should be easy to grasp, and is a setup for disasters that might have been avoided.

What is mildly astonishing is that so many managers who in their working lives are actively and continuously engaged in short-, medium-, and long-term planning do little or no planning for themselves. The dissatisfied manager who has "stayed too long" on a job or with a company or who is "trapped" in work by age and circumstance is all too often someone who could have and should have moved on long before if careful career planning had been part of normal operating procedure.

Our fourth main assumption has been self-evident for decades, but becomes even more crucially important during a period of great and accelerating change. It is that lifelong professional self-development is far more than desirable; it is absolutely indispensable for modern managers, as it is for most other professionals in our time. It is necessary to be able to use the radically new methods of information storage and retrieval that are now available to us; to be able to work with computer professionals; and to keep up with legal and regulatory matters, scientific and technical changes, a large body of specific changes in each company and industry, and larger economic, political, and social trends supplying the context within which other matters occur. And it is always vital to sharpen basic personal management skills and acquire new ones.

In an earlier period we might not have felt it necessary to state our fifth assumption, which is that our economy and political system will remain basically unchanged in the foreseeable future. Were we to accept the inevitability of civilization-destroying atomic war or total economic and political collapse, we would have no reason at all to write this book, and would then be urging "survivalist" solutions—and adopting them ourselves. But that is not what we believe. We think it probable that we will all stagger along together into the next century, doing the best we can to achieve social solutions for social problems, while at the same time trying very hard to take care of ourselves and those for whom we assume direct personal responsibility.

PROFESSIONAL SELF-DEFINITION

Beyond these assumptions are some key ideas that underlie and inform much of the material in this book. Perhaps most important of all is our firm idea that a manager's self-definition as a professional may be crucial to success in the coming decades.

Sometimes, and especially to others, we seem little more than a bundle of skills—oh, a growing bundle of skills as the years go by, but still definable by those skills better than in any other way. After all, if you are in the computer business or the publishing business for 20 years, it seems obvious that your skills at managing and doing business in those industries define your career—and therefore your possibilities. Similarly, you may be seen—and see yourself—as defined by function. A personnel manager works in personnel, a financial manager in finance. That too seems obvious, and it is so for many working managers who stay in one business or function for many years, either starting out there or settling there after an early moving-around period.

This leads us to a very basic matter—that to be a working manager is not necessarily to be a professional manager by trade. To put it a little differently, all working managers manage, but not all are professionals who can move freely and effectively from industry to industry and function to function, unconfined by narrow and limited self-definitions.

The truth is that we are considerably more than—and more valuable than—a bundle of skills. We are a bundle of the right questions; and we are capable of consistently finding both the right questions and several sets of the right answers to those questions, year in and year out, throughout our careers and for the rest of our lives. To see ourselves as less than that is incorrect—and profoundly self-limiting and self-damaging.

In management, more than in most other careers, self-definition plays an enormously important role, for a person is a generalist more because of attitude, and the actions that accompany that attitude, than because of anything else, including formal training and job necessity. And professional managers are, above all, business and institutional generalists, rather than people in a particular business or people who perform a particular function. In operational terms, management is management, and skills and knowledge differ from industry to industry and country to country, but the basic tools of inquiry, the problem-solving techniques, and the people-handling and process-handling skills are general rather than particular in nature.

In personal terms, the question of self-definition is crucial; it is one of those matters that informs a whole career. As professional managers, we pursue a far wider range of insights than we do as people self-defined by business or function. Those who see themselves—and operate—narrowly are prey to all the adverse occurrences possible in a period of enormous technological change and economic shift among industries and nations. Seemingly secure jobs and careers are capable of disappearing without a trace at any time. On the other hand, those who define themselves widely as professional managers, and who behave accordingly, are capable of moving with the times, as professionals engaged in the practice of the widest, most mobile, most secure, and most lucrative of all the business careers. Likewise, those who self-define narrowly can have great difficulty shifting to satisfying later-life careers, while those who self-define as professional managers can shift later quite naturally and easily.

We must also make every attempt to see ourselves as individuals, as bundles of hopes, desires, and attitudes carried with us since childhood. No, we will not indulge in currently fashionable psychobabble, but it is foolish to react adversely to psychobabble and thereby pay too little attention to our own motives. It is true that we go into our careers for a variety of reasons, from the inertia of someone succumbing to participation in the family business because there seems to be nothing better to do, all the way to the great drive of a highly motivated superachiever determined from the first to become president of a major corporation. But it is also true that we continue to pursue our careers because they satisfy us—at least in part; and that in the long run those who are not satisfied either find other lines of work or fail miserably at their current endeavors.

Most of us take into our management careers a rather easily described set of standard motives and expectations. We expect something rather like a conventional three-act play, with a first act consisting of training and the years of starting, moving about, and beginning to move up; a second act consisting of the long, mature working middle management years; and then, in act three, the peak years of corporate level general management and possibly even a company presidency. Then an epilogue: the good years of retirement, with substantial corporate pension in hand and perhaps some teaching, writing, and consulting. Meanwhile a procession of rewards—money, prestige, spouse, children, homes, dogs, cats, horses, cars, boats, travel, hobbies, and all the rest. A long, hearty, happy spring and enduring summer of a life, finding, tasting, and partaking, early and often, of a sumptuous repast consisting of goodly portions of the several parts of the American dream.

It often has been so, and never more than in the middle years of the century, from the end of World War II to the end of the Vietnam War. And just as often it has not been so, punctuated as our lives have been by depression, war, recession, technological unemployment, and now the stagnation of the last portion of the century.

Yet with all the pressures and disappointments that seem so endemic to the practice of management in this period, those early expectations and rewards—which shaped the main body of managers now practicing—continue to provide the emotional context within which we work. It is still true that most American managers tend to be rather sane and pragmatic in approaching daily working lives and personal relationships. And it is also true—and centrally important—that most American managers, like most Americans, continue to hold fast to the idea of personal freedom.

STRUCTURE AND FREEDOM

Related to that is another basic matter, which informs much of what follows—the contradiction between the pyramidal, hierarchical nature of most organizations and the idea of personal freedom. Americans, managers included, have more difficulty subordinating themselves to organizational needs and structures than do many other peoples; nor should they find subordination easy, for much of the American manager's strength lies in entrepreneurial attitudes and independent professionalism. That is why such management style aberrations as "management by crisis," which robs us of professionalism and dignity, and therefore also of freedom, do not work at all. It is why "participative management" is so widespread. It explains why the much-deplored but also endemic American business tendency to develop ad hoc, task force, and permanent committees that meet ad nauseam is more than merely a bureaucratic tendency. It is also why bigness and centralization of function, however sensible they seem in economic and organizational terms, seldom work as well as approaches that seek to liberate the creative energies of entrepreneurially oriented, independent-minded American managers.

The conventional and most widely used structural form in American business organizations is that of the pyramid, with a chief operating officer, who reports only to the board of directors, at the apex of the pyramid, and an unbroken line of superior-subordinate reporting relationships down through management to the lowest ranked first-line supervisor, to whom nonsupervisory workers report. Managers whose jobs fall directly into that chain of reporting relationships are *line*, and those who are not in this sense directly in line, usually performing advisory and supportive functions, are *staff*. At the corporate or organization-wide management level, managers often work to a large extent in group as well as line, and the chief operating officer at the top of the pyramid may come from either a line or a staff background. All of this is substantially modified in practice by the development of informal power structures within all organizations—an inescapable fact—as well as by conscious modifications aimed both at using the creative talents available throughout the organization and at keeping independent-minded managers interested and happy.

But with all the modifications, formal and informal, that basic structure is in continuous and deep conflict with the idea of personal freedom. And from an individual point of view—the point of view taken in this book—the resolution of this conflict in favor of the idea of freedom is critically important. The idea of freedom is so central to Americans, so pervades every part of our daily lives, and so underlies our understandings and goals, that failure to keep our sense of personal freedom in our working lives makes achievement of any kind of lasting career satisfaction impossible. This is particularly true of managers, the best of whom, far from being the gray organization people they are so often thought to be—are pragmatic, self-starting, and self-disciplined entrepreneurs by desire and inclination.

The only truly lasting way to resolve that contradiction in favor of freedom, and therefore in favor of personal satisfaction, is to build a career as a wholly independent management professional, tied in the last analysis to nothing but your own sense of integrity and your own very large bundle of transferable insights and skills. Empty words if you have no financial independence at all, and need to have next week's paycheck lest the economic walls come tumbling in. Empty words if you have not taken the time and trouble to develop that very large bundle of transferable insights and skills. But for those who have those essentials in place, merely a common-sense restatement of what freedom and independence—and therefore self-respect—are about.

But why not turn oneself into the kind of ruthless manipulator so favored by novelists and screenwriters? Well, some do, for a while, or even for a lifetime—usually a rather shorter lifetime than might otherwise have been expected. For most of us, it simply goes against the grain. It makes the cost too high, whatever the material, power, and prestige rewards. Perhaps the most fruitful lesson a young, enormously eager-to-succeed graduate of a "top" business school can learn in the early days of a career is that the "game" you think you see is not necessarily the game that is being played, or the game you really want to play in the long run.

There are games, of course, and some of them are facts of management life: political games, power games, selling games, sexual games, and a whole range of acknowledged

business and modeling games which are part of the para-
phernalia of decision making in the medium-to-large modern
American corporation. In personal and career terms, it is the
informal, unacknowledged games that directly concern us.
Oddly enough, although the term *games* can carry some
rather unwholesome connotations, it is the games element
that supplies much of the day-to-day satisfaction in many
careers, certainly including management. In a sense, the
entrepreneurially minded manager plays a very special kind
of game, much as does the champion runner who runs
competitively against the pack and at the same time against
the clock, attempting to beat a record.

Rigorously speaking, an entrepreneur takes the role of
initiator, main driving force, and general manager of an
enterprise, at least in its formative stages, taking a major
share of the risks and rewards involved. In that sense,
working managers are not entrepreneurs. But the term is
used far more broadly, to describe a much-prized managerial attitude, the kind of attitude that makes a manager a
prime organizational asset. Entrepreneurially minded managers identify themselves with organizational goals, especially when they play a significant role in developing those
goals, and behave as if they were indeed sharing both risks
and rewards. Many companies greatly reward that kind of
attitude and the results flowing from it, and provide a wide
range of incentives aimed at rewarding successful entrepreneurial performance.

It is the independent professional manager who makes
the best kind of entrepreneurial contribution. The independent professional has perspective as well as deep involvement, has a very large bag of skills and insights, and can
bring all the tools of the trade to bear on problems and
opportunities. To see extraordinarily high management performance as a kind of game to identify with, meet, and
surpass organizational goals, and yet to have the kind of
independence and integrity that says, "I can walk out the
door any tomorrow if need be," is the best kind of dynamic
balance to achieve out of the inevitable conflict between

company structure and the idea of personal freedom. This is the essence of the most personally successful and satisfying American management style of this portion of the twentieth century.

That is not to say that other management styles cannot be equally successful in company terms. Paternalism, for example, can work in some situations rather well, with a combination of real concern for employees and almost-guaranteed long-term employment for a favored few. Paternalism, however, makes no sense at all from an individual manager's point of view. It robs one of the ability to sharpen skills and attitudes and to move freely as an independent professional. It ties one to a single organization and to its way of doing things in a period in which the job that looks absolutely secure may disappear tomorrow under the conditions created by economic stagnation, new technology, and foreign competition. Worst of all, acceptance of paternalism as a way of life in the long run tends to destroy self-definition as an independent professional manager.

Similarly, from the individual manager's point of view, there may be some things to be learned from management styles and techniques dominant in other cultures, such as those of Japan, but there is little to be emulated. Whatever robs a manager of independent professional attitudes and status is to be avoided like the plague it is. We do not function in an industrial culture that guarantees lifetime or near-lifetime jobs to its employees—nor will the Japanese, for that matter, if their industrial boom lags significantly, as it well may before the end of this century. But even if we could look forward to lifetime jobs, most of us would not want them—that is the antithesis of the freedom, mobility, and independent professional status we so prize. Indeed, anything that is a major lifetime approach to work and personal style and at the same time "goes against the grain" poses great psychic hazards. A game that you do not want to play, no matter how well played in the short run, will in the long run be played badly and turn very, very sour.

The short-term profits game is one such; it now alienates

hundreds of thousands of otherwise extraordinarily creative, entrepreneurially minded American managers, the management cadre that so spectacularly built the American economy in the two and a half decades that followed World War II.

CHANGING EXPECTATIONS

American managers are quite naturally builders of organizations. Yes, some are "empire builders" in the negative sense, but most reach for organization building as a matter of shared history; we are, after all, the heirs of four centuries of European conquest and expansion into the Americas, and only two centuries past the founding of the American nation. Those are short times, in terms of idea building; and we inevitably carry the idea of growth side by side with the idea of freedom and the entrepreneur's assumption that a single individual can make at least some minimal impact upon current history and a great deal of impact upon his or her own circumstances. These are all very basic ideas, and underlie very basic personal attitudes.

Therefore, the shift away from emphasis on growth and profit to the overwhelming emphasis on short-term profit that now characterizes American business functioning within a stagnant world economy can, if continued very long, produce profound negative effects upon most American managers, and upon American management styles. And there is a very good chance that it will go on for a long time, even into the next century, for the combination of international cooperation and technical application breakthroughs that can change the underlying situation seem, at this writing, very far away.

It seems almost a contradiction in terms to discuss the negative impact of emphasis upon short-term profits, when American managers spend so much of their time making and continually revising five-year operating plans along with their medium- and short-term operating plans. But the truth is, and well recognized in fact if not in open statement by most managers, that most long-term operating plans are treated with less than good-natured contempt by those who make and remake them. Plans that require continual radical revision to conform to short-term realities deserve that kind of contempt; they become mere time-wasting exercises indulged in by people who know that they should be making and working plans that are realistic. And the bitter truth is that we are witnessing the early stages of demoralization as managers realize that yesterday's implied promises of growth and continuity cannot be kept today by business organizations in deepening trouble. The current emphasis upon short-term profits at the expense of long-term organizational building is sure to harm American competitive positions in many industries and sink many American companies. That is not to say that top managements are merely wrongheaded in their emphasis upon short-term profits; a whole constellation of adverse economic factors, including current stock market, stockholder, and conglomerate financial requirements, often mandates the very short-term policies that can only lead to long-term disaster.

For individuals, these conditions pose both practical and psychic problems. Human relations, techniques cannot solve the deeply felt current insecurities or the very real threats of economic personal crisis created by such conditions. There are no easy solutions here, personally or emotionally—only the sharp realization that the main management career game has indeed changed greatly in the latter part of this century, and that independent professionalism is now not merely desirable, but a matter of survival for managers. That has not been so before; it now becomes so as the contradiction between expectations of stable growth and the reality of instability, accompanied by emphasis on short-term goals, becomes sharper and sharper.

The last two decades have produced other kinds of changing expectations as well, with deep impacts upon personal matters and life styles. But here it is not a matter of deepening contradiction between personal desires and corporate needs and styles; rather, it is a partial coming together of personal and corporate approaches to such problems as "workaholic" behavior, the handling of stress, and alcoholism. The enormously hard-driving, near-suicidal, near-psychopathic executive so often featured in post–World War II movies is still sometimes with us, but in far smaller numbers than during the forties and fifties. More important, it is no longer a favored, or in many instances even a tolerated, management style. We certainly have large numbers of hard-driving managers in the American management cadre, but today there is a new emphasis upon sanity and health, even during the most stressful situations. That can be taken for granted by modern managers; it should not be, for as a mass phenomenon it is very new on the American management scene.

This new emphasis and the advent of the movement for women's liberation and equality are underlying reasons for the widespread and increasingly successful resistance to the thoughtless and foolish practice of moving managers and their families many times during the course of their careers, whether or not such moves are even desirable from management's point of view. From a manager's point of view, that sort of moving about can be terribly damaging, particularly in regard to family relationships and the emotional health of spouses, children, and self. What has not always been so clear, though, is that such moves can also be extremely damaging from a career point of view. Professional mobility depends to a considerable extent upon financial independence and a network of career contacts. The manager who moves about a great deal has a very hard time achieving either. There can be no advantageous investment in local business real estate or in a local business when you move so often that you never have a chance to sink economic roots in an area. There is no easy professional movement among business friends of long standing within a major metropolitan area if you cannot stay put long enough to make real friends outside your company. There are only standard financial instruments; the hidden but very real costs of moving, which are never fully compensated; the spouse and children who may be increasingly alienated from you and a succession of unwanted new communities; and the very narrow circle formed by the people in your own company, who are as rootless as you. A personal career move of one's own, in pursuit of personal and professional goals, in concert with family, is one thing; a forced move to suit the company's whims of the moment is quite another, especially when often requested. As always, financial independence is the key. If you have no reserves, no ability to "walk away" if you must, an insistent relocation demand from your company becomes an offer you can't refuse. If you have planned well and have developed reserves, you can be serious about a refusal to move. Happily, such insistent demands to relocate are encountered less frequently, but they are still encountered. And, unhappily, adverse economic circumstances may increasingly force relocation decisions upon many managers for different reasons, as companies move to relocate and consolidate operations.

Yet currently adverse economic circumstances and the multifold personal hazards accompanying a career in management are, for most managers, only matters to be taken into account while pursuing their careers, rather than reasons to change career choices. For some, a real understanding of the context within management as practiced today will indeed mandate career changes; for most, that is not so. The professional practice of management will continue to be attractive and satisfying to most, given the material rewards possible, and the psychic rewards available to those who, by their very own natures, reach for the kinds of activities central to the pursuit of a management career.

What the new circumstances of these years do mandate is the kind of professionalism made possible either by a combination of excellent and complete early training, rounded apprenticeship, and continuing professional education, or the same kind of professionalism on the part of working managers whose training has, in the main, consisted of practical experience and continuing education. Managers arrive in the profession in a variety of ways, and those who arrive as MBAs out of prestigious graduate schools have a leg up—but only that. Many who arrive in other ways continue to prosper in their careers, generally through proper professional self-definition and continuing self-education. Although an MBA from a leading business school is increasingly a prerequisite for entry on a fast promotion track, most professional managers today do not have MBAs, but instead have a wide variety of other undergraduate and graduate degrees, and these include the chief executives of most medium and large American corporations. Self-definition, practical and entrepreneurially minded experience, and continuing self-development continue to be the keys to successful independent professional careers in management.

CHAPTER 2

MASTERING
THE ESSENTIALS

Self-definition as a professional manager helps the development of professionalism; professionalism leads to continuing, wide, and deep professional self-development. And self-definition, professionalism, and self-development make mobility, independence, and personal freedom far more than empty dreams.

Of all the career-building essentials, professional self-development is by far the most important. We use the term *professional self-development* rather than *professional education* deliberately. The latter has come to be widely used as synonymous with *formal* professional education, that which is *taught*, whatever the teaching form adopted. And from a personal point of view, that tends to stand the matter on its head, to the detriment of consistent and lifelong self-educational efforts, the success of which must be measured by what is applied successfully in life, rather than by what is taught. To say this does not denigrate the role of the teacher of management or of the school in which teaching takes place; it is only natural for institutions to measure success in their own institutional terms, rather than to attempt very seriously to go deep into the subsequent

practical careers of their students to try to measure what has
been learned. In truth, that would be too much to
expect—institutions can be expected, alas, to self-justify,
rather than self-criticize, for that is intrinsic to their natures.

From the individual's point of view, all management
education is self-education, whether secured formally or
informally, and at whatever stage of one's career. Whether
you follow a course of study eventuating in an MBA degree,
take a refresher course in or out of your company, or accrete
on-the-job experience, the extent of your development
depends upon how well you learn the material at hand.
Putting it a little differently, it is quite possible to take
courses, secure degrees, gather experience, and learn
relatively little. It is also possible to spend relatively little time
in formal courses, gather experience, and learn a very great
deal. Although modern management does require some very
significant hard skills that are best learned formally, it
is still, and will be in the foreseeable future, largely an
apprenticeship occupation, with many of its most important
skills and approaches learned on the job.

We should distinguish here between education and
credentials. A bachelor's degree is a necessary credential; it
is a prerequisite for entering management at any level above
that of first-line supervisor, and more and more it is a
necessary credential there, too. But that degree, by itself, is
nothing more than a credential; its holder may or may not
have acquired much that will prove useful in the pursuit of a
management career. One who has an MBA degree is likely
to have learned a good deal that will prove useful while
pursuing a management career, in addition to having
acquired a credential that is in most instances valuable early
in a career in direct relation to the prestige of the school
granting it and the academic record achieved while in
attendance there.

Later in a career, these early academic credentials
become much less important, for then practical experience
and a "track record" consisting of a series of increasingly
responsible and well-paid jobs becomes far more important

than entering credentials. This reflects the very real long-term primacy of work experience; if it were otherwise, we could fill top management jobs by competitive examination.

In a period of swiftly changing management-usable technology, particularly in the "hard" skills areas of financial management, mathematics-based modeling, database use, and computer technology, early and lifelong formal education is particularly useful. The new MBA graduate is likely to be up to date in many of these kinds of matters, while the experienced manager is obliged to do a great deal of catching up, often with inadequate grounding, but obliged nevertheless, if current professionalism is to be maintained. In this, the working manager is roughly equivalent to the accountant who must keep up with new accounting conventions and changes in tax law, or with the doctor who must keep up with advances in medicine and medical technology.

Early formal education has been extraordinarily useful in another way, as well. Those holding MBAs have tended far more readily to see themselves as professional managers, capable of working in almost any industry or function, than have working managers with less formal management education. That is partly because they have more useful and better developed entry skills; but more than that, it is because of self-definition as professional managers achieved during the period of formal education.

But early formal education is not necessary for self-definition as a professional manager. That kind of self-definition can be achieved by any manager who understands the need to do so—and doing so is extraordinarily important for every working manager.

Professional self-development, then, is a combination of lifelong and continual formal education in a swiftly changing set of hard skills, whether or not developed on top of a graduate or undergraduate degree in management or a related discipline, and equally sustained lifelong attention to the self-development that can come from day-to-day practical experience, if that experience is properly seen and ingested. Both the formal and practical side are indispensable for the kind of professionalism that comes from continuing self-development.

For managers, it is clearly the experience that teaches most—if that experience is seen as a source from which learning can flow. If, on the other hand, day-to-day experience is treated so pragmatically that generalizations are not habitually drawn from it whenever possible, very little learning results. Then it scarcely matters how much formal training is joined to practical experience, and little personal development takes place.

It is not really usual for us to think this way as working managers. We tend to think of ourselves as problem-solvers, doing our best to achieve and exceed mandated goals. Learning is all too often for the classroom; the practical world is somehow different. That, too, is only natural. After all, most of us spend our early years embedded in educational establishments that develop that point of view, with very little opportunity to develop self-generating learning attitudes. Yet, as working professionals, we desperately need self-generating learning attitudes if we are to grow as we can and should in a fast-changing world. That central contradiction between early educational modes and lifetime educational needs haunts most of us all our lives. It need not; but clear understanding and considerable initiative are required to surmount our early disabilities.

LANGUAGES OF BUSINESS

Language is the great carrier of human knowledge. And self-development starts with understanding and using the changing languages of management. In a wide sense, both English and mathematics are languages, and both must be understood generally and specifically, as necessary, by working managers.

As a personal and practical matter, managers must have

excellent reading, writing, and speaking skills in standard (sometimes called *university*) English. Let us hasten to add that we are not practicing elitism or "cultural imperialism" when we urge this. We strongly urge those who for good reason want to be expert in such special languages as Black English, the several regional English dialects spoken in the United States, and for that matter the different languages spoken by the many ethnic groups composing our culture and people to pursue that goal, agreeing that plurality and diversity are essential to the unfolding of the unique American experience. At the same time, we must very strongly say that the language of management, as well as most of the other professions, is standard English, and will be standard English for the foreseeable future. All the main ideas expressed by managers, all the main information exchanged by managers, and all the sublanguages developed by managers use standard English. All memos, reports, studies, proposals, letters, and promotional materials are written in standard English, and evaluated by people who accept standard English as "correct." The manager who does not have a wide vocabulary and flexible command of all the modes of expression in standard English is, in professional terms, considerably disadvantaged. The manager who has poor standard English skills must either sharply improve those skills or be substantially—perhaps fatally—disabled professionally.

There is considerable change in the language of management, even from year to year, as old techniques and objects are described in new ways, and as new processes and technologies call for new descriptors. Much of it is ephemeral, here today and changed tomorrow, and it is tempting to dismiss most of it as "gobbledegook," and the new terms as "buzzwords."

That is a mistake, for new language, however ephemeral, must be learned, if only for purposes of communication with those who use it, even if only pretentiously. And very often new language does usefully describe new processes and technologies, although sometimes several different terms will be used to describe the same thing, as language evolves.

For example, a generation ago the term describing marketing efforts directed at selling goods and services to discrete, determinable, and relatively small markets was *special interest marketing*. That became, in due course, *special marketing*. At this writing, the main term describing exactly the same thing is *narrowcasting*, with some also using the term *segmented marketing*. In dealing with two generations of managers, all four terms are worth knowing, and any one of them is useful in describing the marketing processes involved.

Or take some terms out of the special sublanguage of computers, that fertile source of new and often terribly awkward synonyms for perfectly usable existing terms. During the course of a single meeting, or in a single communication, you may be exposed to any one of the following related terms: terminal, computer terminal, editing terminal, layout terminal, video-editing terminal, videotext terminal, video-layout terminal, video display terminal, cathode ray tube, VDT, or CRT (these initials are used even more often than video display terminal and cathode ray tube, for which they stand). The problem is that all those terms may be used imprecisely and cause complete confusion. For a video display terminal (VDT) is a kind of cathode ray tube (CRT), which is often familiarly called a terminal or somewhat more formally a computer terminal. All the other terms are possible video display terminal uses, depending upon the programming involved. Later on, more sophisticated and therefore much simpler language will evolve; right now, you have to be able to communicate with the imprecise and overlapping terms available.

You must be able to move easily in standard English and through to the appropriate sublanguages. You must also have a couple of good reflexes. One is the dictionary reflex. When an unfamiliar term comes up, that reflex calls for turning to a large standard dictionary, a general business dictionary, or a special dictionary for the appropriate industry, business, or function. And they should all be right behind your desk; a dictionary reflex cannot develop if the right dictionaries are somewhere else in the building or at home.

A second reflex is the keeping-up reflex. One of the most important functions performed by current business and general periodicals is to keep you abreast of relevant current language, language that is so new that it is not to be found in the dictionaries you consult. Very often, language that new is not really defined in the periodicals you read, but its meaning can easily be figured out from the context of the work in which it appears, and then it can be used and understood in other contexts.

An old saw has it that understanding the jargon is half the battle in any field. Taking away the wryness implicit in the observation, and replacing the term *jargon* with the word *language*, that old saw has it exactly right.

But in management there are two languages to understand; the second is the language of mathematics. Balance sheets, profit and loss statements, flow-of-funds statements, operating budgets, sales forecasts, capital budgets, five-year projections, break-even analyses—these and all the other instruments that summarize the essence of the managing and controlling functions are cast in the language of numbers and use the concepts of mathematics. Rather complex mathematical concepts underlie such common activities as modeling, forecasting, and other planning functions. Along with standard English, a modern manager must have the language of numbers or be fatally disabled.

Managers need not be mathematicians, any more than they need to be grammarians. We need not be able to perform all the calculations and program all the computers ourselves. What is vital is to understand the mathematical concepts expressed by numbers; in short, managers must have a "numbers sense." Modern managers can use all the mathematics they are capable of ingesting. While the actual mathematical work may be done by specialists, the more mathematics we know, the better we can evaluate and apply the analytical results. This is especially important with the small computer revolution bringing mathematics ever more firmly into management offices.

Using Machine Intelligence

Increasingly, modern managers satisfy their number-handling and other mathematics needs by turning to computers. The day of laborious work with columns of numbers is long past; the advent of the desktop calculator saw to that, starting in mid-century. Now, as we approach a new century, we turn to machine intelligence programmed by human specialists for the satisfaction of such needs.

We are also beginning to turn to computer memories for storage and quick retrieval of business information. For now and for quite some time in the future, retrieval will be in mixed forms, with information available simultaneously through computer terminals and in print forms. In the future, data will more and more be available directly through desktop terminals, whether it is generated in-house or stored in large databanks in remote locations, and in the long run, specific bits of information will in general be more available on screen than in print, but that will be a very long run indeed; we will be using print media to satisfy data needs for many more decades.

It is quite apparent that computers offer great advantages to managers in both mathematical and information retrieval areas. Looking back in 50 to 100 years, we will view this time as the beginning of the period in which machine intelligence was introduced into human culture, with now-incalculable consequences that will only then become apparent. That is the promise—and perhaps the threat—of the computer, perhaps better called the machine intelligence revolution.

But focusing on the future can blind us to current realities, and computer promises should not be allowed to blind us to their current limitations. In our time, computers are extraordinarily useful tools, but only that; calling them machine intelligences does not alter this. There will probably come a day when they are companion intelligences, but that day is highly unlikely to come while those born during the first 60 years of this century are still practicing management. We cannot prudently assign any major decision-making or conceptual functions to computers or to narrow computer specialists who are not also generalist managers, for if we do we will be letting key management skills atrophy, and our current and future work will not come out well. Using the computer to develop alternatives for us in such areas as budgeting and market modeling is a fine idea—as long as we bear in mind that nothing ever therefore becomes "automatic." We plug our best estimates as to sales and costs into budgeting programs, and it is the quality of those estimates that determines the quality of our forecasting, not the sophistication of our computer programming. We plug our best guesses as to market acceptance into our new product computer modeling efforts; but success is as much a matter of existing marketing power and art as it was in earlier times.

Our concern here is with the management career opportunities and hazards opened up by the widespread introduction of computers into the business world. *Computer literacy* refers to the ability of working non-computer-specialist managers to fairly fluently use preprogrammed computers to work rather sophisticated numbers and retrieve rather complex data. That is all; you need not be able to program and design systems, or to understand programming languages. That was necessary not long ago, but is not really so anymore, since computer programming, or software, has become easier to use—that is, more "user-friendly."

You do need some knowledge of the special business sublanguage used by computer specialists; as always, knowing the jargon is half the battle. You have to able to talk with computer people intelligently about the uses and limitations of programs and computers, on the one hand to gain maximum advantage from full use, and on the other hand so that you will not be misled by the endemic overoptimism of computer specialists, who very often are so entranced by long-term possibilities that they have some difficulty seeing short-term operational hazards. That kind of sublanguage facility comes with time and conversation with specialists— and with full development of the dictionary habit.

It is also desirable to be able to work a computer keyboard, which for some managers means acquiring the ability to type. For most managers' needs, it is not necessary to learn rapid touch-typing, though that is useful. A reasonably quick "hunt-and-peck" technique will do for most people.

Note that office computer use has some potential physical hazards that should be looked out for and adjusted to as necessary. Beware of eye strain when engaged in protracted use. Some models are worse than others in this regard, but almost all can be expected to produce a certain amount of glare and cause some strain. Also beware of back and neck strain, because most models are not properly adapted to standard office furniture heights and styles. Pregnant women should definitely be concerned about possible radiation damage to unborn children. This is by no means certain, but caution is much better than imprudence in this area.

Managers use computers now and will use them more and more in coming decades for a wide range of planning, forecasting, and analytical functions, and for retrieval of needed data from what are becoming enormous bodies of computer-accessible information. At the same time, many managers often feel as if they are being buried under an ever-increasing mass of computer-generated paper, and are in the process of learning how to control and best use that mass of paper. Computers are tools, to be used freely to identify problems, seek solutions, and perform indicated tasks. They can help enormously, but only if they are viewed analytically and skeptically, rather than with wide-eyed and uncritical enthusiasm.

When inquiry, skepticism, and reaching for central processes in each situation become reflexes rather than efforts, consistent and lifelong self-development becomes inevitable. That is, after all, the key to it all; it is no less a key for managers than it is for scholars—only the means of learning and the applications of that which is learned differ. This is hard to teach, yet it can and is learned by some in each new generation, as they emulate the best of those around them and simultaneously read and follow the thought processes of those whose work they are reading. It is one of the main goals of a liberal education, and yet it occurs very frequently outside educational institutions, out in the world of life and work. For managers, who by the very nature of the work performed must be generalists, the cultivation of lifelong learning and therefore self-development reflexes is as natural as breathing. To have "an inquiring turn of mind" is sometimes seen by others as a somewhat engaging but usually annoying personal trait—a little thing. But it is not a little thing—it is a central thing, shared by all who innovate, and in our culture not least by the entrepreneurially minded professional manager.

THE INFORMATION EXPLOSION

We are to a considerable extent what we eat, intellectually as well as physically. And there is no proper inquiry without information, lots of it, and on an extraordinarily wide variety of matters. Some of these matters are directly concerned with current work; they necessarily take priority, and are often the materials that swell our briefcases and provide a great deal of our very large quantities of after-dinner and weekend reading. Other matters are less directly concerned with current projects and matters, but are still directly job-connected; we must keep up with people and developments throughout our organizations. Still others are industry- or function-connected; personnel or financial managers, for example, who do not keep up with key developments in their fields soon fall behind and are then less valuable on the job and less competitive with their peers. We also need to keep up with contexts. The generalist planner—in a sense that is what every professional manager is—who does not keep up with intertwined national and global political and economic developments suffers greatly in the long run. And we need to keep up with management as management, a body of attitudes and skills transferable to a wide range of industries, functions, and institutions; that is a matter of indispensable self-definition.

The aptly named information explosion that started after World War II and has since continued to accelerate has created several career necessities. The chief day-to-day result of that information explosion—and of the accompanying explosion of internal paperwork in management—is that managers today read, and read, and read. All day, every day, evenings, weekends, and on holidays, we read, scan, skim, find digests, access databases, do everything we can to ingest as wide and deep a mass of material as possible. It is never enough, can never be enough, for as we try to keep up, the mass of material increases. Yet we must do so; our current and future functioning depend in large part upon our current state of knowledge, and so do our careers. That imperative, in turn, causes us inevitably to select that which we consider most important, and to severely limit the rest. Alas, that also very often makes us far narrower and duller people than we would like to be—and than we need to be if we are to develop as generalist professional managers. Once again, professional self-definition, in the long term, most profoundly affects the course of a career.

For it is not enough to keep up with matters relating to job, company, kind of business, and kind of function. In the long term, no professional manager can pursue a proper course of self-development without the other two essentials: broad and deep contextual information, and the attitudes and skills of management as management.

For broad contextual materials, managers can profitably turn to such periodicals as the *Wall Street Journal, The New York Times,* the *Financial Times,* and the *Times of London.* The last two, published in England, are enormously valuable for their wide windows to world economic, political, and social matters. The two American periodicals are basic, and provide national and international coverage, but very often from an American point of view. The British periodicals have traditionally taken a much wider view of international matters; not of British matters, though, where their views are at least as insular as those of the American press.

Such periodicals are for skimming, scanning, clipping, and copying, rather than for extended reading; time needs preclude that. Occasionally, though, there will be thoughtful, broad-gauged articles well worth reading in full and keeping. Some of these you will want to circulate to others in your organization and among your network of professional friends. Most such articles will, however, originate in magazines and professional journals, rather than in newspapers. Such magazines as *Fortune* and the *Harvard Business Review* will sometimes be useful in that regard. Once again, though, time pressures will necessitate a good deal of skimming and scanning.

Such newspapers and magazines are also useful for locating those few among the tens of thousands of books published each year, on both sides of the Atlantic, that you will have time to read carefully and completely. There are some that should be read that way, and sometimes those are selected by reviewers and thus brought to your attention. Unfortunately, some of the best books available each year are not so selected; then all one has to fall back on is word of mouth, advertisements, and browsing visits to business-oriented bookstores, of which there are several in most major cities.

Keeping up with information on management as management is equally difficult, and there are fewer good vehicles available for doing so. As a result, periodicals in the field take on a significance considerably beyond the value of their contents. Management periodicals, as well as industry and functional periodicals, are the vehicles through which readers are alerted to new sources of information and insight, through book reviews, critical articles, and advertisements. Subscription lists to such periodicals are rented widely to those seeking to reach audiences for their own publications and services, so that subscribers can expect to receive catalogues and solicitations of all kinds—but especially in areas of interest, resulting from subscription to such special-interest periodicals. True, there are so many of these that the temptation is to throw them all away unread, as "junk mail." But those who do so cut off a valuable source of information. In these ways, then, the special-interest periodicals serve as needed conduits of information and insight, far beyond their own editorial content.

PERSONAL REFLEXES

But lifelong professional self-development is far more than reading, no matter how voracious and astute a reader one may be. It also stems from several personal and interpersonal reflexes. Each of these by itself on any given day may seem like a little thing, but all of them together and over the course of a lifetime become extraordinarily significant.

The first and most essential personal habit of all is listening. Just listening. Listening to what people say, and doing one's absolute best to understand what they mean. This is not for purposes of persuasion—though listening is by far the most important early step in the process of persuasion—but for purposes of learning. Listening to learn, with as few preconceptions as possible, whatever the working hypotheses you have adopted, and whatever other information and insights you have—or think you have. To write about such a basic necessity in a book directed to an audience of professional managers might almost seem insulting, but the truth is that very few people, including professional managers, know how to listen, and do listen reflexively and well.

And questioning. Not adroit interrogation—merely the asking of questions aimed at eliciting answers that inform and clarify, sometimes as much from the way the answer is supplied as from its content.

And therefore also watching. Watching the entire communications pattern, both verbal and nonverbal, of those with whom you are speaking. Also the interplay between all the members of a group you are in, a kind of watching that seems difficult to those who do not reflexively do it, and quickly becomes second nature to those who learn to do so.

And therefore also empathizing, that is, "putting yourself into the shoes" of another. That is the key to persuasion, and therefore also to all selling; it is also vitally important for self-development. Much of a manager's most important knowledge is of the probable state of mind of others; much of what must be learned about the management of institutions is about how people inside or associated with those institutions feel and react in the basic situations that repeat themselves over and over during the course of a working lifetime. Those who characteristically have trouble with people handling and situation handling are usually people who have not learned how to empathize. Often, by the way, that is not so much an intrinsic flaw as it is a strength carried to fault. Many hard-driving, entrepreneurially minded managers are perceived by others as having handling problems, when in fact the problem lies in their lack of control of that drive. To run roughshod over foes and friends alike is the hallmark of the improperly seasoned professional manager.

The habit of cool, unsparing, unsentimental self-analysis, extended over a lifetime, is an invaluable aid to self-development. "Don't look back—someone may be catching up," may be fun to say, but it is some of the worst advice ever seriously tendered. Only by reflexively looking back—and sideways, for that matter, while in the middle of a situation—can we hope to learn consistently what we need to know, generalize from our own experience, and meet new situations better. This, too, is so axiomatic it scarcely seems necessary to say, but it is a habit more honored in theory than in practice by professional managers, among others.

In this area, the technique of the "postmortem" can be particularly effective, especially if there are like-minded people to work with. And in the long run, like-minded people can be developed, as the efficacy of the technique is proved in practice. It is as simple as meeting the "morning after" a

negotiation, a sale, a training meeting, and asking yourself
and others: "How did we do?" "What could we have done
better?" "What, if anything, was left undone?"

Useful insights can come from all sorts of seemingly
unlikely sources, if we are habitually open to communication
from others. Even those interminable committee meetings
can be useful sources of information, and sometimes of
insight, beyond the stuff of the meetings themselves. It requires developing the habit of acute, almost unconscious
listening, though; the defense mechanisms set up by many
managers to counter the effects of too many dull, repetitive
meetings and lunches are often so massive as to nullify the
listening reflex in all but the most devoted self-developers.

PERSONAL RESOURCES

People in our own organizations can be immensely valuable
sources. We are all part of informal and formal power and
reporting structures within our organizations, and those we
work with are quite naturally also our best sources of information and insight regarding matters within our organizations. But they can be much more, as well, for in the course
of their careers they have experienced and analyzed much,
and have much to offer, just as we do for them. Early in our
careers, those who are more experienced and reflective than
we are have a great deal to offer us, if they are properly
perceived as potentially excellent sources rather than as
"dinosaurs" patiently waiting for retirement. In truth, even
many of those who are pacing out the years until retirement
have a great deal to offer, if listening and empathy are
properly tempered with one's own analysis.

Self-definition as a professional manager has some interesting and beneficial side effects. One of them is that those
appearing from outside your organization—newly arrived
managers at your level or above, eager youngsters, the
occasional consultant who arrives with an unspecified
charge and may make recommendations that shake up the
whole company—are greeted by the professional as fresh

sources and opportunities to learn, rather than as enemies. A consultant can be a tremendously valuable source of both state-of-the-art information and industry and function insights. Consultants also get around a great deal, and may be sources of favorable job recommendations both inside and beyond your own company. A new manager can be someone who becomes a bitter antagonist, but is more likely to be someone whose interests run together with yours, especially when you are recognized as a professional manager. Those mutual interests may extend far beyond a single company and a single working relationship. They may span whole careers, with both of you working together, recommending each other to successively higher levels of responsibility, and forming a network with others like yourselves for decades.

The executive recruiter, or *headhunter* (the somewhat pejorative current term), can also be useful as a source of career insights and possibilities. No matter how happy you are at your present work, it never really hurts to talk to an executive recruiter who seeks you out, partly because you can never know what your alternatives are until you have explored them, and partly because whether or not you take a proffered job, you can learn a good deal from the recruiter. For one thing, you may learn that you can get more pay and responsibility than you thought possible. That is valuable information whether or not you decide to stay in your current job. It is valuable when deciding whether or not to attempt to negotiate increased pay or responsibility. It is valuable in providing a potentially useful career contact in the executive recruiter and the recruiting organization. If you go as far as interviewing with other companies, it is valuable to have deeper insight into how other companies work, from the inside. It is also valuable in assessing when is the right time for you to make a move.

Most long-term professional self-development proceeds best on an individual basis, fed by self-definition and inquiry. But although there is no substitute for such self-development, group endeavors and formal courses have a substantial part to play.

Professional and trade association memberships are

most often seen as career-building tools; they can also be self-development tools. The extent to which that can be true varies greatly. An individual chapter may be moribund, or it may be an active organization, with useful exchanges of ideas and experiences and with interesting speakers; in the long term it may provide a good deal of valuable material. A national organization may do little other than run a showy convention once a year, or it may run a large body of continuing professional education meetings, seminars, and large formal courses, by itself or in conjunction with colleges and universities. Alert modern companies normally encourage their managers to participate actively in appropriate professional organizations, and often pay membership fees, encourage attendance at meetings and conventions at company expense, and act as sponsors of association educational activities. Alert modern managers encourage their companies in this, and participate actively themselves, as part of both continuing professional self-development and career-building.

Such organizations are particularly useful for interpreting current regulatory material and technical changes. Most managers keep up with such material by subscribing to newsletters, looseleaf reporters, and other periodicals, often retrievable from computerized databases as well as in print. But the give and take possible at a meeting, between speakers and audience, cannot be duplicated by the periodical forms. A tax or labor law change, a new kind of machine or process, a major new application of existing technology—all need both detailed study in print and the kinds of wider discussions made possible by association meetings and other continuing professional self-development forms.

CONTINUING EDUCATION

Many professions in this period are faced with similar continuing professional self-development needs. In some professions, such as medicine, that need stems from the enormously swift pace of change in medical science and related areas; the doctor who does not keep up may lose patients who might otherwise have been saved. In other areas, such as law, it is the interplay of legislative, regulatory, and judicial materials that makes it absolutely necessary for lawyers in many substantive areas to keep up or fail to represent and advise their clients properly. In profession after profession, it becomes increasingly clear that competence depends much upon continuing professional self-development. For some professions and in some jurisdictions, such professionals as doctors and lawyers are legally required to take continuing professional education courses; California is one state that has pioneered in this area.

Professional managers, as of this writing, face no such legal requirements. But management shares, with other professions, the momentum created by both an accelerating pace of change and rapidly developing public attitudes as to the desirability of continuing education. That is why continuing education is such a widespread movement in American management, with many organizations offering it in various forms, including the American Management Association, a large number of graduate and undergraduate colleges and universities, and several thousand independent educational organizations of all kinds, which offer everything from hard knowledge courses in computers, mathematics, and financial analysis to highly questionable courses and traveling seminars on the latest fads in the manipulation of yourself and others.

Once again, it is desirable to distinguish sharply between credentials and useful learning. In the area of continuing professional education, the overwhelming emphasis is upon learning; yet even here credential-seeking often plays a part. One who takes courses part-time for a business degree can and often does pursue learning and credentials simultaneously, with completed courses—even if well short of a degree—counting considerably toward promotion on a present job as well as in a resume. One who secures an MBA often finds doors opened, even on a current job, that were closed before, although the level of knowledge and professionalism achieved the day before the degree was earned is much like that the day after. The degree in that respect then becomes a matter of status—not your perception of self, but how you are perceived by others.

Many courses yield credits called continuing education units. Such credits do not, at this writing, lead toward any kind of generally recognized degree, in the sense that bachelor's degrees and master's degrees in business administration are widely accepted degrees, granted by institutions of higher education, operating within a whole accrediting and legitimizing apparatus. Courses are given by thousands of organizations unaffiliated with accredited institutions of higher education. Many of these courses are very useful indeed; some are not. Yet even in this area, credentials are often gathered, with companies viewing current and prospective employees more favorably if such courses are part of a work history and resume.

As a practical matter, however, the relative utility of such courses is the most important thing about them. The manager who takes a relevant professional education course is very often informed and made more valuable to his or her company by that course. Such courses are particularly useful where practical experience has been light, and you are not a recent business graduate who has recently taken relevant courses. The manager who, after ten years, wants to move from personnel administration into finance, for example, must somehow show current interest, aptitude, and knowledge, no matter how strong early credentials in financial management were. Conversely, the manager who wants to move from financial management into personnel management is well advised to take some courses—which may or may not be terribly useful in practical terms—in the several areas that constitute human resources administration.

A very practical and personal note here. Many companies will finance or help finance continuing professional self-development efforts on your part, all the way from the company that routinely sends top and middle managers to a

Harvard—or other business school—summer seminar, all expenses paid, to the company that matches your tuition contributions in pursuit of a graduate business degree. Company practices in this area are important to explore when considering a job offer. And such matters can also be part of the substance of negotiation between you and a prospective employer or your current one.

The discussion so far has been within the context of a career spent working full-time in medium to large companies owned wholly or largely by others. But sometimes our dreams of freedom and independence take us in other directions. And all of us can reasonably look forward to living and working far beyond our corporate careers, even though we pursue those careers until "retirement."

This is why self-development as a fully rounded, entrepreneurially minded professional manager is useful in far more than management career terms. It is also vitally important for those who strike out on their own during their earlier years and for those who continue to work, often in their own small businesses, in their later years. Many experienced managers fail in their own businesses because they do not realize until it is too late that they do not have some of the basic skills, approaches, and up-to-date knowledge they need. The marketing manager who confidently goes into a business without first developing financial skills all too often experiences early, complete, and avoidable failure. A few courses in financial management during the marketing career and a small period of apprenticeship in the desired kind of business can mean the difference between success and failure. Putting it a little differently, self-definition as a rounded professional manager, and the securing of the skills needed to back up that self-definition, are as indispensable for alternative and later-life careers as they are in the course of your career as a working manager.

In career-building terms, then—and even in alternative and postcareer terms—lifelong professional self-development is the most important single kind of activity in which one can and should engage.

PERSONAL QUALITIES

There are other key career builders, as well, having to do
with your personal characteristics as seen by others, notably
those others with whom you work within the corporate
hierarchy. Note that we are not here discussing "image
building"; that may work for advertised products, but does
not in the long run work very well within our own organizations. Those who work with us know us, sooner or later, just
as well as our families do. We spend so much time together,
in so many situations, and communicate so much, both verbally and nonverbally, that it is almost impossible for us not
to know each other well. No, not image building; rather
personality building. Not what we would *seem* to be to
others, but what we really are to and with them is what
matters in the long run, in personal and in career-building
terms.

The standard constellation of personal qualities we
would wish others to have, and wish to have ourselves as
professional managers, usually includes brightness, quick-
ness to learn, consistency, sound decision-making ability,
good people-handling talents, excellent problem-solving ca-
pability, flexibility, balance, and several other characteristics
indicating our ability to do anything that needs to be done as
well as or better than anyone else.

Sometimes we include integrity, because it is important
to us for personal reasons, even though it is sometimes
perceived as something of a drawback in a corporate world
seen—sometimes properly—as a "jungle."

But when we think of others as possible colleagues and
subordinates, we think first—and last—of people whom we
can trust, "stand-up" people, people who will be there when
we need them. In short, we think of people of integrity. All
the other positive things, too; but personal integrity most of
all. For all our talk of jungles and corporate warfare, we
value integrity most—oddly, even while occasionally doing
some things ourselves that give the lie to our cherished self-
images. It therefore seems apparent that personal integrity is

the most important career-building personal characteristic of all. You are both what you are and what you make of yourself; the person who has a well-deserved reputation for integrity has the most important image a professional manager can have—and as actuality, not merely image.

That kind of assessment sometimes seems hard to square with perceived corporate and marketplace realities. Advertisers routinely overstate, lying routinely by omission and exaggeration, and often by outright misstatement as well. Many books and articles counsel a wide range of cunning stratagems and artifices, claiming to instruct on how to play all the possible games one can encounter in life or in management. Some claim to have the keys to "powerful" professional and personal relations, others to foolproof negotiating and persuading methods, and yet others to sure ways to move ahead with enormous, unchecked speed and momentum.

Those who sell professionally face to face encounter the same kinds of advice. They are urged to engage in a whole set of practices adding up to cunning manipulation of buying motives and buyers—to close deceptively and hard again and again, to use "every trick in the book" to make a sale. Nonsense, of course. Those who buy are inured to tricks and deceptions, and the professional seller who develops a well-deserved reputation for being "slippery" and "tricky" soon needs to find another line of work. That is easy to see, and sound sales professionals know all about the unique importance of integrity.

Yet some of those who manage professionally do not so easily see this. But the truth is that all of us read the same books and articles, live in the same business and personal world, know the tricks as well as we know what we had for lunch ten minutes ago, and desire nothing quite so devoutly as to work with people we trust, who do not play manipulative games—precisely the games we are urged to play by some bogus experts. Most fully seasoned professional managers know better than to habitually play manipulative games, recognizing the professional and personal harm they can do themselves and others; a few do not. Some inexperienced people are taken in by bad advice, and do try to play them, harming others in the process, and doing themselves no good professionally at all. Certainly there is tactical maneuver in the real world; certainly we do not always reveal everything we know to others; certainly we do things that hurt others—that is the inevitable result of decision making. But habitual game playing is extraordinarily counterproductive personally and for organizations, and the manager who is seen by his or her peers and superiors as lacking in personal integrity has nowhere to go but out, if personality and image cannot be repaired in place.

EXCELLENCE AND POSITIONING

Astute career development, as we have so far discussed, rests on bedrock comprised of self-definition as a professional manager, lifelong professional self-development, and perceived personal integrity. And now another bedrock matter—perceived excellent performance. Doing a job that is seen by peers and superiors as excellent is considerably more valuable in career-building terms than all the manipulative tricks and tactics in the world. How hopelessly old-fashioned that sounds in a world like ours—how true it still is and will be.

That is why, except at the corporate level where it matters less, "line" is still in general a better place to be than "staff." It is far easier to produce measurable results in line than in staff. Doing an excellent job is basic, whatever responsibilities are carried, but in career-building terms, that excellent job must be visible to superiors and peers. Those performing line functions are easily seen as receiving definable revenues and incurring definable costs; therefore they are capable of being treated as sources of profit or loss—as "profit centers." Those performing staff functions are far harder to treat in this way, although many modern companies make some attempt to do so.

And since excellence is basic, but for career-building

purposes must be perceivable by superiors and peers, the manager who can produce definable results in line is usually far better positioned for advancement than most staff managers. This argues strongly for attempting to direct a career into line management rather than staff management positions.

That is a matter of positioning, which is a key career-building idea and strategy. A wise staff manager may well take a sidelong transfer, with little or no increase in pay or responsibility, if it means entering line management in a rather visible position, in which excellent performance can be expected to result in promotion. A successful line manager may well resist promotion if it means moving into a staff job, or into a line job with smaller possibilities. For example, a line manager may do extraordinarily well running an operation that is, by company standards, very small or not central to company plans; although in line and doing well, that manager is not well positioned, and is in a virtual dead end. Career building may then require a move into another, more fruitful line, or even, in extreme circumstances, a move to another company.

As in every other human endeavor, excellence develops the habit of excellence. And settling for less than excellence often enough can seriously erode the habit of excellence. That, too, is still a bedrock truth, whatever the demands placed upon professional managers in difficult times such as these.

And that is a problem. For these have been difficult times for most American managers for well over a decade now, and may continue to be so for a good many more years. And the habit of personal excellence is quite likely to come into conflict again and again with business realities, as troubled times continue.

In the absence of massive national and international economic initiatives, most American businesses of all sizes will continue to find themselves forced to focus on short-term profits rather than on that combination of profits and growth that characterized much of the American economy in the period that started with the end of World War II and ended in the early 1970s. In addition, national and international competitive pressure will in most industries accelerate that process of adulteration of materials and shoddiness of workmanship (known as *hidden inflation*) which daily debases American products and services. To expect American managers to continue the habit of excellence and to build excellence upon excellence under those conditions is, to put it gently, somewhat unrealistic. American managers have, in fact, very unhappily presided over the dismantling of substantial portions of the American industrial system, and have watched in far-from-mute horror as financial managers took over decision-making powers that had in a healthy economy been exercised by competent and sometimes world-class American line managers.

This is not to enter one side of the argument between line and financial managers over who should make these decisions. That argument quite misses the point. It is very easy to see that financial managers pursuing short-term goals have not been making corporate policy in a vacuum; the American economy has been so sick for so long that it scarcely matters who makes and executes the short-term yield decisions. When substantial publicly-held companies are as vulnerable to takeover as most American companies have been in this period, there is little choice left but to maximize short-term profits and hope that takeover can be averted. When conglomerate owners regard their resources as pools of capital to be moved from one opportunity to another to achieve maximum short-term yield—in a very real sense as pools of "hot" capital reaching across the world for quick profits—then it scarcely matters whether top management is led by someone with a financial background or someone with an operating background. Orders are orders, and must be carried out. Worse, orders can be anticipated, and goals can be set that reflect short-term profit desires. And so a whole economy, in both private and public sectors, fails to renew its industrial base and large portions of its infrastructure, and becomes in several very important ways antique and uncompetitive.

It may get worse; it may get better; but it will not change

very substantially for quite some time. Yet, at the same time, there are some healthy American industries as well as many sick ones, many healthy American companies, and many opportunities for career building in management. But opportunities are harder to find, and they cannot be taken for granted. It is no longer realistic to expect to work for a few companies early in a working life, one or two more in your thirties and forties, and settle into a major job in your late forties or early fifties, to move only if you are then moving about a bit at the corporate level. That can happen; it will happen for some who are working in healthy industries and companies. For most, it is far more realistic to assume that one who enters upon a career in management also enters upon a perpetual consideration of multiple job opportunities, inside and outside of current employment.

That means considerably heightened sensitivity to career opportunities and pitfalls than was necessary two decades ago, when the perceptions of those now in senior management were formed, which in turn means that some mentors, who have kept up with new realities, can continue to be enormously useful, but that others should be looked upon with new skepticism. It means that executive recruiters, who yesterday might have been thought to be terrible time-wasters, should be looked upon today as indispensable adjuncts to astute career building. That professional meetings, courses, and contacts of all kinds take on a new career-building significance, for each is also a job mart. That one burns no bridges at all, if at all possible. That the need to build a web of long-term business friends—now called networking—is more important than ever. And that the interpersonal and political skills underlying all this must be kept sharper than ever before. Upward career mobility can happen almost by accident, a happy combination of being in the right place at the right time and doing an excellent job. But it is, as it always has been, rather unusual for it to happen that way. Normally, it takes a good deal more than that. And today, as never before, it takes careful and constant self-assessment and astute opportunity-seeking to protect and nurture your career.

CHAPTER 3

ASSESSING CAREER GROWTH

Opportunity seeking starts with knowing what you wish to seek and how you wish to seek it. Putting it a little differently, we face the same basic career direction questions all our working lives: "Where do I want to go?" "How do I want to go about getting there?" The contexts and answers certainly change a great deal for most of us during the course of a life and career, but the basic questions remain the same. As age, experience, and accomplishment grow over the years, some of us come to prefer these questions cast in terms of processes. "What do I want to be doing for the next five years?" "The next ten?" "For the rest of my career?" "For the rest of my working life?"

After basic career choices have been made, many or perhaps most working managers do not ask those kinds of questions systematically and repeatedly. If faced with personal or career crises, they may be forced into a reexamination of basics. But systematic and repeated reexamination of career choices is not a habit that develops out of circumstances; it is a matter of conscious planning, a habit that can only develop out of a set of self-analytical reflexes. Yet without the repeated asking of those basic questions, there can be no serious career planning, only a reach for each successive promotion or seemingly advantageous job change, even though our personal desires and needs may change enormously over the years, and even though career survival itself depends on careful, long-term analysis and reanalysis of goals and personal situations.

Managers have a wide variety of career and personal goals, and the two are intertwined. The young MBA determined to subsume all to career is merely failing to see personal goals. Even the youngster who announces that he or she is determined to make a million dollars a year and preside over a major corporation usually carries a rather romantic view of corporate and personal power, prerogatives, and status, and secretly wants to impress his or her loving family and all the kids on the block.

These basic goals questions underlie all the rest. The answers to the host of questions that add up to "How am I doing?" must always be related to the basic goals questions if they are to make any sense at all. Personal goals change in a rapidly changing world; grabbing the brass ring on the merry-go-round does not mean much if you have decided that the merry-go-round is not where you want to be. That promotion in the home office of a New York–based company may not really turn out to be what you wanted if, between the time you started trying for it and the time you received it, you decided that New York is not the place for you and that the Southwest is where you want to put down roots and stay. The decision to put down roots anywhere may change the basic corporate game for you so much that you want to reexamine some seemingly basic goals. Maybe you want to find a company headquartered in the Southwest and settle into it, with a view toward developing your own enterprises there in later years.

Sometimes your choice of industry will restrict your mobility, overriding other concerns. Perhaps you above all want to work with books, even though you know that many areas of the publishing industry are desperately sick, that many companies will not survive, and that you could make a

lot more money now and have far better future prospects as
a professional manager in another, healthier industry. Then
the decision to stay in publishing, which makes no sense at
all without the desire to stay with books, may be not only
defensible, but the only one you should make. You will still
look for a relatively healthy company to work with, and try to
build it as best you can under considerably adverse
circumstances, but your basic decision has been to stay with
books, and try to get where you want to go in an admittedly
difficult vehicle, the publishing industry.

People have all kinds of reasons for developing and then
changing these kinds of basic desires as the years go by.
What is indispensable is to develop the ability to recognize
your own basic desires, assume the ability to reach them,
and continue to reassess them as they change, for change
they will. Concentrating as Americans do upon personal
relationships, it is easy for most of us to see that relationships
change quite naturally as life patterns develop. We easily see
that marriage relationships, sibling relationships, and all
kinds of other personal and family desires and relationships
change. What is not so easy to see is that, by the same token,
it is entirely natural that career matters are also deeply
affected by life experience and changes in personal goals.
Yet it is so. The key is to recognize the attitudes and assess
the changes in them that do occur. How? By engaging in
more or less continual self-analysis. By that we do not mean
psychotherapy, but rather developing the habit of
continually asking oneself the right questions, again and
again, throughout a lifetime. "Where do I want to go?" then
properly becomes, "Where do I want to go as I see myself
and my needs and desires now?" "How do I want to go about
getting there?" then properly becomes, "How do I want to go
about getting there as I see myself and my needs and desires
now?"

In business, we routinely develop five- and even
ten-year development plans, revising those plans yearly or
even every six months. And we routinely do rolling yearly
forecasts as budgets, reassessing those budgets quarterly,

sometimes even monthly, or whenever extraordinary business developments make such reassessments necessary.

A career cannot be planned quite as easily as that. Yet it can be planned. The principles of periodic and systematic questioning and reassessment are the same. The need to do a rolling revision of plans based on current outside and inward realities is the same. So, too, is the need to recognize the connection between the "How am I doing?" questions and the more basic "Where do I want to go and how do I want to go about getting there?" questions.

This leads us to the whole body of questions that, for serious and continuous career building, must be asked of oneself periodically. (By periodically, we mean at least yearly in a formal sense; as a practical matter, these are the kinds of questions that should recur reflexively and quite naturally as career and personal events occur.) Once we get into the habit, these are the kinds of matters that are under perpetual review as we do whatever else we normally do. All are in a very real sense "How am I doing?" questions; all are inextricably intertwined with the basic "Where do I want to go and how do I want to get there?" questions.

REVIEWING CAREER STATUS

Most career-related questions cannot be answered in hard, precise ways; in this they differ greatly from corporate budget performance and personal financial growth questions. That is a key reason for focusing first on the easiest-to-answer and therefore easiest-to-assess career questions: "How am I doing financially?" and "How am I doing in terms of responsibility?" While progress in these areas, year by year, is not necessarily a crucial determinant, in the long run money and responsibility tell us a great deal about how we are doing. In a very real sense, we sell our time and talent in an overlapping set of national and world markets, composed of all those who might buy the use of that time and talent. In

the long run, therefore, marketplace supply-and-demand
factors tend to deeply affect levels of pay and responsibility.
Comparative pay and responsibility within an industry, and
among those doing similar jobs in different industries, provide most revealing information as to how we are doing in
the national and international management marketplaces in
which we work. In addition to comparative pay and responsibility, we can measure how we are doing in real dollars,
very specifically and unsentimentally.

During the last 18 years, prices as measured by the
Consumer Price Index have just about tripled, meaning that
the dollar we spend today is worth about one-third of what it
was worth 18 years ago. (As you read this book, those basic
facts may have changed somewhat, but they are unlikely to
have changed very much for the better.) Therefore, a manager who is now making $60,000 per year is in real pretax, or
gross income, dollars earning about as much as a manager
who was making $20,000 per year 18 years ago.

That is a pretty staggering fact; it means that many
managers who have spent their whole careers moving up
from $20,000 to $60,000—or whatever the equivalent tripling
of income has been—have in fact turned out to be marking
time financially; even though they may carry far larger
responsibilities now, they are making no more real money
than they did 18 years ago. It was not quite that simple, of
course; many made real gains until the mid-1970s, and then
lost all their gains and often much more as the pace of
inflation leaped ahead of increases in most management
incomes.

Others, who did not keep up with the pace of inflation as
well as this, have suffered quite substantial losses during
most of the 1970s and 1980s. A middle manager who is now
making $40,000 is—in the real dollars of 18 years ago—
making $13,000 to $16,000. The "fast track" young MBA
entering the work force deeply in debt for undergraduate
and graduate education but starting at $30,000 to $40,000 per
year is not really doing much better than an executive
trainee of the mid-1960s starting at $10,000 to $15,000 per

year. And that executive trainee often had only an undergraduate degree and owed nothing to anyone.

These are difficult facts for many managers to face. But without facing them, there can be no realistic answer to "How am I doing financially?" That a manager received a 10% increase in pay last year may signify a real increase in income—if the inflation rate last year was 6%. But if the inflation rate was 10%, that was only a cost-of-living increase. And if the inflation rate was 12% to 14%, that was no real raise at all, but a loss, no matter how large the congratulations that came with the seeming raise.

If all those working in the American economy gained or lost equally, this would be an empty question. But that is not the way it works; varying rates of real increase or decrease occur, often relating less to individual merit and progress than to company, industry, and career choices. A company that is doing badly may not be able to significantly raise the pay of even its most meritorious managers; it may indeed require pay cuts, which have multiplied impact in periods of rapid inflation. Today many whole industries are sick; managers working with those industries are often disadvantaged vis-à-vis managers in other industries. Sometimes whole professions are more or less advantaged than others. For example, managers as a group have not kept up with the incomes and tax-advantaged professional practice-building possibilities of those in the health care professions, but they have stayed well ahead of the general income levels of people in such professions as social work, urban planning, and writing. The balance between opportunity and risk that in the last generation tipped decisively for many in the direction of management careers may for many managers now seem to tip in the direction of entrepreneurship and the attempt to develop businesses of their own.

With all that in mind, "How am I doing financially?" is a little harder to answer. Certainly, if your cash compensation is growing at a faster rate than that of inflation, you are at least making some progress. In more sophisticated terms, more important for those with higher incomes, if your total

compensation package is growing significantly faster than
the pace of inflation, you are making some progress—but
that is somewhat harder to assess than the rate of increase of
direct cash compensation. What a pension or profit-sharing
plan will be worth at some future date is often hard to
evaluate, especially in difficult times; and whether today's
strong-looking company will be there to honor its long-term
commitments when you retire may be questionable. With
cash compensation needed more than ever, and with tomorrow's ability to honor today's promises shakier than ever, it is
surely most realistic to look hardest at cash compensation—
cash in hand now—when assessing financial progress in your
career each year. Cash compensation is therefore by far the
firmest and most determinable single aspect of career progress in this period.

That emphasis on increasing the amount of real dollars
you are paid each year has some very significant career-
building implications. Among other things, it means that a
job move within one's current company that does not result
in significantly higher immediate real-dollar income is to be
regarded very warily indeed; we can no longer expect that
moves into line from staff, or moves to greater responsibility
within line or staff, will more or less automatically result in
higher real incomes, even when they are accompanied by
moves to higher compensation grade levels within a company. More than ever before, higher compensation in current companies under these conditions becomes a matter of
negotiation rather than acceptance of a presumably beneficial status quo in terms of established salary and organizational structure. For we are now in a time when many
companies can reasonably be expected to strongly resist
routine real-dollar salary increases, making every attempt to
substitute status for money and promises for real dollars
now.

As managers are very much on their own in salary
negotiations—the very thought of collective negotiation is
anathema to the overwhelming majority of American managers—a new stress must be placed on job mobility. Cer-

tainly job mobility is a must for defensive purposes, in difficult times; it is also a must for managers of considerable
talent and skill, who can do better elsewhere than in their
present companies. Putting it a little differently, we are in a
period in which many companies are not willing or able to
hold their best people with real-dollar salary increases, so
each manager must be ready to move to other companies for
real-dollar compensation gains. Under these circumstances,
moving from job to job rather frequently is no longer as
clearly inadvisable as it was in an earlier day; instead, it
becomes a necessity for many managers, as companies and
whole industries falter and become unable to move their
people up as rapidly as do other companies and industries.

No, we do not suggest moving every year or two to a
different company; that is still properly described as sterile
job-hopping, leaving you with too little time to really build
anything anywhere, and raising a serious question as to
whether you are capable of doing so. We do suggest a far
more serious attempt than ever before to keep other company and industry job options wide open, to spend time
adroitly increasing those opportunities, and to regard job
moves as quite natural and healthy for professional managers, rather than fearing each move as a step off into an
unknown world full of hazard. But never burn a bridge. The
number of companies that see former employees as somehow disloyal grows smaller every year, as current business
realities change old attitudes. More often than ever before, a
move to greater real pay and responsibility in a different
company or industry ultimately results in a return to a
previous company at a higher level. Somehow, those who
could not see you for a desired promotion when you were an
employee can easily see you for a job two steps up from that a
few years later, when you are returning from a more responsible job in a different company. The career-building logic of
our time is not, "Stay put, and grow it where you are," but,
"Move, move, and keep moving until you find something to
grow unless you are lucky or skillful enough to find that early
in your career."

Responsibility, usually measured by budget sizes and numbers of people controlled internally or as outside vendors, continues to be a substantial measure of progress. The manager who in the course of any year substantially increases the size of his or her operation or moves up to a position of greater responsibility may be doing some real career building, whether or not real-dollar pay increases directly result. If increased responsibilities result from a move to another company, a substantial real pay increase is also quite likely. It is less likely, in these times, if they occur within the company. But whatever else they bring, operations growth and responsibility increases are excellent resume items, and provide an enhanced basis for advantageous moves, within or outside of the company.

REVIEWING COMPANY STATUS

The next career assessment question would, in other times, have been the question of one's own excellent performance. But in these times, a prior question is, "How is my company doing?" Excellent personal performance, even if well perceived, no longer can be relied on to bring desired rewards; companies and portions of companies must be doing relatively well to reward excellent performance. It must often be seen even more narrowly than that, down to, "How is my group doing?" and, "Does my division head have the power to reward my excellent performance, or is he or she in such difficulty that I am likely to be swept away in the debacle that is about to occur here?"

In a way, the larger questions are rather easier, although most of us do tend to stick our heads into the sand and refuse to recognize when our companies or operations are in trouble. For example, American industry is full of managers who have had the experience of working within a company that was losing money, or was clearly vulnerable to takeover because it was not making enough money, or was about to be sold by owners anxious to retire—and who refused to recognize that their business environments were about to change, dramatically and sometimes adversely, because of a change of ownership. It is not so hard to study company balance sheets and operating statements to see how your company is doing relative to other companies in its industry, or to keep up with your company's stock, as it fluctuates. It is very easy to keep up with ownership possibilities in a family-owned company, or with acquisition and divestiture movements within a larger corporate structure. It is only a little harder to study carefully your own divisional operating statements and keep up with divisional performance, even in areas in which you do not have directly budgeted responsibilities. And for your long-term career it is essential that you do all those things. If you are doing rather well, and everyone else is doing very badly, you may be seeing opportunity—but you are far more likely to be seeing a disaster shaping up in which you will be deeply involved, unless you take steps to distance yourself from current division management in the eyes of top management, to transfer to another division, or to leave the company. Not that what you do, or try to do, will always be correct or work out well; but the worst possible error is to become an uninformed ostrich caught in a corporate sandstorm.

It may be hardest of all to recognize that you are associated with a failing management and will be unable to change the main course of events. It happens often. An executive vice president who has been closely associated with a fired president is also fired, even though performance over the years has been superb; or a marketing manager goes when a divisional vice president goes, unjustly blamed for divisional shortcomings. It is quite natural that this failure of analysis should occur; those who are most deeply involved in attempts to save or turn around a situation are often the last to recognize that it has all gone past the point of no return.

There are no easy answers in this area. Good managers become identified with their own operations, and develop group goals and loyalties, whether or not things are going well. It is the rare manager, indeed, who is able to stand back and coolly recognize that the situation all are trying so hard to save is in fact unsavable, and that it is time to distance, transfer, change jobs—in short, to move on. It usually happens far too late, when choices are already severely limited. Yet, in career terms, it is desirable to cultivate just that sort of analytical ability in all seasons, no matter how deeply involved one is in the efforts of the moment or period. And in this season—a season of prolonged and intractable economic and therefore company difficulties—that kind of analytical stance becomes an absolutely necessary career-building and career-saving tool.

How your company is doing and how it is likely to do in the near future are important assessments to make. You are best able to make job moves when you are doing very well, in a company that itself seems to be doing at least rather well. When a company is visibly doing badly, it often becomes much harder to move up out of it, to the kind of job that provides a substantial promotion and increase in real-dollar pay. Your desirability and therefore your negotiability are always best when moving from a strong company, and almost always weakest—unless you have recognizably unique or valuable things to offer—when moving from a troubled or failing company.

REVIEWING MANAGEMENT SKILLS

And then, in estimating how you are doing, there is you, your attained level of management skills, and demonstrated excellence of performance. Learning how to manage increasingly well is a lifelong enterprise, and one that continuously refreshes those who practice management. How that ability is developing is terribly hard to measure, and is far more a matter of subjective analysis, of "feel," than something that can be measured in a hard and quantitative way. What is required, rather, is to develop the habit of self-analysis, of taking a long, cool, critical look at personal performance, day by day, year in and year out. "I'll do that a little better next time" requires the ability to make some pretty informed estimates as to how well you did it this time, within the bounds imposed by the situation.

Excellence of performance is in some respects the same, but, in career-building terms, it is quite a different thing. We are best advised to be our own worst critics; that is the way to excellence. But at the same time, our performances as managers are also measured by how well we meet and exceed budgeted goals, how well we demonstrate entrepreneurial attitudes and skills, how tight and smooth are the ships we run. We want to perform excellently in all those ways, and we want our excellence to be recognized by our superiors and peers. That requires first of all goal-setting skills, for ourselves and others, from the main forecasting or budgeting skills necessary to set up adventurous but workable business goals to the people-handling skills necessary to help others set and reach goals within our overall forecasts. And making sure that our excellence is recognized is partly a matter of politics and positioning within an organization.

How one is currently doing within a company is more than that series of basic and indispensable matters having to do with real pay, recent promotion, increased responsibility, and setting and reaching budgeted goals. Those things are musts; without them there is no progress possible or discernible, and no amount of skill in personal maneuver is likely to prove very helpful in career terms. There are exceptions, of course; only the blind would maintain that American business is free of nepotism, favoritism, sexual exploitation, and assorted bigotries. Yet they are exceptions. The general rule is that at least recognized competence and more often demonstrated relative excellence are "openers" when dealing with questions of management career advancement in most substantial business organizations.

Yet once those basic matters are in place, a substantial number of what can only be called political skills come into play in every organization, as formal and informal organizational structures interpenetrate to form the real motor forces at work in every organization. Therefore, "How am I doing in my current company?" must also be answered in terms of essentially the same kinds of questions asked by those involved in any other kind of political life. These are the questions involving business friends, mentors, rivals, influences, promises given and received, formal and informal spans of control and reporting relationships, and the whole web of relationships generated by the ad hoc committees, permanent committees, task forces, and study groups that generate the incessant meetings that characterize American business life in this period.

Political skills are part of the apprenticeship side of management, as they are in other professions. The curricula of our colleges and universities are strikingly deficient in this regard; while Machiavelli is seen and taught as a historical figure, little or no attempt is made in any of the professions to develop those indispensable skills that have to do with motivating and moving those we work with and our own organizations in desired directions. We teach a little about propaganda, something of selling, sometimes focus in speech departments on the techniques of persuasion, but we touch hardly at all on intraorganizational persuasion and the skills associated with that practice. It is an enormous gap in the formal education offered the overwhelming majority of professionals, managers among them. True, the skills involved are hard to quantify, graph, program, and otherwise massage with mathematical tools. And true, these skills are all too often rather sanctimoniously viewed by many in academe as somehow indecent, often as the unwelcome "underside" of American public, commercial, and professional life. But they are indispensable skills, nonetheless; without them, one cannot in the long run function very effectively in a world full of emotional, self-interested, often irrational people, who carry all sorts of conflicting attitudes and interests—in short, ourselves and our co-workers.

In this context, "How am I doing in my company?" requires a sober periodic tallying of friends and foes among peers and superiors, and an equally sober comparison of current relationships with those of a former time, probably a year ago. And along with that tallying, some questions: "Have I maintained and strengthened relationships with my friends?" "Have I done anything for them in this last period, or they for me?" "Have we continued and strengthened our information sharing and mutual day-by-day support?" "Have I paid attention to their wants and needs as I would want them to pay attention to mine, or have we let our relationship slip somewhat, assuming quite erroneously that we will 'be there' for each other when needed?" "Have I added any friends?" "Have I acted as a mentor for others?" "Have I, in short, properly recognized that friendships must be worked at and continued to strengthen mine within the company?"

The same sorts of questions apply for superiors, some of whom may be your long-term in-company sponsors, champions, and advisors—your "mentors." All lasting relationships are two-way streets, matters of give and take, of caring about those who care about you, and that applies to those who at first glance might seem to want or need nothing from you, while being willing to help you in any way they can. With a mentor, it is often as little as a smile; a little seemingly irrelevant talk about the weather and current state of each other's health; a baby picture; a golf score; a restaurant recommendation; a shared complaint about the air conditioning—a set of tokens, signifying that you face your world together, rather than quite apart and at arm's length. It may also involve such matters as information sharing; many a wise corporate-level old-timer understands the value of networking at least as well as younger and less experienced people who are rapturously discovering, applying, and writing about the technique. Early, sound information delivered by those we trust can and often does make all the difference between timely action and far-too-late attempts to piece things together after a costly set of errors. And those who deliver timely information coupled with their own sound insights are demonstrating excellence and are seen quite properly as "comers" by astute managers further up the corporate line.

A subsidiary question that should accompany this kind of periodic personal evaluation has to do with hard-to-assess positioning matters. Determinable growth in one's own operations and formally recognized accretions of responsibility are clearly career-builders. But to a lesser degree so are appointments to key temporary and permanent committees, task forces, and the like, often because they bring contact with matters important to our organizations and their top managements, and considerable personal exposure to top management, as well, exposure that may be worth as much as any other accomplishment in any given year. Therefore, further proper questions are: "Have I had any kinds of fruitful or potentially fruitful special assignments and exposures?" "How have they worked out, in career-building terms?" "If they are still in progress, what should I do to help them work out to best personal advantage?"

CAREER MOVES

The answers to all these kinds of questions make it possible to arrive at a reasonable evaluation of how well you and your company are doing now and as compared with the last such evaluation. They provide the necessary basis for asking such questions as: "Should I be actively seeking an in-company move right now?" "Am I doing all that I can to build my career in this company at this time?" "Is this still the right company for me, given my own changing wants and needs—and given internal company, industry, and general economic developments?" "Is it really time to move on, to very actively seek affiliation with a different company, in view of current possibilities in my present company, my demonstrated skills and performance level, and the level of opportunities available elsewhere?"

The answers to these kinds of major career questions

rest in part upon your answers to some other questions that deal with somewhat wider professional and personal matters.

Here we return to lifelong professional self-development, seen now from the viewpoint of practical career mobility. It is when you encounter questions like these that you really begin to see the importance of keeping up with the industry and function within which you are currently working, with the broad contexts within which you and all other managers are working, and with the profession of management as management. When you make a move, you may hold yourself out as expert in field or function; of at least equal importance, you hold yourself out as a wholly mobile professional manager to whom "management is management." And to the extent that you have consistently pursued lifelong professional self-development, you are able—by demonstrating who and what you are to a prospective new company—to back up your central claim to being a professional.

That is particularly important when moving from field or function to the corporate level, often from a position in middle management in a relatively large company into corporate management in a smaller company, as when a marketing executive for a leading company in its field becomes the executive vice president of a smaller company in the same or a related field. No matter how well middle-management functional responsibilities were handled, if the middle manager did not handle corporate-level responsibilities in the past, the question of corporate-level suitability must inevitably come up. Then all the questions about in-house and outside management courses, MBA degrees, professional association activities, and the breadth of view demonstrated in that all-important set of face-to-face hiring interviews come up; the question of lifelong professional self-development becomes central.

When we are considering the big question of whether or not to try for an intercompany move, we also find ourselves exploring how well we have pursued our network of outside contacts during our current employment. And it is extraordinarily important that we do just that, quite formally, at least once a year, as part of a substantial "How am I doing?" evaluation. Unless carefully scheduled, this question can and does easily get away from many managers, who quite naturally focus on current colleagues and job-related matters, rather than making the effort to keep up with and further develop a wide network of career friends and contacts far beyond their present companies. The manager who does let this kind of networking activity slip away is in a very poor defensive position should anything go seriously wrong with current employment. Even if a decision to move has been made from strength and the realization that better opportunities exist elsewhere, such a person is in a seriously deficient job-seeking position.

This is when you test the network of professional friends you believe you have built up over the years; find out whether the potential job contacts you have cultivated are really worth anything; see if the executive recruiter who sought you last year meant it when he or she begged you to get in touch if you ever changed your mind and decided to make a move. This is when you find out that you should have developed a network, cultivated job contacts, and talked to executive recruiters, if you had previously not done so.

When the will to do so is present, a network of potential career-builders is very easy to build, the ways of going about it very easy to see. Many of our best lifelong career contacts are those with whom we have previously worked, people who were part of our internal networks over the years and who have moved on to other companies. It is often as simple and direct as following a mentor to another company; the new company president reaching back into a previous company for key personnel is a common phenomenon in the business world. Often the connections are considerably more circuitous, however. The peers who once worked together and have remained friends over the years may inform and recommend each other for job after job in an ascending spiral for decades.

Excellent career contacts can also come from outside professional education courses and association contacts. Managers who spend anywhere from a week to two months living, working, and solving business problems together in a university-sponsored professional development seminar may become lifelong friends who may do business together for their companies, get together professionally and socially, and ultimately find their way into the same company, as opportunity arises. Similarly, managers who find themselves sharing and enjoying a weekly or monthly table at a periodic professional luncheon quite often expand their contact and become valuable professional friends.

And then there are the executive recruiters—not the ones who will take anywhere from several hundred to a couple of thousand of your dollars to run tests and perhaps help you find a job if you are involuntarily unemployed, but the ones who are engaged by companies to find excellent managers to fill vacant or soon-to-become-vacant positions, and therefore call you. They are all too often pejoratively described as "headhunters," the implication being that they will do anything to "steal" good people from their loving companies. Nonsense; let yourself be "headhunted," recruited, or whatever you want to call it. There is no better way to turn up good opportunities. You are never in a better negotiating position than when a company comes to you regarding a new job, rather than vice versa.

Even if you have no intention of making a move, it never really hurts—and can help a good deal—to talk to executive recruiters. In immediate terms, you may find yourself comfronted with an offer too good to turn down, which you had no idea at all you might receive at this stage of your career. Also, you may very possibly learn a good deal about pay and conditions in other companies and throughout your own and other industries. Executive recruiters come to know a great deal about many things that managers—and especially excellent managers who do not move about very often—may not learn so easily in any other way. And in less immediate, but often even more important terms, every executive recruiter you talk to is a potential job contact should you decide to make a move in the relatively near future. By all means take the time to meet and talk with executive recruiters. Let them talk; listen hard; ask questions. Each such contact can, in the long run, amount to a considerable expansion of your network of job contacts.

Executive recruiters can be particularly valuable for a very special reason having to do with the difficult nature of the times. Many of them do tend to specialize in one or two industries, but many work in and keep files on several industries. In today's world, characterized as it is by faltering companies and even whole industries in trouble, when managers very much need to be able to reach into other industries as well as into other companies for stable jobs, executive recruiters can play a considerably enhanced role. An experienced recruiter who knows you and believes in your experience and demonstrated talents can in these times become a prime career-building asset for you, as are all the key people in your network of business and personal friends and contacts.

CHAPTER 4

MANAGING YOUR TIME AND WORK

For many American managers, the times seem more than a little out of joint, and nowhere is this more apparent than in the day-to-day practice of management.

The contexts have changed; that is the essence of the matter. It is a period in which the seeming "givens" no longer apply. It is a period in which yesterday's rather "fat," growth-oriented, heavily staffed, investment-minded company is today's "lean" company, fighting for short-term profits, cutting staff and compensation, often struggling for mere survival under terribly adverse conditions. It is also a period of considerable disarray, with the kind of top management confusion that leads companies to continue reflexively to waste much desperately needed management time in constant revision of five- and ten-year growth plans that cannot possibly bear fruit while everyone must strain for short-term profit.

At the same time, and coincident rather than intertwined with the adverse economics of the time, it is a period in which a historic change in the area of management tools is taking place, as computerized and computer-assisted management systems come into full play and machines created by humans both replace and make new accomplishments possible for humans in management, as in every aspect of our world.

It is also therefore a period in which you may on one day be working in a company committed to management by objectives, participative management, and human resources coordination, and be hip-deep in an unending series of meetings and people-handling activities, while trying to keep up with a massive and ever-changing body of computer-generated materials; and the next day be working with a lean company, operating quite informally and seemingly rather autocratically, while coping with an entirely different set of ever-changing computer-generated materials.

This is a period of great teaching and publishing activity in such areas as time management, people handling, negotiation, persuasion, and how to handle meetings of all kinds. That is quite understandable. Managers, among others, are experiencing considerable difficulty in handling matters that in different times seemed far more a question of developing good working reflexes than of learning whole new bodies of techniques.

The emphasis on new techniques really clouds the issue. In practice, managers need only develop the same body of basic skills they have always needed. What is new is that we must develop our skills into excellent reflexes in a considerably changed and widened set of work and home environments, and we must pay far more attention to the contexts within which we work and live than ever before.

In the area of time management, for example, it is always very tempting to start by pointing out that there are only 168 hours in a week, then to set forth a series of mechanisms that will in aggregate help us to use our time most effectively and finally to embellish lovingly what are essentially a series of simple techniques with scores of checklists, charts, graphs, and other visual materials designed to help drive home the simple points made. Useful, certainly; but by itself utterly misleading. Without a deep analysis of your own personal and business goals, and of the organizations within which you are to a considerable extent encased, these simple techniques will take you nowhere, no matter how effectively and attractively presented. In this instance a picture is not worth a thousand words; quite the opposite. A few well-chosen words reflecting your own hard analysis and illuminating the nature of your goals and environment are likely to be worth a thousand graphs, checklists, charts, and cartoons.

Our main long-term goals—or strategic goals, a synonym as here used—are least likely to change as circumstances and working-style alternatives change. To put it a little differently, day-to-day techniques and tactics and medium-term strategies may change, but we will continue attempting to keep our home situations stable, maintain our physical and emotional health, build our skills and careers, make our organizations successful, and provide for our later years, no matter how much else changes.

Except for relatively brief periods, as in the early years of management practice, or in such unstable periods as those of marital breakup, most of us will insist on trying to develop and grow healthy home situations, no matter what the demands of our work. That is not new; the extent and bedrock nature of that insistence is new, though, and reflects the expectations and emphases developed by two generations of concentration upon such matters as mental health and sound interpersonal relations. It is even quite likely to be true of the "liberated single," who, beneath appearances, is very often a rather traditional American man or woman who demonstrates the need for stability by attempting to build long-term relationships out of some very unlikely material and situations.

For managers, that bedrock insistence often seems in sharp contradiction with professional needs and job demands. For the truth is that most managers do not work even nearly the hours they seem to work. You may work 35 hours a week in your office, but aside from holidays you are highly unlikely to have devoted as few as 35 hours a week to

the practice of your profession in all your working life. There
is always work to take home, much of it vital to job success.
There are always networks to be cultivated for career-
building purposes, on the job and also most significantly on
your "own" time. There are professional publications to read
and assess, and professional organizations that quite
properly require a good deal of attention. All these on
"personal" time.

"Personal" time? Nonsense. That is the conceptual error
that creates the seeming contradiction between the very real
50 to 80 hours a week you spend pursuing your career as a
professional manager and your bedrock insistence on a
sound personal life. To think of the time spent in your office
or on the road directly involved in your company's affairs as
paid work time and the rest of your professional time as a set
of unpaid and deeply resented encroachments upon your
personal life is purely and simply to set yourself up for a life
of continual personal resentment and abrasion at
home—and for a foredoomed lifelong attempt to somehow
cut your outside-the-office professional time demands as
close as possible to zero.

PROFESSIONAL LIFE

It just does not work that way. It never did. A professional
manager can no more avoid outside-the-office professional
responsibilities than can a lawyer, who must keep up with
current professional developments and cultivate and sustain
client relationships for much of each working week, far
beyond the time actually spent in office, court, or library. Or
a doctor, who must keep up with professional developments
and association activities, even though an actual working
week may be as long as 50 to 70 hours, sometimes even more.
Or a sales professional, who may seem to others to be
spending very little time actually selling, but who in truth
spends enormous amounts of time traveling, on the tele-

phone, planning, and handling masses of paperwork, often in ill-lit motel rooms late at night.

Putting it that way, there is no reason to expect that a manager's professional life should be less busy than the lives of other kinds of professionals. Real adjustments must be made between professional and home matters, but they need only be adjustments, rather than the kinds of seemingly unmanageable contradictions that stem from misunderstanding the nature of a professional life. A manager does not simply sell time, on an hourly, weekly, or yearly basis, but pursues an entire career, with office time and current compensation only part of that career. With that understanding clearly in mind, expectations can be realistic; so too can moves aimed at improving total effectiveness, saving valuable time, and increasing control over both professional and personal life.

In any event, managers should expect to spend a good deal of their most valuable working time at home, on the road, and in some cases while commuting to and from their offices. The nature of working in organizations makes it so, whether those organizations are fat with meetings, reports, and ad hoc committees, or lean and hungry, with quick meetings, fast decisions, too few people to do all the things that need to be done, and a great deal of personal short-interval scheduling. Either way, the working day is going to be full of people, paper, telephone calls, computer printouts, and lists of priorities that grow and grow. No matter how well you plan—and excellent planning is essential even for survival, make no mistake about that—your office is quite unlikely to be a place to think a long thought, create a medium- or long-term business strategy, seriously evaluate a subordinate or peer, or make major career-building plans and moves. Oh, you may occasionally be able to "lock yourself up" to work on a report that must be delivered in a few hours, or arrange a luncheon meeting that accomplishes some real planning moves, but those are prudently to be regarded as exceptional situations—bonuses snatched from the maelstrom that is any manager's predictable work week.

To put it a little differently, you cannot expect to dream, plan, and do other things that require blocks of open-ended time during your normal working day; but these things are essential and must be part of your normal working week and working style. Therefore many of the most important things you routinely do must be done outside your office; your away-from-the-office work is vital and normal, and to be planned for, no matter how effective your office working style may be.

Once the professional practice of management is seen this way, the seeming and real contradictions between business and home life comes into focus. The real contradictions remain; they are the same time choices caused by the practice of any work requiring long hours and close attention. However, the seeming contradictions—and these are the ones that cause so much trouble at home—disappear. They are replaced by recognition of the need to organize effectively that part of the work that is properly done away from the office, so that it may be done well and within time bounds you have consciously set, rather than expanding to fill and thereby destroy your own personal life and the lives of others with whom you live.

That requires most of all the will to do so, which can only come from shared understandings. It does not matter how efficiently you may have set up an office at home if those you live with expect your almost undivided attention. For example, a woman in management whose family expects her to come home to cook, clean, nurse, and in general watch and ward for them during all the rest of her waking hours is a woman whose career and home life are probably in disastrous conflict. Not because she is spending "too much" or "too little" time with either business or personal life, but because her family does not understand that her profession demands that she continue to practice it at home as well as in the office.

Similarly, a man or woman who is heavily and continually criticized at home for "not spending enough time with the family" may indeed be a compulsive and self-destroying person—but rather may be simply a working manager trying to practice that part of his or her trade that must be practiced at home, under terribly adverse conditions. There are work compulsives, of course; but there is also widespread misunderstanding of when and where the profession of management is practiced. A manager who works 60 or 70 hours a week, and sometimes even more, including many hours at home, may be a "work compulsive" who is in the process of destroying home and family; but he or she is far more likely to be a quite normal, terribly harassed American manager, trying to pursue a difficult profession in the twin maelstroms of home and office.

And there is the key. You have to be able to think a long thought somewhere, whenever you want to. It is a must; it is indispensable to the practice of the profession. Most managers cannot depend on their offices for this; it must be done before or after hours, and elsewhere. Usually that means at home. Usually—but not always. Some who travel a lot accomplish a great deal of "office" work on the road, and some who commute accomplish much while traveling to and from work. Some managers arrive very early or stay very late at their offices, in an attempt to create controllable time of their own. Unfortunately, that time all too often becomes filled with leftover details, rather than becoming available for strategic purposes, or, even worse, becomes filled with even earlier and later meetings as others become aware of their availability.

OFFICE AT HOME

In the long run, therefore, most managers need an office at home. Nothing else will do. A *real* office, as carefully organized and equipped as any other office in which a manager practices. For most managers living in their own homes, that is not terribly hard to accomplish, with a little investment and foresight in home selection. For those living in crowded city or suburban apartments or condominiums, that is often much harder to accomplish; harder, but not less necessary.

A real office for a practicing manager working at home is a separate space, preferably a separate room, as isolated as possible. It is a dedicated space; offices at home having nothing to do with kitchen or dining room tables co-opted for work while families either continue their normal activities and thereby make it impossible to work properly, or tiptoe about resentfully, making it impossible to have a normal family life.

Beyond the basic understandings that management is practiced both at home and at the workplace, and that an office at home must be private and dedicated to its working functions, offices will vary as widely as do working styles, mechanical skills, needs, and available technology. For some managers, an office at home may be a very small room containing little more than a desk, a filing cabinet, good lighting, a telephone, and a dictating machine of some sort. Some will add such machines as calculators, typewriters, and personal computers, or will be tied into substantial computer systems through terminals at home. Some, where such possibilities exist, may choose to set up working quarters in separate structures, much as an artist sets up a studio in a barn or other outbuilding. Whatever the office setup adopted, the physical requirements are basically the same at home as at work: an adequate table or desk; such other surfaces as are needed; letter- or legal-size files; good-to-excellent lighting—a must; decent heat and ventilation; high-quality machines that work consistently (no, a little, light, manual portable typewriter really will not do in the long run); a comfortable rolling chair; adequate book space; and a reasonable set of office supplies. In addition, if you work on the telephone out of your office at home, you will probably want to install a separate telephone line for your business calls, hooked up to an answering machine for handling calls that, in the office, are handled by others. That will enable you to separate professional and family activities completely, even though they are carried out under the same roof—and that is important. Much unnecessary abrasion can be avoided over such situations as your incoming calls continually disrupting the lives of others, or their calls continually tying up lines you need for business purposes.

Note that many modern companies—even in difficult times—clearly recognize the stake they have in making it as easy as possible for a manager to pursue job-connected matters in a well-equipped office at home. Such pieces of equipment as computer terminals tied in to large main frame computers and distributed databases, minicomputers, dictating equipment, answering machines, typewriters, office supplies, and even some items of standard office furniture are routinely supplied by some companies. Other companies will supply these kinds of goods and services if you take the trouble to ask, and press the point, along with your coworkers. Still others will do so only if you have made it part of the whole body of items negotiated when you took the job. These items should not be regarded as fringe benefits, by the way; they are essential working tools for managers who are doing their jobs properly, and should be supplied as readily to offices at home as they are to offices on company premises.

A manager working at home cannot always tightly schedule and ration time spent on business matters. On the other hand, it is quite possible to set aside recognized periods in which others can expect you to be working at business matters, and to stay generally with the patterns established. Your work at home then becomes expected and mostly predictable. Without that kind of predictability, a manager working at home is always cast in the role of a villain who can be relied upon only to frustrate family plans, and any work you accomplish at home seems to be done at the expense of others and against strong family resistance.

These may easily be seen as trivial matters; taken one by one, they may be. But proper understanding and handling of professional work needs and of work at home are central to good relationships with others and to the satisfaction of our own lifetime goals and expectations.

When seen clearly, such matters as long-term work time commitment and bedrock insistence on a healthy family life are most fruitfully perceived as processes, whether or not so stated. There are milestones along each of the intertwined paths on which our strategies work themselves out; shorter-term goals achieved or not, desires reached or not, battles won or not. That much of your professional life will be pursued at home must be a shared long-term understanding with those you love, whatever the changing physical and time arrangements over the years.

Similarly, and intertwined, is the question of focus. Or, to put it a little differently, the question of at least apparently unbalanced focus.

A standard and only occasionally valid bit of folk wisdom is that if you spend most of your time at home focusing on work-related matters and perhaps an unnecessarily large part of your time traveling, you are conveying a clear signal that something is very wrong with your personal relationships, and that you may be getting ready for a change of partners. Perhaps; perhaps not. It is at least equally likely—in the early years, anyway, before one-sided focus really can destroy relationships—that you are in the process of being caught by a set of job and professional needs, in a set of games you may not know how to play terribly well. After all, winning objective after objective does not bring you any nearer to the end of the professional game; only time does that. While the game is being played, and that is for a whole career, it can expand to fill every bit of time in your life, if you let it.

Except for that other bedrock personal goal, so sharply demanded by the people of our time and place: insistence on trying to find and build long-term personal relationships. For we are, in the long run, desolate if we are unable to do so, and almost equally distressed if we are unable to do so in our work. All of which sets a considerably amended set of contexts within which we pursue our careers in this last portion of the twentieth century, and helps explain our focus on such matters as interpersonal relations, time management, and several kinds of people-handling matters at work, as well as the preferred management styles of the period, focusing as they do upon participation and a measure of democracy, even though such approaches are structurally difficult.

The current focus upon time management is quite appropriate, seen in this set of contexts. For without excellent personal organization and priority setting within a clearly understood body of long-term goals, all of life can very easily become the maelstrom that is the normal modern office, as experienced by normal modern managers, and few, if any, long-term personal or business goals can be consistently pursued.

The main thing is to keep those goals firmly in mind, continually assessing and reassessing them in light of events. Beyond that central and indispensable activity, there are a few simple techniques for handling time, people, and tasks that can make life easier and enhance efficiency considerably, if they are developed into habits. None has to do with time alone, for all are inextricably intertwined with tasks, people, tactics, and strategies; as is usually true in life, time saving and efficiency are means rather than ends in themselves. All are simple enough, as sophistication is simple; all taken together add up to cultivation of a set of excellent working reflexes that begin to make it possible to consistently translate long-term goals into the stuff of everyday life and work.

ORGANIZING YOURSELF

The most important working reflex of all is to develop the habit of continually putting to oneself two related self-management questions, and of having the answers to those questions before you constantly, written down in the form of ever-changing lists of tasks and priorities. The questions are: "What do I want to get done?" and "What needs to be done?" And implied in each is, "When?"

These are the essential self-organizing questions. Note

that they do not lead to exploration of a wide range of alternatives; that is part of longer-term decision making and planning. In contrast, day-to-day effective self-management requires limitation of alternatives and development of current action from proven skills and strength. A list of possible actions, rather than a list of specific actions to be performed, is likely to be quite useless—a waste of time to prepare, and a worthless self-organizing tool. A good deal of effective thinking must precede preparation of a list of things to do; it is the process of preparing the list that is the key act of self-organization.

Very few managers need to be convinced that listing is a necessary device. It is axiomatic that no one can remember more than a modest fraction of all that needs to be done in business and personal life; it is equally axiomatic that five undone things bouncing about unlisted inside your head feel like fifty undone things. Indeed, the best way to convince someone of the value of listing is to go through the process. Almost always, that person's "I always seem to have so much to do" results in a far shorter list than he or she had imagined. The listing process also often turns up vital matters that had not been on that person's mental list.

Listing always seems simple enough. You take a sheet of paper, or a notebook—or a personal computer, for that matter—and write what needs to be accomplished. You include everything from "get haircut" to "explore job change" to "do new product report—due 30 days." Then, as things get done or proceed toward accomplishment, entries are crossed off or updated; and as new items develop, they in turn are listed. The result is an all-inclusive, undifferentiated list; it takes the least possible time to prepare and update, and you do not have to spend half your time listing, updating, excising, adding, and thinking about lists. It is simplicity itself; but not nearly adequate.

For listing is a key act of personal planning, and many of the matters with which you routinely deal are not intrinsically simple and easy to accomplish. Oh, you can and should keep the trivia of the day and week before you at all times on a running list; given the complicated lives most of us lead, to do otherwise can be maddening. But if all you do is keep an undifferentiated list, you are quite likely to find yourself dealing superbly well with trivial matters and perhaps filling your life with nobly handled trivialities, while missing the main matters with which you should be dealing, except as they are forced upon you by outside events. "Get haircut" is easy; "prepare report" is a lot harder and more time-consuming. You will certainly prepare the report—but unless you plan well, you are likely to prepare it under extreme last-minute pressure, and less well than you might have. You may even succeed in developing long-term rationalizations for poor planning. Management is full of bad planners who stoutly insist that they work best under deadline pressure.

The main thing to understand about listing is that it is only the basic and indispensable start of effective planning. Certainly you will start with a relatively undifferentiated mass of items, but you will need to develop several special-purpose lists adapted to your particular needs. Once these are in being, you may quite routinely update and study several lists simultaneously, perhaps as you sit down on a Sunday night to plan your coming week's work, rather than making a single list and then transferring items to special-purpose lists. As you proceed through each day, you are quite likely to enter items on several running lists, although some people prefer to keep an undifferentiated list and transfer items once a day to special-purpose lists. For many kinds of items, such as meetings, appointments, and dead-lines, you will routinely use such calendared devices as small appointment books and desk diaries. If you travel a great deal, such lists must first of all be portable and sturdily housed; if you travel little, you will develop somewhat different tools. And unless you carry a single set of lists with you routinely, you will need to conform running lists carried at the company office, the home office, and on the road. That, by the way, is why lists kept on personal computers are so

difficult to use. It is a physical problem. You need to be able
to carry lists into many different kinds of places and situations, and plain old paper and pen or pencil are better for
that than computer screens. That may change in coming
decades; later on we may all find ourselves carrying small
computer devices hooked into remote memories. But that
kind of change will be measured in decades, not in years; for
now, lists are best done on paper. You will develop a series of
lists and listing tools that suit your personal preferences and
needs so lists and listing devices will vary considerably
between managers.

But whatever the mechanical devices used, well-organized managers are likely to find themselves using three
general kinds of lists, with considerable overlap among
them. The first will be a day-to-day, rather undifferentiated
item list, containing mostly trivia, but also including recent
additions not yet added to other special-purpose lists. That
list is probably best carried separately and constantly, as on a
pad or looseleaf memo book. For managers who move about
a good deal—and most do—such lists should be pocket-sized,
and therefore easy to carry and use in most situations. When
something occurs to you in an elevator or train, on a street or
in a restaurant, during "working" hours or at other times, it
is important to be able to jot it down, to capture and set the
thought. That is true whether what occurs is a task to be
listed or some other thought you will want to pursue later;
you will therefore want to be able to use a single memo
device that allows you to add to a running list or make other
notes.

This is a raw list, in some ways like the list you might
derive from a brainstorming session. Some of the items you
add will be crossed off on reflection. Others will prove to
duplicate items already on this or other lists. No harm. That
will become apparent when you stop to consider the items
you have added, which you certainly should make every
attempt to do daily. A caution—do not triumphantly excise
items as soon as you think they have been accomplished; all

too often you have accomplished only part of an item, or must verify later to make sure that something has, in fact, been accomplished. Premature excision can cause you to lose items; that is, at least, a bother, and sometimes can cause real problems.

Some managers carry these kinds of raw lists in their desk diaries. That may work for you, but the sheer mass of trivia often causes unnecessary duplication of a different kind, with many items carried over and rewritten day after day, until accomplished. On balance, it seems more efficient to carry the raw list separately, making or updating diary entries only if timing elements are involved, either from the start or at various stages of accomplishment. For example, "get haircut" will be part of a raw running list either until it is done or until you make an appointment to get it done. If done, it is removed from your list. If an appointment has been set, it leaves the running list and is put in place in your diary, at the time indicated. Similarly, "do marketing report by June 30" may first go on your undifferentiated running list and then, at the end of the day, be put on a separate project list. It will also be put into your diary, probably in more than one place, as you indicate not only the June 30 deadline but several timed milestones on the way to successful conclusion of the project.

Effective planning demands that projects be listed separately, not just in those raw and calendar lists through which they enter and are worked out within your planning system. No matter how active you may be, or how overworked you may feel, it should be possible to place every one of your substantial projects on a single ever-developing major planning list, with key elements and project status always in clear view.

And that project list must be viewed and reviewed continuously and critically, for that major planning list is one of the key differences between the entrepreneur and the time-server. It is a device through which you can place business, personal, and career-building tasks and goals side by side, all in one place, continuously evaluating progress, making connections that work for you, and setting and resetting your view of the context within which you are functioning.

A project list will certainly include "prepare marketing report" as well as "hire assistant" and "start budget workup." It will also include such skill-building items as "develop better computer literacy—explore AMA and other possible sources," and such career-development items as "become more active in association this year"; "cultivate Mary, Joe, Tom re: opening in Department X"; and "explore and consolidate executive recruiter contacts—weak here." This is a comprehensive, personal, and very private project list, and should be for your own eyes only.

Your project list should be all in one place, and if possible on one sheet of paper, to help you to reach and hold most easily a complete view of your personal situation and priorities. At the same time, it needs to contain outlines of the main tasks to be done to help make projects move along. That can usually be accomplished with a combination of your own abbreviations and appended materials as necessary. This is a list that provides an overview, but it is also a working list, and you must have enough detail to be able to note progress and revise as you go.

As a working list, your project list will indicate priorities, often by the order in which you place projects and also by your appended comments. Similarly, you will probably use such marks as asterisks and underlining to call attention to priority matters. Priorities change; so will those marks and comments.

You will need to provide yourself with a fresh copy of this list periodically, as your neat, clean copy gradually turns into a mass of hand-scribbled additions, updates, and excisions. How frequently you will need to do so will depend largely upon how actively you pursue your projects. Planning tools, like lists, are meant to be worked with. If any of your lists are as clean at the end of the week as at the beginning, your progress in the areas covered by those lists has probably been negligible.

The third kind of general list is the calendar, which may occur in such various forms as Day-at-a-Glance or Week-at-a-Glance desk diaries, pocket-sized appointment books, loose-leaf memo books, "pop-up" files or "ticklers," and desk and wall calendars. Whatever form or forms you use, you will want to provide ample space for note taking and changes, for the most efficient way to handle timed matters is to attempt to put them all together in one place. For example, a single page of a day-by-day desk diary, with one page for each day, may contain business appointments, personal appointments, deadlines and interim deadlines, personal and business trivia, and personal and business events, such as professional meetings, birthdays, trade shows, anniversaries, and due dates of several kinds.

With that kind of information in hand, all in one place, it becomes possible to do what should be done and to avoid the kind of surprise and dismay that so often occurs when you forget things important to others—and sometimes to yourself, too. That argues strongly for keeping a fair-size day-by-day desk diary, with enough space to hold all those items, and the accompanying inevitable mass of changes. You may also keep more complex tools, as dictated by preferences and job needs; some managers buy and use quite elaborate planning board devices as necessitated by their work, and tack many other items onto their planning boards. Some do use computers to help them master their timing needs, and expand such uses to include personal and business planning materials. Most of us, though, will find the desk diary enough—if we use it well and consistently.

That desk diary should travel with you, from home to road to office and back again. With you, and not in your luggage, by the way; its loss would be a small disaster. It is as much part of your personal equipment as a watch or glasses, and is far more important than either, for watches and glasses can easily be replaced. Note that it is wise for your

secretary or assistant to have a duplicate copy, carrying at
least your appointments, so that when you are away others
know your schedule.

MONITORING PROGRESS

The desk diary technique makes some extraordinarily important self-analysis possible, for it enables you to track
consistently how and with whom you spend your time. And
keeping track of your time on a regular basis is one of the
most valuable planning-related activities in which any manager can engage; it can help you convert or partially convert
a seeming whirlpool into a set of manageable sequences in
your company office and on the road, and help you maximize
productivity in your office at home.

Let us stress the central importance of consistency here.
As elsewhere, consistency is essential when you seek to turn
well-reasoned approaches into good management reflexes,
and repeated actions into habits. It really does not do to log
carefully your time at the office once in a while; to make a
few remedial moves to attempt to make better use of your
time; and then slowly to sink once again into a sea of trivial,
time-consuming chores and boring meetings that seem to
take up all available time. That is all too often the norm.
Repeated, it is disheartening and can become demoralizing.

In some ways, the counselors on time management may
be contributing to the problem, rather than the solution. The
difficulty lies in the complexity of the self-analytical material
and techniques offered, and the special attention that must
be paid to them. If, to manage your time effectively, you must
develop and learn how to use new and complex tools, replete
with forms and flowcharts, the odds are that you will not do
so. If complex materials are needed, then the odds are that
you will read a book, take a course, or both, and apply what
you have learned only very briefly, if at all. The application
will seem to help, though you will not be sure whether that is

because the techniques are helping or because you are momentarily paying close attention to time management matters. But it will not help enough for you to make the extra effort needed over a long period of time to develop it all into habit. It is usually too special, too complex, too time-consuming.

It is far more to the point to use a time-oriented tool already at your disposal for other purposes: your desk diary. If you develop the habit of noting in it precisely how you spend your time, day after day, throughout a career, you will be able to begin exercising as much control of your time as is possible in your specific circumstances, whatever your job, company, and personal contexts.

That means using your diary as both planner and time log, not only at your company office, but also at home, while traveling, and perhaps while commuting. Your whole time situation can come into proper focus when you record all your time expenditures; to record only what you do during your office working day is to miss much of your professional life.

It is impractical to suggest logging every minute of every day of the year, but it is entirely practical—indeed, vital—to do exactly that at stated periods throughout the year. You can very easily pick one week in each quarter of each year for close time logging, note those weeks in your diary at the beginning of each year, and then proceed in very orderly fashion to do just that, as the prescribed date pops up in your diary. That, too, is a good habit. If scheduled, it is anticipated and easy.

For most of the year, your diary will serve as a basic time log, if you get one that devotes at least a full page to each day, and breaks up the day hour by hour. During close time-logging periods, you may need a little more space than that, adding additional space and entries as necessary, or even keeping your time log separately. But do try to keep your time log in your diary, if at all possible, even during such periods, however you must compress your notes to do so.

No matter how long and consistently you record your time expenditures, you are likely to find each successive time log reevaluation rewarding and surprising. Very few of us really know how we spend our time, and most of us, when asked, will respond with substantially inaccurate estimates. When closely analyzed, "another day of boring meetings" generally turns out to have been a few mostly fruitless meeting hours, a few more hours on the telephone and in brief conversation with casual drop-ins, lunch, an hour or more fighting traffic, and an evening spent wrestling with moving inessential paper. Or "a day well spent" becomes a day in which as much as two or three hours were well spent, with the balance of the day following the routinely wasteful patterns above. Much of our most fruitful work is accomplished by a few seemingly almost random informal telephone calls, some brief face-to-face conversations, and a little quiet work with paper and print at home and office— even while the rest of the day's activities seem to have simply recirculated institutional debris. The time log, when studied carefully and consistently, shows it all quite clearly, helps us make connections, and begins to illuminate how to expand those small amounts of well-spent time in the company office, and how to develop the substantial blocks of time you need at home and office to really move matters ahead.

With your strategic goals in order, and a full personal and business project list before you, thoughtful time-log analysis can yield excellent—though not necessarily unpredictable—results. Most of us find ourselves wasting enormous amounts of time on trivial matters; spending far too little time on projects; barely touching some of our most important long-term strategic goals, particularly in career and skills-building areas; and tending to fill our personal lives with the same kinds of trivial business matters that occupy so much of our workdays. No matter that much of the trivia is generated by the institutions in which we are to some extent encased and the people with whom we are surrounded; our job is to manage our time and work so as to minimize that waste and maximize both effectiveness and the satisfactions to be gained from living rewarding personal lives.

That takes a great deal of thought and attention, and often necessitates sharp limitation of some kinds of time demands placed upon us by our situations and by others. All the personal planning, replanning, listing, relisting, logging, and analysis we have been discussing takes much valuable time, and it is in the long run only worthwhile if it can be made to pay. That requires a good deal of action, some of it not always immediately acceptable to those around you.

Much of it requires controlling the seemingly uncontrollable, in a sense taking a "zero-based" approach to the items and activities that fill your normal working day. That is nowhere more apparent than in the area of telephone control.

TELEPHONE CONTROL

Telephone control? It seems unlikely; most of us spend hours on the phone every day, no matter how hard we try not to do so. There always seem to be dozens of calls that really must be taken, from superiors, allies, aggrieved customers, government regulators, lawyers, accountants, consultants, subordinates with very real emergencies, husbands, wives, children, lovers, friends—and the plumber working on a plugged drain in your house who has just inadvertently severed the oil line leading to your furnace and is ankle-deep in the thick oil that is now flowing into your basement office at home.

More than anything else, it is the telephone that fractures the day and creates the whirlpool effect that so characterizes the office life of many otherwise effective managers. There is the call that will take "just a moment," and instead takes 15 minutes or even more, or the seeming emergency that causes you to make several calls of your own and forces a couple of quick, informal, unanticipated meetings before you determine that it was not really an emergency, or the

five phone calls that you must make to set up a meeting—
except that before you are done, you have called each of the
five people you seek an average of twice before you and they
actually spoke; have found yourself juggling six schedules,
including your own, to set up your meeting; and have spent
more time setting up the meeting than the meeting itself will
take.

It is not just the company office day that can be fractured
by the telephone. Many managers spend a good deal of time
on the phone at home, as well, talking with people in far-
away time zones and others who are unavailable during
normal company office hours. A necessary late-afternoon
call from a co-worker in California, following a day-long
meeting with a customer or vendor, will reach you in a New
York office long after the close of business for the day, and
must be taken at home. But so will an unnecessary call from
a subordinate who has managed to see an emergency where
none exists.

You will not control the telephone completely; not if you
are a good professional, who understands that some literally
uncontrollable matters must be dealt with in timely fashion to
be dealt with effectively. But most managers can succeed in
significantly cutting the amount of time they spend on the
telephone, and in controlling when that time is spent, so that
scattered calls do not effectively dominate much of each
working day.

No matter how effective you are once on the phone, all is
lost unless you are first able to exercise some measure of
control over which incoming calls you will respond to and
when. The worst reflex you can develop, unless your entire
work consists of handling a large volume of calls, is to hear
the phone ring, automatically pick it up, and speak your
name into it, thereby identifying yourself to your caller and
opening yourself up to whatever then comes over the phone
before you even know who is calling, much less what the call
is about.

In your company office, by far the best way to handle
incoming calls is to very carefully train your assistant or
secretary—and each succeeding assistant as necessary—to

take your calls; find out who is calling and if possible what about; handle what can be handled without your involvement; take messages if you are unavailable; and put the remainder through to you—then or later—only after consulting you. That is standard, rather old-fashioned operating procedure. What is astonishing is that so many managers adhere to it in theory but not in practice. It is appalling, for example, to see an otherwise competent manager wait for someone to pick up a ringing phone, and then along about the fourth or fifth ring, shrug apologetically and pick up the telephone. What has happened is that a secretary or assistant is on some sort of errand down the hall, or perhaps is out for the day, and backup arrangements, if any, have broken down. Or an assistant is on another line, and has not yet picked up this incoming call. Then the great American telephone reflex takes over, and a manager, who should no more be picking up an unscreened call than going out to sit at the reception desk, picks up the phone, says, "Jane Smith," and enters into what may be a wholly unnecessary, distracting, and time-splintering discussion.

Train others to pick up the phone and screen your calls. Provide for adequate backup, so that someone is highly likely to be available for at least pickup and some screening at all times. Build the availability of such backup into your office setup plans. Avoid the very private, nicely isolated office setup, with corridors and doorways ensuring that, if your assistant is not available to pick up an incoming call, no one else will be able to get to it in time.

If no one but you is available to answer an incoming call, and you are not expecting an important one, let the telephone ring. Don't answer it. Indeed, develop a non-answering reflex, no matter how disagreeable that may be to you while you are learning not to pick up reflexively. That may be difficult. Most of us are so habituated that we regard any ringing, unanswered telephone as an abomination to be avoided at all costs. Develop the nonanswering reflex, anyway, however difficult it may be. It is very much worth the effort.

If your telephone system comes through an internal

operator and switchboard, your failure to answer the ringing telephone should be picked up by the operator and your caller asked to replace the call, or, if your office is so organized, your operator should take the message and convey it to you. Either way, an adequate screening device exists. That is usually also true if you are part of a telephone system that supplies you with a unique number and allows outside calls to come directly to you. In that instance, unanswered outside calls are normally, after a specified number of rings, switched back to the company switchboard, and handled there.

Internally generated calls, however, just ring and ring, until the caller gets tired of waiting and hangs up. The unanswered internal caller may be your immediate superior, or perhaps your company president with a magnificent new job for you; nevertheless, do not pick it up unscreened as long as you have something better to do, as you almost always will. Internal calls can be extraordinarily time-consuming and unproductive, for a great many of them concern matters that can easily be handled directly by your assistant, or that should be directed elsewhere.

Your assistant will need to know which calls are routinely to be treated as priority calls, and in what order of priority. That knowledge will come with experience, but in the early stages you can help by preparing a list of priority callers. There will also be temporary priority callers; you should inform your assistant if priority calls are expected. Beyond these standard and temporary priority callers, standard operating procedure should be that all calls are to be carefully screened and handled, whenever reasonably possible, by your assistant. It can happen that an overzealous and perhaps empire-building assistant may shield you too much; that does not invalidate the working assumption, but rather obliges you to clarify what calls you want.

Among the calls you do take, many will be properly referred to others. Some will be referred back to your assistant, perhaps with special instructions, and many to other people within and outside your organization. Effective referral demands knowing enough about a matter to refer it properly; effective time conservation demands going no further with a discussion than you need to go. There is little point in pursuing a matter once you know that it will be referred elsewhere, particularly if that referral will be to another fully responsible manager. If the referral is to your assistant, however, and the matter is not routine, you may want to go a little further, on the theory that your assistant may later need some help in handling the matter.

Many—all too many—calls start out small and grow. And once started the temptation is to keep on talking, so that you will not have to go over the ground all over again on a return call, with the hazard of making several tries before reconnecting. That is an entirely valid approach and set of concerns. On the other hand, an unplanned half-hour call may scramble a considerable section of your day, even though it is physically possible at the moment. There is no easy rule or trick to handling this one; your decision as to whether to break off and call back later will rest upon the circumstances of the moment, the importance of the matter, and who the caller is, in terms of organizational position and probable later availability. All other things being relatively equal, however, it may be useful to lean in the direction of the return call, if you see early that a call is likely to expand; you may even prefer to schedule a quick, informal face-to-face meeting. Either way, you will then be better able to do it at your convenience, and therefore with minimum adverse impact on your activities.

TELEPHONE HANDLING

We spend so much time on the telephone that we tend to ignore the fact that it is far more difficult to communicate effectively by telephone than face to face. The telephone robs us of the ability to communicate nonverbally as well as verbally; face to face, our "body language" very often carries the main burden of communication, especially when our main aims are motivating and persuading others, as is so often true for managers. In other periods, that caused many managers to talk far too long, in an attempt to use an inherently inferior instrument as an effective substitute for face-to-face communication. But today's pressures have caused many modern American managers to develop quite different telephone-handling problems. They become terse, and even combative, in their attempts to cut the time they spend on the telephone. It is not at all unusual for a harried, otherwise skilled manager to respond to a routine opening, "How are you?" with a sharp, "Very busy," which is guaranteed to start any conversation off on the wrong foot. The rationale for this kind of error is usually attempted telephone time control; in fact, the manager who does this sort of thing has no control, and piles insulting telephone behavior on top of inability to manage time effectively. It is far better not to take the call and to call back when you have full command of your faculties and can conduct a conversation with common courtesy. Poor and unskilled telephone behavior conveys lack of control to others. It also clearly conveys the message that you care neither about others nor about how you look to others. It can be, and is for many, a career-harming reflex; as such it should be carefully avoided. It is also simply discourteous; the old axiom has it quite correctly that those who give no respect deserve no respect.

Skilled, courteous telephone handling gets things done and also builds careers. We cannot meet face to face with even a large fraction of those with whom we work on the telephone; time and geography preclude that. Sound professional managers must limit access to themselves by telephone and intelligently plan their own calls, but when they do get on the telephone they must handle it well.

That starts with getting the mechanics right. The telephone instrument should be placed to the left of those who write with their right hands, and vice versa, with the wire coming from that side, rather than trailing over your desk from the wrong side and impeding your prime reading and writing area. Writing materials and desk diary should be next to your writing hand, rather than requiring you to stretch every time you want to write during a telephone conversation. The telephone instrument should be easily reached, held a few inches away from your mouth, and you should speak into it naturally and easily, rather than raising your voice. If you find it comfortable, by all means get a shoulder cradle that lets you have your hands free, or a desk microphone, that lets you speak and listen without using a receiver, if you find one that works well enough. Such advice is simple and basic, certainly. But it is honored only in theory by many thousands of managers, who pay less attention to organizing the mechanics of personal telephone handling than they do to buying a tennis racket, even though they spend hundreds of hours each year on the telephone.

Beyond mechanics, it is vital to realize that your telephone is an extension of your persona, an instrument through which you convey who and what you are. It is simple enough to respond to "How are you?" courteously, and move into either business or personal talk with something like, "Well, thank you. And you? How are things going down there?" Your tone, your verbal pace, and the nature of your responses will convey your attitude toward caller and conversation very well, if you take the trouble to cultivate good reflexes. The length of the call will depend on what you and your caller are trying to accomplish; if you seem to be going further afield than you wish, one or both of you will have to take the call back on track. With the basic communication established, you can usually shorten the call without damaging its usefulness.

When on the line with a time-waster—more often than not someone who has been a time-waster on other occasions—you are likely to know it rather quickly. That is when you make it clear that you are late for a meeting, or working on a deadline, or whatever it takes to close the conversation courteously and firmly. A caution here, though—some seeming time-wasters need listening to and drawing out. There are really no rules in this area, but rather the "feel" you develop with good reflexes, and your persona on straight.

Impatience and frustration are the great enemies of effective telephone handling, because of the inadequacy of the instrument. It is so much harder to communicate effectively by telephone than face to face, and it often takes so much longer, that it is quite natural for both impatience and frustration to develop and be inadvertently communicated, so that it then acts as a bar to further communication. Brevity is a virtue on the telephone, but only when something can be briefly communicated, as when a fact is asked for and supplied, or a meeting date is agreed upon. When brevity acts to abort effective communication, it often would have been better had no communication been attempted at all.

That is one of the reasons it is desirable to "stack" outgoing calls; the other key reason being, of course, that stacking allows for far more efficient use of your time than the kind of occasional and periodic calling that can make hash of your working day. Many calls need not be taken as received, but can be very efficiently held, categorized, and returned in orderly fashion at a time of your own choosing. No, not between four and five in the afternoon; if everyone stacked calls and made them at the same time, everyone's telephone would be busy at the same time and nobody's calls would get through. And not all together, once a day. But it is desirable to pick one to three blocks of time, depending on the day's other needs, and make your return calls then.

When you do set out to return calls, and to make some kinds of other outgoing calls, it will be useful to make them in priority order. That is very easily accomplished if the incoming calls are taken on individual slips of paper or cards. Standard operating procedure should, in most instances, be for your assistant to make the calls in sequence, as you indicate that the call you are on will soon be over; an experienced assistant working near an open door to your office will come to know that without an indication from you, or a buzz from you inside a closed office can indicate when it is time to place the next call. Many calls you return will not result in conversations, which can result in a kind of telephone ping-pong, as you and your caller go back and forth trying to make contact. That is an annoyance; it is also

unavoidable. Having your assistant make the calls can help
save you that kind of time-consuming nuisance.

Some of us routinely make calls we should not be making, as when we do a round robin of calls trying to set up a
meeting. It is well worth the time to train an assistant to make
those kinds of calls, as well as a wide range of information-
seeking calls. For example, most managers know enough to
train others to make their travel arrangements. Some do
not—an elementary error. The manager who routinely
spends valuable time making travel arrangements has developed a reflex well worth excising.

A surprisingly large number of managers do not return
their calls for days and days. That is pressure. There often
does not seem to be enough time to return them all. Wrong;
as wrong as can be. There is always time to return calls in
timely fashion—but you do not always have to return them
personally. It is relatively easy and very efficient to train an
assistant to attempt to return all calls before the end of each
working day. The system will fail only when your assistant is
unexpectedly out for the day and your backup is untrained
for this kind of activity. Your assistant will be able to handle
some kinds of return calls directly, as when the caller seeks
available information or requires referral elsewhere. If your
assistant cannot handle a matter, you can then call later or
the next day. When you are unable or unwilling to return a
call that day, and your assistant cannot handle it, the caller
can be told that you will be unable to return the call today,
but will try to call tomorrow.

All of the foregoing can add up to a significant measure
of telephone control, which is so essential if you are to
exercise some control over your working life. It all requires
time, attention, training, and the assiduous cultivation of
good working reflexes; it is well worth all that, for without
considerable telephone control your working life is indeed
likely to become a whirlpool.

Your office-at-home telephone requires control, as well.
Without close control and careful handling, your business
calls at home can both damage your personal life and frag-
ment those large blocks of time that are an essential compo-

nent of your working life as a professional manager. It is not difficult to prevent an uncontrolled flow of business calls into your home, calls that must be answered by you or other members of your family at times that may be very, very inconvenient. That is where a separate line that rings only in your home office and an answering machine is so valuable. Together they can completely insulate your family from your business calls, guarantee that the time you need is kept inviolate, and make it possible for you to take calls only when you wish, stacking the rest and returning them at your own convenience.

Get a machine that can be set to ring only once; better yet, look for one that can be set not to ring at all. And get one with a monitoring device, so that you can listen to incoming calls if you wish, and decide whether or not to pick up before the caller finishes putting a message on your machine. Don't worry about people who are uneasy about talking to answering machines; they are fewer and fewer, especially in the business world. You may also want to get a machine with a remote device, so that you can call from outside for messages without bothering your family or depending on family members to be home when you call.

Telephone control is one very significant aspect of what must be a lifelong drive to control the seemingly uncontrollable, to manage effectively in what can all too easily become a maelstrom of ringing telephones and demanding people, an avalanche of meetings, and a storm of paper, punctuated by frequent, exhausting business trips, themselves maelstroms of vehicles, hotels, meals, meetings, telephones, paper, and people. Effective telephone control succeeds in significantly limiting and organizing your exposure to others.

OFFICE CONTROL

It is equally vital to exercise control in face-to-face situations. We spend most of our company office working days awash in a sea of people; our effectiveness as managers depends in large measure upon our ability to swim well in that sea.

As with the telephone, you must find the way to control—and that usually means to limit—the timing and extent of others' access to you. It is useful to have an "open door policy" most of the time, signalled quite literally by keeping your office door open, but that cannot be allowed to mean that anyone can come through that office door at any time and expect to have your full attention for as long as it takes to discuss whatever business or personal matter is on his or her mind. To have any real chance of working well, an open door policy cannot mean a wide-open-door; it works best as something much more like a half-open-door policy.

Your assistant can be of some help in this area, but cannot provide the kind of tight screening that is possible on incoming telephone messages. The effectiveness of the half-open-door policy depends mostly on your behavior, your positioning inside your own office, the body language you use to signal receptivity or something less than that, and, if necessary, the firmness with which you indicate that, at least for the moment, the open door is about to close.

Physical positioning itself can mean a good deal. It is nice to be able to see whoever comes to your office door, but not if it means that anyone passing by can also see you, and make an on-the-spot estimate that you are relatively unoccupied and available for a discussion of yesterday's meeting or tennis game. Try to place yourself so that you can see, but others cannot see you without coming through your door and actually into your office. If that is not possible, try to place yourself so that you do not directly face your office door, especially so that no one passing by will be able to make eye contact with you easily and then move into your office. Your aim in having an open-door policy is to make yourself accessible to your co-workers when appropriate; the half-open-door policy aims at discouraging the casual, often time-wasting visit.

Your assistant can do some screening, if you make it clear by a consistently conveyed attitude that you really are not available for time-wasting trivia, although always available for all else that matters. Very few people habitually burst into the offices of those who have made it clear that

casual, undirected drop-ins are not appreciated. It becomes
quite natural for an incoming, unexpected visitor to stop at
your assistant's desk and ask if you are available. And a
competent, well-trained assistant will soon come to know
whom to wave on in, and whom to call you about. Such
screening will probably not apply to your closest associates,
however. You and they will have to work out relationships
and priorities according to your own special circumstances.

Once a conversation has started, how it goes depends
upon how you handle it, both verbally and in terms of body
language. If someone comes to you with a matter that you
agree should be taken up on the spot, your attitude and
conversation will make that clear. If someone starts a discussion you quickly see should be handled at a different time, or
elsewhere, you will say so, with little need for subtlety. But if
a conversation is started that you want to discourage, your
attitude, as expressed by your body language, will have to
carry the burden of extricating you from the situation for, in a
way, any overt rejection of a co-worker is a handling defeat.
You and your colleagues have to live and work together;
beyond that, what is raised today may be trivial and time-
wasting, but what is raised tomorrow may be essential. That,
after all, is what the open-door policy is all about; we cannot
consistently discourage others from coming to us and still
hope to manage well.

Rarely, very rarely, confrontation may be necessary.
There are people who just go on and on, and will not take a
hint, no matter how many times and how openly it is conveyed. But it is safe to assume that, if you are faced again and
again with situations in which you ultimately lose patience
and must openly or nearly openly ask people to leave, the
problem is yours. The odds are that you are conveying—
perhaps quite unintentionally—considerable interest with
face and body, even while you think you are conveying your
desire to return to work, and the conflicting signals you are
generating are probably causing the problem.

Once a half-open-door policy is firmly established and all
know what to expect from you in this area, there is no harm

at all in physically closing that office door occasionally. Although managers must expect to do a great deal of planning, writing, and reading away from their company offices, sometimes it is very desirable to "lock yourself up," take no calls, and generally behave as if you are not even on the premises. When you do decide to do that, though, be sure to have someone outside, ready to handle the telephone and physically repel face-to-face boarders. There are those, after all—and they are often located just down the hall or up on the next floor—who will call once or twice, become frustrated because no one is picking up, and then come charging around to transact whatever business they had in mind. Far better for your peace of mind and your peer relationships to have your assistant available to take calls and arrange for later callbacks.

At home, it is a little different, especially when children are involved. There, it makes sense in most instances for the policy to be a closed-door policy. You must be flexible, of course; when a child cuts a finger and you are the only adult in the house, you will want to be summoned, no matter what you are working on. It is wise to want your family to know about your work, the more the better, but that is best accomplished at times of your choosing, when there is ample time to explain, answer questions, and relate your working life to theirs. A closed-door policy, a separate telephone line, and an answering machine can together play a substantial role in making both work at home and family life happy and productive.

PEOPLE PICKING

Underlying all attempts to control the seemingly uncontrollable aspects of a working life in management is the need to develop, maintain, and grow effective working relationships. That is a lifelong need, having everything to do with finding the ways to free your own creative energy and that of those around you, and then moving that energy into appropriate

channels. To a considerable extent, that need antedates and
provides much of the basis for profit and growth.

It has very little to do with *people handling,* especially
with that construct's inevitable manipulative connotations.
Nor does it have much to do with *negotiation* and *persuasion,*
two of today's most widely discussed and thoroughly misused
techniques. People handling, negotiation, and persuasion
are the language of manipulation, of covert and overt confrontation, and directly oppose the creation of increasingly
effective group endeavor. For no matter how vital it is to
build your own career, move ahead independently, and plan
to take care of yourself and those you love, it is also vital to
work well with others to conceive, reach, and exceed organizational goals. In the private sector, there is no real personal
possibility without growth and profit. In the public and nonprofit sectors, there is no real personal possibility without the
building of excellent, goal-satisfying organizations.

On the working-with-people side, an excellent professional manager has to be a sound people-picker, good
trainer, motivating leader, and skilled organization-devel-
oper, who can and does work well with peers and superiors
as well as with subordinates. Tall order; you can be a pretty
good manager without having all those qualities and skills.
But you will not be an excellent manager unless you have
them all. You may indeed be highly successful, though sadly
deficient in your people relationships, but the odds are
against that.

Far and away the most important of all the people skills
is to be a good people-picker—not just a good hirer, though
that is essential, but also a good picker of advisors, superiors,
and peers, with whom you mean to spend a working and
mutually supportive lifetime, perhaps in one place but more
likely through a succession of affiliations.

As we discuss in Chapter 9, job seeking is in considerable part a selling process. Not entirely; you choose as well as
being chosen. Seen from the other side of the table, when
you hire subordinates and associates to work with you, you
are involved in a buying process, which relies for success

partly upon any personnel specialists who may screen for you, but largely upon your own buying skills. You screen, or have others screen, for work history and demonstrated skills—for track record. But once those basics are established, you must assess compatibility with yourself and the others in your group, for each new personality and set of skills changes your group. Substantial abrasive possibilities are a red flag; other qualifications and potential benefits must be very large if personality problems or the probability of group disruption clearly exists.

Key elements to consider are work history, track record, compatibility, high energy level, intelligence, will to win (otherwise called motivation), entrepreneurial approach, skepticism—and above all integrity. We hire managers and assistants for the qualities we respect in ourselves, and try as hard as we can to hold them by supplying considerable opportunities for advancement.

We also hire within the pool of possibilities we find, for we hire in a real world. That does not mean settling too soon for someone less suitable than we had hoped for; it often does mean settling for someone we think stands a good chance of learning how to do the job we want done, rather than someone who can do that job superbly from the start. It should never mean hiring someone clearly unsuitable, no matter how shorthanded and overworked you and others in your group are. That only guarantees throwing good time after bad, wasted training time after failed hiring time. It is far better to work shorthanded than to bring in people highly unlikely to work out.

Much the same skills are brought to hiring as to job seeking; in personal terms, hiring is job seeking in reverse. You seek the widest range of qualified applicants; derive as much information and insight as you can before and during face-to-face interviews; reach for emphathetic understanding of the applicant; attempt to assess the benefits that hiring an applicant can bring; soberly assess possible drawbacks; and ultimately compare a few remaining applicants and go on to make a decision to hire or not.

At the end of the process, that applicant who has "sold" you successfully will seem the logical or even the inevitable choice for the job. But it is here that people-picking skills and experience count most. It is wise to take a deep breath, and take enough time to make a sober and at least relatively objective decision. With the process completed, everything you have learned about the applicant can still only help limit possible errors; in the end the positive decision rests upon your "feel" of the applicant and situation. People picking can be learned, but it is extremely difficult to teach. If you go for integrity, skeptical intelligence, basic abilities, and probable compatibility, you will seldom go wrong. Beyond that, sound people picking in hiring is largely a matter of the accretion of closely examined experience.

Those key qualities are wisely sought in associates as well as subordinates. A career web is a network of like-minded, compatible people; it works well in the long run only if many of them are also effective, growing professionals, so that all in the web can move ahead more or less together over the years. Similarly, a superior who can be pushed along and who will simultaneously pull you along is the kind of person most desirable to work with. You should carefully choose and cultivate your network of associates throughout your career rather than allowing accidental associations to play too important a role in your working life.

Training and Holding Good People

Beyond people picking, there is the matter of training. As in all teaching, training is a matter of time, patience, skill, and providing a model to emulate: you. If you habitually apply your skeptical intelligence to the task of finding the right questions to ask, so will those who report to you—if you encourage them to do so. On the other hand, if you lead not by example, but by pronouncement, you are quite likely to find yourself leading a group of bland time-servers and failing.

Finding good people may be extraordinarily difficult, as

we all know so well. All too often, we must settle for someone who has a little less potential than we had hoped for, after scores of potential applicants have been screened by others for us or seen personally. But whether we find someone exceptional—that is, a competent self-starter—or someone a little less promising, it is extraordinarily important to put in the time needed to train and develop new people. Unfortunately, time is usually in shortest supply when new people have just been brought on. That is true whether your former assistant or subordinate is staying on long enough to train someone new or whether you have had a break between people and must train the newcomer entirely by yourself. Either way, for the first couple of months you are likely to be spending what seems like far too much of your limited office time training a new person on routine paper-, people-, and telephone-handling matters, and will be unable to delegate much of the work you are accustomed to delegating.

It is worth it, though. More than that, in the long run it is vital for you to have competent and experienced people around you, people who in many ways can act as an extension of your persona on a wide range of matters. At the same time you must know well which matters you should be handling yourself. That is standard wisdom, but in today's working world it is wisdom all too often ignored. Too many American managers have developed a sort of shell-shocked negative reflex as to the possibility of getting and holding the kind of people who make a real training and developing effort worthwhile. It goes something like, "If you are going to have to spend many relatively unproductive months every year training new people, and never get to where you can really begin to reap the benefits of the time you spend training, why bother?"

And so many don't bother, rationalizing their foolish expediency by telling themselves that there is no point in trying. Wrong? Yes, obviously. But it is also quite a widespread attitude. It results in self-fulfilling prophecy. The ill-trained person is bored and ineffectual, learns little, complains much, and soon moves on, while the manager who has not done the training job glumly interviews all over again, and inveighs against the current state of the business world.

There are no easy answers here, no way to secure an unending supply of bright, self-starting, overqualified people who will stay on for two-score years. For nearly a century, many extremely competent women were trapped in subordinate office roles when they were well qualified to move into more responsible positions after a few years. No more. Our world has begun to move more toward equality in the workplace. But it is still possible to find and hold good people for some years, if you take the time and trouble to nurture and appreciate them, emotionally, organizationally, and financially. That means training them, helping them develop their educations inside and outside the company, raising their pay in place, and finding ways to promote them internally when they are ready, after using them to train their successors.

One of the main ways you will hold good people, and at the same time derive truly enormous benefits from their activities, is to begin to delegate responsibilities to them as soon as is reasonably possible, and expand those responsibilities in a planned way throughout their tenure with you. No, that is not to be freely translated as, "Load them with work!" That is all too often the net result; but when that happens without adequate training and preparation, you only guarantee failure, and the delegated work is returned to you often mishandled and requiring much time to redo.

When you delegate, you hand over something that is essentially your responsibility—or your trivial chore, for that matter—and look forward to being informed or check to see that it was done, and done well. Delegation has nothing to do with permanent shifts of responsibility. If you have worked it properly, however, many kinds of matters that are your responsibility may be done by others for years on end, and such confidence may develop that your checking is minimal, as is their need to inform you that all is going well.

That is especially true of a good assistant. For a good assistant will control the telephone, and will gradually take over such matters as arranging meetings, securing information, checking timely receipt of reports and expense statements, handling travel arrangements, and holding the fort on all kinds of miscellaneous matters when you are on the road or vacationing. It is when all those things are happening that even repeated training and development time turns out to have been worthwhile.

That is, of course, the essence of motivational leadership; it is what all the many theories in this area boil down to. Similarly, this consistent pattern of training and delegation, which releases the creative energies of those around you, is basic to the development of your own closely knit, superbly functioning organizational unit, which is often at the heart of success in management.

MEETING CONTROL

No list of seeming uncontrollables in a manager's life would be complete without meetings. Meetings at breakfast, in trains and automobiles on the way to the office, in the morning, at lunch, in the afternoon, over drinks after office hours, at dinner, by telephone during the evenings, on weekends, in gyms, at country clubs, sometimes even in washrooms, when participants are all of the same sex. Life in an extraordinarily large number of American companies and other institutions seems to be composed of a little office time and an unending series of meetings, some of which accomplish a little, and most of which seem to accomplish nothing perceptible at all.

Some meetings are necessary; not many. Meetings are to some extent matters of style and organizational structure, reflecting top management's organizational approaches. To an even greater extent, however, their quantity and lack of quality are more attributable to bureaucratic ineptitude than to design.

Yes, bureaucratic ineptitude; yours, too, if you habitually initiate and carry through large numbers of worthless meetings over the years. It is very easy to call a meeting

when you do not really have a plan, or are too lazy or
unskilled to think through and write an explanatory memo. It
is even easier to go along with scores of meetings called by
others so as not to "make waves" by resisting the worthless
meeting. And it is easiest of all to call or go to a meeting that
has been ill-prepared and can therefore come only to
naught, even though it might have been useful if well prepared. Why bother to prepare for a meeting if no one else
will, and if the meeting is therefore bound to come to nothing? Clearly, the prophecy becomes self-fulfilling, setting a
disastrous bureaucratic pattern that is very, very hard to
change.

Several kinds of meetings are wholly unobjectionable, if
adequately prepared for. Such ceremonial affairs as stock-
holders' and board of directors' meetings must be held at
stated periods, and can serve useful organizational functions. Wholly informational meetings, such as those to orient
new employees or introduce a new pension plan, are often
indispensable adjuncts to written materials supplied, and
allow useful discussion of matters that should be discussed,
rather than confined to one-way communication on paper.
Periodic sales meetings, which so often combine exhortation,
carnival, information, and training, can be necessary and
useful, if they use management time productively, rather
than being loaded with management people who yawn their
way through—and often bore—the very salespeople they
are supposed to be motivating, informing, and training.

It is also true that some of these kinds of meetings can be
time-consuming and at least seemingly fruitless. It is more
than annoying to spend two weeks preparing a major presentation to a board of directors, only to find upon entering
the meeting that your allotted time has been cut from 45 to 15
minutes, and then to be told after 10 minutes that everything
is fine and the chairman of the board has a plane to catch
back to Minneapolis or Chicago or wherever the home office
(and perhaps the chairman's country club) is located. More
than annoying—but less than a disaster. Those who are
seemingly ignored are very often those in rather good condi-

tion; those who face tough questioning are more likely those in trouble.

Is This Meeting Necessary?

There are two kinds of meetings that cause the most trouble, however, and make the day, week, and year seem to be an unending series of meetings: the periodic meetings held because they "should" be held periodically, and the working meetings that do not work. Both waste huge amounts of valuable and irreplaceable time. Most meetings that "should" be held should not. Some working meetings can be made to work; most cannot. For most working meetings that do work, the tasks would have been handled more economically and efficiently without any meetings at all, or with the barest minimum of expended meeting time. Many of the few meetings that work do so because some or all of the participants have settled most of the main questions before ever stepping into the meeting room.

What does all that add up to? That some periodic and working meetings may be desirable and a few even necessary, but that an effective manager's working assumption should be that the burden of proving the desirability or necessity of a meeting rests heavily on whoever initiates that meeting. In modern management jargon, that is a "zero-based" approach to each meeting, and to the general question of the desirability of meetings within each organization. A previous generation of managers called it asking the question, "Is this meeting necessary?"

Take, for example, the Monday morning meeting, so dearly beloved and almost wholly unexamined by some generations of American managers. The truth is that it is almost guaranteed to start the week with a yawn, and that it normally accomplishes the precise opposite of its organizer's main intention. For instead of focusing all attention sharply on main priorities, informing everyone equally so that sharp focus can be achieved, and motivating everyone to move ahead with verve and "team spirit," that meeting normally merely succeeds in delaying the start of the work week for all participants and most of their subordinates and assistants while thoroughly familiar matters are reviewed ad nauseam.

The number of times in any year that the initiator of a Monday morning meeting comes in with a new insight that will galvanize everyone into frenetic and productive activity usually may be counted on the fingers of one closed fist. Open the hand and a vehicle exists for counting the number of times anything really new and interesting is discussed, from any source. Sometimes information is conveyed; almost always the information is better conveyed in writing. Sometimes clarifying discussion is needed; far better to accomplish that in place, as needed, during the week. Monday morning is the least likely time of the week for illuminating discussion of any kind.

Yet, the team is gathered; the meeting is held, again and again . . . and again. The verbose discuss, the climbers do their best to demonstrate promotable virtue, and the effective wonder what in the world they are doing there. What indeed?

One of the most interesting and revealing things about the Monday morning meeting and other such routine meetings is that, once examined, it becomes clear that no elaborate mechanisms are needed to replace them. No time-consuming long memos; no series of short but cumulatively long and wearing meetings with subordinates and peers; no unending series of telephone calls and difficult face-to-face conferences because of the problems caused by the uninformed. None of these; only a work week that works better because some of the routine meetings cluttering it up are gone, as are many of the subsequent meetings heretofore generated by those routine meetings. Make no mistake about it; meetings generate meetings, rather than in any way diminishing the need for them. You do not eliminate many smaller meetings by getting everybody together periodically. Instead, you greatly increase the need for additional meetings—and for that matter, for more informal contacts and memos.

The "lean" companies now becoming so much a part of the American corporate scene are instructive in that regard. They tend to be lean of necessity, unfortunately; many would be operating in far less adverse circumstances than they now do if they had been lean by design in good times, and thereby more profitable and readier to meet and successfully deal with more difficult times. In such companies, there are fewer managers than there used to be, and when fewer people are all charged with doing more than they used to do, somehow the need for the routine meetings seems to disappear. Monday mornings tend to start with a hard charge instead of a dull and fruitless meeting. The ten-minute coffee break and walk down the hall become an informal and quite productive meeting. Decisions tend to be made by those who must make them, with informing memos circulated after the fact; some possibilities for abrasion exist here, but nothing that cannot be handled well by skilled people in a hurry. There are fewer consultants around to meet with, if only because there is not so much money available to pay them. Likewise, there are fewer interviews, meetings, follow-up meetings, extended reports, and "final" meetings that only serve to generate more committees and more meetings after the consultants have gone. There are far fewer ad hoc committees and task forces, with their voracious hunger for management time, and their tendency to generate meetings that discuss previous meetings and prepare for more meetings. And, as a practical, and sometimes personally very regrettable fact, there are fewer staff people; with fewer staff people, there are fewer meetings, for the very nature of staff work generates assignments that, in turn, generate meetings—large quantities of meetings.

Meetings That Don't Work

Ah, the ad hoc committees and task forces! And the working parties, conference calls, brainstorming sessions— all that passes for participatory management, while chewing up enormous amounts of valuable time in working meetings that don't work. Much of the descriptive jargon is taken from military and political bureaucracies; the activity it describes is equally unproductive there, unless it is used in some of its original senses. A task force, for example, will probably be capable of making a serious attempt to carry out its given objectives, if it is—as originally intended—a substantial body of warships setting out to engage an enemy battle fleet or to scar what had once been a lovely island in the South Pacific. But if it is a group of harried managers asked to investigate the possibility of "getting the company into" some new line of business, it is quite likely to be dead in the water shortly after inception, having started with imprecise objectives generated by muddy thinking.

This is usually the root problem with meetings that don't work. You cannot get to your destination unless you find out and state precisely, very early in the game, where you want to go. Then you need to develop a sound set of ideas— working hypotheses, in jargon—as to how to get there, and a very, very precise idea as to who is charged with the responsibility of leading the way. You cannot go about it halfheartedly, either; a great deal of skill and preparation are needed before and alongside conversation. Without that, the conversation is empty; it all goes nowhere.

As in so many other areas of activity, people going into a meeting or series of meetings must, first of all, think that something can be accomplished. That basic belief is so often absent that it is sometimes hard to perceive as a live necessity. An extraordinarily large number of American managers are shell-shocked when it comes to working meetings, and enter them with precisely the wrong self-fulfilling presumption: that the meeting is "just another," and that the only business that really counts will occur outside the meeting room. For most of us, whether we admit it or not, even to ourselves, meetings are to be endured rather than made to work.

The only way to radically change that destructive notion is to initiate far fewer working meetings than we routinely do; to think about and prepare for them far better than we normally do; and to make a far higher percentage of them work to achieve objectives that are seen far more clearly than is usual. Clearly, that is an unlikely prescription for American management, in an environment still largely characterized by "fat" company thinking and with tens of thousands of instant staff people, rather than embryo working managers, being turned out of our business schools every year. But it can be done, and is very much worth trying to accomplish.

Hard, original thinking is very seldom done in groups, any more than good painting is done by committee. That is particularly true as regards the working hypotheses from which basic working meeting objectives are drawn. Putting it a little differently, successful task forces, working parties, ad hoc committees, and the like—groups aiming to achieve a desired end—are in most instances going to depend heavily on the hard premeeting thought of a single initiator, whether that thinking comes to the group directly or is filtered through a previous group. Six people sitting down together to consider a fuzzy hypothesis, or hardly any hypothesis at all, are highly unlikely to be able to develop a sound hypothesis to explore. Generally they proceed to engage themselves in a series of terribly wasteful meetings aimed at developing one or more such hypotheses, unless they assign one or more of their number to do so, which should have been done before the first meeting was ever called.

But a working hypothesis is often harder to achieve after, rather than before, a group is called together. People come to a meeting with perceived and partly perceived interests, and therefore with unspoken and often only partly perceived agendas of their own. The term most in use for this right now is *hidden agenda,* but that term is rather misleading, since it implies a well-thought-out alternative agenda and set of goals. In practice, these rarely exist. At most corporate and other institutional meetings, lack of preparation and ineptitude are the general rule, rather than the high degree of preparation and near-conspiracy implied by the existence of a hidden agenda. The term can be useful when used in the diplomatic world, and sometimes in the board-room; in the day-to-day world of the working manager, it is usually merely pretentious. People at meetings do respond in terms of their own interests, though, as they see or come to see them, which means that they can argue for hours about what should be minor agenda items, and spend meeting after meeting discussing what should be the proper area or areas of inquiry.

They also play for position, whether real or imagined, and whether reflexively or for achievable personal purposes. There is nothing more disheartening than to sit through a committee meeting or two and gradually come to realize that nothing is being accomplished because two or more individuals or groups are locked in a long-term political battle, with the stuff of the meeting only part of the weaponry with which that battle is being waged. There's nothing much you can do about that, unless you have either considerable authority in the situation or the patience of a saint and the political skills of a successful urban mayor. It's hardly ever worth it to try, when you find yourself so trapped; early extrication is usually indicated, if possible.

Meeting attendees also engage in legitimate and predictable career building, in which they seek to make favorable impressions and develop worthwhile working relationships with their peers and superiors. That is to be sharply distinguished from destructive political infighting, for it is one of the motors that can move a working committee along successfully. The excellent report that is acted upon, the searching and helpful questions, obviously the fruit of excellent preparation, the responsibility taken and handled skillfully and productively—these are some of the things of which successful internal career moves are made.

Meetings That Do Work

But all this makes it vital to sharply define objects of inquiry—working hypotheses—before a meeting is called, for those meetings that you seriously want to make work. The main context within which a meeting or group of meetings is to be held is best and most easily cast early; it is far harder to do this once the working group has been convened. The group will certainly develop goals and sometimes modify them substantially as it proceeds—after all, it is testing hypotheses and trying to turn them into productive actions—but it is then much less likely to bog down before it even gets fairly started.

After a sharply defined set of working hypotheses, the key need is a reasonably strong and considerate leader who will think through and suggest an agenda aimed at getting the group where it wants to go. The aim is to develop—often, in a sense, to negotiate with the group members—an amendable-as-you-go working agenda. The leader is then needed to time and stay with that agenda, amending general timing, item sequence, and the agenda itself as needed, but with a strong bias toward staying with the agreed-upon agenda, and strong resistance to unfocused discussion.

For a meeting to be effective, all of this needs to take place within the context of careful preparation. That means careful development of the information that will go to meeting participants beforehand, including both working hypotheses and backup materials; without such preparation, it is seldom worthwhile to hold the meeting at all. It is far better to cancel an unprepared meeting until it can be held with well-prepared people than to go ahead with it and hope it will somehow come out all right. The odds are that it will not, and that you and your colleagues will have wasted valuable time.

Preparation continues as long as the task proceeds. Each step along the way creates the need to set down, usually best in writing, what has so far been accomplished, what remains to be done, and what further materials, if any, need now to be examined. It really does not do to assume that everyone who attended a meeting last month, or last week, for that matter, remembers what went on; or that their recollections of what went on are even nearly the same; or that they shared similar perceptions of what was going on while the meeting was in process.

Do by all means supply people with written materials long enough before meetings for them to be able to study what you have given them. Most of them will then come prepared to move ahead intelligently. Some will not read whatever you give them on time, of course, which is why it is useful to briefly review each previous meeting at the start of each succeeding meeting, so that those who are unprepared will not slow everyone else down too much. All elementary; all far more honored in the breach than the observance, as evidenced by too many barren meetings, and too many managers with very bad professional reflexes in this area.

Yet even with good professional reflexes toward the possibility of creating sound and productive working meetings, and even with success in so doing, it remains true that most of us will be able to seriously affect the conception, conduct, and success of only a small portion of the meetings in which we find ourselves entrapped. Of necessity, then, much of our attention in this area must be directed toward limiting the negative effects of unproductive meetings. First of all, that means avoiding as many as possible of those meetings you think likely to be unproductive. And it means repeatedly asking yourself and others whether a planned meeting is necessary, and attempting always to limit the number of participants in meetings.

It also means understanding and taking full advantage of the informal operating structures that exist in every organization, just as you routinely do when networking and otherwise career building. Many a needless meeting or group inquiry can be headed off before it starts with an informal meeting between interested parties. Many decisions that might be made with the help of consultants, task forces, and ad hoc committees can very easily be made by skilled people without that kind of help, after a few astute questions and comments from you and other responsible people. You may also find that many decisions you feel a little uneasy about making yourself are better made without going through all those time-wasting meetings. It is quite probable that you really do not need a consultant to tell you that you are right to want to make a certain move, or a group of your subordinates and peers to tell you to go ahead and do something you already know you want to do.

Meetings surely are not wholly controllable, any more than the telephone or the door to your office. But, like the other "uncontrollable" elements of your working life, they turn out to be significantly controllable, if understood and properly approached.

PAPER CONTROL

The blizzard of paper and print in your life can be controlled, too. No, you are not likely to control the quantity, but the way you handle it can make the difference between being overwhelmed by all that paper and using it efficiently and productively.

Twentieth century managers have always had significant amounts of paper and print to move. Today, however, two devices have increased paper flow tremendously: the high-speed computer printer and the copying machine. When daily, weekly, and monthly reports had to be typed by hand on as many carbons as a typewriter would take, or in some instances reproduced on some kind of printing press, they tended to be rather small, by modern standards. When the same kinds of reports can be programmed and generated in any quantities desired, they tend to be large and extremely detailed. When most internal memos and reports had to be hand-typed and hand-corrected on carbons, you can be sure that they were distributed sparingly; the copying machine has made far wider distribution the norm. When customer correspondence was keyboarded one letter at a time, the quantity generated was relatively small; now that letters can be moved through word processing equipment, hundreds of personalized letters are created out of a single writing and a single hand-typing.

The net of it all is that a river of paper flows across most of our desks. We are queried, informed, and reported to as never before. We are hooked into management information systems within our own companies, and into massive remote databases of all kinds through desk terminals that are part of distributed data processing systems. Even if the river of paper slows down a little as more print is carried on screen— though there is so far very little evidence that this is happening—we will still find ourselves inundated by what often seems to be an exponentially expanding mass of data. We are indeed in the middle of both computer technology and information explosions, and will be for quite some time.

It is necessary to be able to handle it all well, while never losing sight of the fact that you are a professional manager, rather than a paper-shuffler or number-cruncher. Entrepreneurially minded problem-solving generalists—that is, successful managers—use paper, print, and computer terminals for their own ends, rather than letting such devices fill their lives, just as they use and control telephones and face-to-face work with other people.

By far the most important keys to this matter are selectivity and timing: selectivity in what you handle yourself, what you short-circuit before it gets to you, what you pass on and to whom, what you write, what you read, and how you read it; and timing of the handling, writing, and reading of various materials.

Unless your job involves unusually large amounts of public contact, you will probably want to see all or almost all communications addressed directly to you, and a good many broadcast internal communications as well. You may also want to see a good deal of the mail solicitation material sent to you; such material often helps keep you informed about new products and developments in your field. On the other hand, you are highly unlikely to want to see some kinds of nonpertinent mail solicitations routinely sent to millions of managers, among others, for such items as office supplies, desert land, or erotic magazines. You also will probably want to see certain portions—usually the summary sheets, at least—of the massive computer printouts that have become so much a part of working life in recent years. But there is no particular reason to pile your desk high with huge and detailed computer-generated reports that you will use as reference material only occasionally, rather than for everyday information purposes.

Once again, a competent and well-trained assistant can help supply a significant measure of control by exercising prior selectivity to your specifications and thereby sharply cutting the quantity of paper that arrives on your desk. You should not be sorting through mail solicitation material to find what you might want; your assistant can very easily do that for you. Your assistant can also separate out those portions of computer reports that you want for current information and file the rest for reference access.

You can be helped far more than in those very basic ways, of course. Your assistant can and should sort incoming material by content and general priority, so that a closely reasoned two-page letter from either a customer or peer is not mixed with a series of small items that can be easily disposed of.

Dispose whenever possible. Selectivity does not mean handling highly complex and difficult matters first, and routine and easily handled matters afterward. Just the opposite. It means moving what can be moved quickly right off your desk. Some of it you may handle quickly and easily yourself, but much of it will go back to your assistant's desk immediately, for handling there or for delegation and transfer elsewhere. If 20 pieces of material, of all shapes and sizes, come in addressed to you on a given morning, you are doing something very wrong if all 20 arrive on your desk in an undifferentiated mass. You may appropriately get ten of them; pass three back to your assistant for handling; pass two more along to others through your assistant; handle three yourself, quickly and efficiently; and effectively start your main working day with only two of those 20 pieces of material on your desk. There will, of course, be times when you find yourself with a lot more to handle than you had expected; you may get 30 pieces and start your working day with ten of them. But in any event you should not find yourself handling and holding a mass of items you have no real business with. Selectivity means screening incoming material and thereby directly receiving only what you want and need to receive. Then it means moving what can be moved off your desk quickly and effectively, making it possible to concentrate on what is left—and on the real business of management, which has very little to do with all that paper.

There are very seldom so many high priorities and difficult matters to handle that a desk must be piled high with paper. Editors and writers, whose business involves masses of words on paper, may quite reasonably expect to pile all available surfaces with paper; managers should not. A manager who is drowning in paper is quite likely to be one who has not even understood, much less mastered, the art of selectivity, and who has not been lucky enough to find—or skillful enough to train—an assistant who does. If you examine the sea of paper on the desk of the drowning victim, you will inevitably find a large body of superfluous reports and trivial matters that could and should have been handled earlier.

A proper working assumption here is that most of what arrives on your desk can be handled easily, largely because it represents kinds of matters and situations you have previously thought through; there are, in this sense, precedents to follow. A much smaller body of incoming material requires more attention, some of it much more. That is what should be put aside for the short time it will take to handle the easier matters.

The potential trap here is what you wind up handling a great deal of time-consuming trivia and do not get to the more difficult and sometimes more important matters. Well, in part that is what your office at home, and possibly your commuting time, are for; but in even larger part that is what your assistant and others about you are for.

Selectivity requires both you and your assistant to exercise good judgment; timing requires even more, and all on your part. You cannot expect your assistant to know which indignant or angry letter you should answer today, and perhaps by telephone, to defuse a potentially explosive and easily complicated situation, and which equally indignant or angry letter you will want to put aside to think about. Some situations are best handled quickly, and some benefit from what may to others seem like neglect. That is your judgment to make, and yours alone.

Most situations certainly do not take care of themselves; on the other hand, some do, especially as regards your participation and therefore time involvement in them. For example, you may choose to make a major—and time-consuming—issue of a too slowly generated report in order to solve the problem it is creating for your far-flung field staff; or you may choose to reassure your staff with a brief broadcase memo and wait for improvements you have reason to believe are coming soon. The one thing you should not do is spend much valuable time making a major issue of the matter when you have good reason to suppose that the matter is well on the way to solution, unless you have other strong reasons for doing so. Political infighting reasons, by the way, are seldom good reasons for spending large amounts of time on a matter; personal pique and undesirable escalation all too often make infighting counterproductive.

Along similar lines, the "hot" reply to the "hot" memo or letter is to be avoided like the plague it is. Pride dictates quick and devastating response to the stinging attack. Mature judgment insists upon a measured response, with open battle not joined but avoided if possible. If, after careful thought, you feel that you must do battle, then let it be as limited as possible, and as little wounding as possible; managers who must work together in the same company, however far removed by geography and function, should make every effort to avoid abrasion. Of course, if you work in a management environment characterized by megalomania at the top and an atmosphere of continual crisis throughout the organization, abrasion and open battle will inevitably occur; such organizations are worth avoiding, if possible.

Go as far as you reasonably can on those matters that can be handled quickly and well, holding no such items in piles of paper in and around your office. Go as slowly as you feel you must on those matters that require considerable thought or that benefit from deliberate handling. A professional manager is neither fast nor slow, but rather is someone who understands and properly uses selectivity and timing.

Activity generates activity. Isn't that what organizations are about? Not quite. Organizations are not about activity but about *effective* activity. Meetings, telephone calls, and written communications all generate more of the same; that places an extraordinarily high premium on careful thought and puts the cost of ineffective motion in a more realistic light.

That is nowhere more true than in the area of written communications, for the mystique of writing is such that they demand response. And in this area you often get what you give. This means that if you write a clear, sharp, needed memo, you stand a reasonable chance of eliciting a cogent, useful response, but that if you write a spongy, ill-timed memo, you are highly likely to get a useless response or one that asks for clarification, continuing the interchange, with paper generating more paper.

The rules established in the days before the copying machine and word processor still apply very well in this area. A sound and sanity-seeking professional manager must master the brief, clear, and quite-to-the-point communication, whether memo, letter, or report; the effective and if at all possible informal response to another's communication; and the look-before-you-leap reflex in assessing whether there need be any written communication at all. That you can dictate many memos in a short time or write a long report does you little credit. Thoughtful brevity is a far more important skill.

Many managers working in large organizations feel the weight of bureaucratic practice in the area of written communications. They learn early that not to "lay a paper trail" can be hazardous, and quite reflexively generate considerable masses of formal communications aimed not so much at developing a useful record for later analysis as at self-justification should anything go wrong later on. What they tend not to realize is that they are also wasting substantial amounts of valuable time sending and receiving large amounts of unnecessary paper. Laying such a paper trail may be a survival reflex for people caught in a bureaucratic maze; it is a very bad reflex for working managers. Certainly, all relevant communications, whether generated as telephone conversation notes, meeting notes, or written communications, should be carefully kept and filed. That is vital in that it saves valuable rethinking and redoing while the interchange is in process and allows proper evaluation later on. But that is all; the long memo, inspired by political infighting and written more for the file than for getting the job done, is a time-waster.

Self-Analysis

Your time log helps you to assess periodically *how* you are spending your time. Clearly, it is no less valuable to go a little deeper than that, to assess *how effectively* you are using the time. Too seldom is that assessment a part of the periodic time-log evaluation process, especially regarding written communications. While we tend to note the content of our telephone calls and meetings, to be evaluated during our periodic assessments, we tend not to look back at what we have written during that period. The memos, letters, and reports for the period in question tend to move right into our files, with our orderly movement of paper in this way defeating our analytical intent.

That can be a significant error of omission, for we write just as wastefully as we meet and telephone. It is wise to hold aside everything you write during a time-logging and reevaluation period, so that you can see your work as a whole. You can file your written communications after you complete your evaluation—but only then, for that body of work is otherwise effectively lost for evaluation purposes.

A close analysis of what you have written during a one- or two-week period, conducted twice a year, can yield a wide variety of insights that will help you save time and enhance your effectiveness. For example, you may find memos on seemingly pressing matters that need not have been sent; on analysis, many such matters turn out not to have been so pressing, and you may conclude that you could have resolved the problem better and in less time if you had handled it a bit more deliberately. You may also find broadcast information memos that need not have been sent, or should have been sent more selectively, and that generated a good deal more paper in response than was necessary. You may find letters you answered yourself that might better have been handled by your assistant or others. You may also find longish letters and reports that you thought at the time worked out rather well, but that on reexamination you feel could have been done shorter and better, could have been handled informally, or need not have been handled at all. It is the rare re-examination of this sort that does not yield considerable fruit, if you are willing to spend the time to do it and have the strength to put what you learn into practice.

Periodic re-examination of what we read for information and insight is also important, if we are to keep up with germane current developments and expand our knowledge in the middle of an information explosion, while attempting to take advantage of the possibilities and avoid the hazards opened up by new information technology. For example, ten years ago you might not have been much interested in periodicals focusing on business uses of computers and development of management information systems, thinking them best directed only to computer people. Today, it is quite clear that every professional manager should have continual updating in these areas.

As new technology makes it possible to place information into computer memories, it will become easier and easier to find and use desired bits of information, summoning them up, whatever their sources, on a terminal in your own office. It hardly matters to the user whether that information is carried in a massive single memory and remotely accessed, or on a disc or cassette that is supplied periodically; those are economic and competitive matters now being addressed by computer suppliers. When transition has occurred, it will be as reflexive to reach for the controls of your screen as it is to reach for a book.

But having information available in both forms may save only a little reading time, for the main reading that managers engage in, aside from such directly work-connected vehicles as memos, letters, and reports, is for updating and career development purposes. In those areas, you may be able to get some of what you want on a screen without as much page-flipping as before. But you will probably often find yourself still reading print on paper, because periodicals and books are far more portable and easy to handle than computer screens—and a great deal easier on the eyes. Whatever the new information technology, most managers will still feel the need to read a great deal more than they can possibly manage, and will be reading far less of the kinds of thought-provoking, long-range works that generalists should read.

Keeping up and growing calls for and will continue to call for selectivity and constant reevaluation. A manager may carefully read the *Wall Street Journal; Time* or *Newsweek* or both; perhaps the *Harvard Business Review* or some other major management periodical; possibly a financial magazine or two; and the key trade journals in his or her current field of business. Such a manager may take pride in the amount and variety of reading done, but still not be accomplishing anywhere near the updating required, while cutting off the possibility of reaching beyond this series of redundant publications to find deeper and longer-range analyses. It is far better only to scan some or all of these, reaching into a relatively limited number of columns and articles for basic updating needs, and reserve as much as possible of your valuable time for reading the kinds of key works drawn on for insight by the writers of all those articles. The periodicals can help you to identify some of those key works; that is the purpose of their book review columns.

USING TRAVEL TIME

There are time-expansion possibilities to be explored, as well as time-saving possibilities. One such possibility comes, ironically enough, with the length of time it takes so many to get to work. When it takes an hour, sometimes even two, to commute to work, and you are not doing the driving, you find yourself with two or more hours every day that are not otherwise committed, in which a great deal can be accomplished. That woman or man who works hard to and from work every day, rather than playing cards or sleeping, is not necessarily a compulsive worker. What the card-players and sleepers—when they wake up—see every day may be a very effective manager, using what might otherwise be dead and boring time to read, write, and think in what can very easily be made into a totally private environment, with no ringing telephone, swinging office door, or quick and disruptive meetings. As many managers have found over the years, you can get an enormous amount of work done during commuting hours, if you see your career commitment needs properly.

To work successfully while commuting, all you need is a supply of relevant materials to carry back and forth; a hard, flat surface to write upon, such as a briefcase; and basic writing (or dictating) materials. And a seat. All is lost here if you have to stand on the way, which makes unremitting agitation for adequate commuting facilities far more than a matter of comfort. If you cannot sit, you are being robbed of a productive work opportunity for from two to four hours a day, and that is a few hundred to a thousand hours a year, depending on the length of the commute and the away-from-office travel time. Not a small amount, and the work many can accomplish while commuting is not a small matter.

So, too, the work that can be accomplished while "on the road" is a potentially significant matter. Many managers spend substantial amounts of time traveling on company business; the time-saving and time-expansion possibilities thereby opened up are well worth noting. This is an unusual view of "the road." Travel away from the office is generally viewed by working managers as very nearly unproductive, except as regards the specific aims of the trip. It is also usually regarded, with considerable justification, as tedious, disorienting, and exhausting, and most of all, boring. There is nothing quite like waking at 4:00 A.M. suffering from jet lag, exhausted but unable to sleep, in an airport motel with no facilities open, with a television set that presents only a blank, buzzing face when turned on, and without a working radio. Or the first jaggedly disorienting time you find yourself walking down a windowless corridor in a hotel or motel and realize that you haven't the slightest idea what city you are in, or for that matter what time of day or day of the week it is. Travel, if you let it, often becomes little more than an endless series of meetings, punctuated by too many drinks with too many people, with each day containing a too-large lunch and a too-large dinner and concluding with a series of unnecessary and really unwanted nightcaps, all accompanied by a continuing ocean of pressure-filled business talk, before a return to a plane or hotel room and further boredom.

Not much fun—and far from the lush executive life conjured up by the almost uniformly bad movies and books that touch upon the world of the modern manager. All that sex, power, and intrigue . . . well, it is expensive, all right, but that's about all it is. Much of the time and expense often seem like pure waste.

Quite right; the evidence supplied by your senses and assessed by your skeptical intelligence is overwhelming. Much of what passes on the road for necessary activity— because "everybody does it"—is so much waste. A waste of time and a waste of money; of time that must be looked upon as working opportunity, and of money that can and should be seen as the stuff of profit and investment.

Business traveling time is as controllable as any other business-related activity—not more, not less—with the keys to control being once again selectivity and timing, and the prizes to be gained including large blocks of prime, usable time, a measure of control over a seemingly uncontrollable aspect of our working lives, and a sane and healthy approach to this aspect of life and work.

Selectivity starts with the decision itself—to travel or not to travel. The trip to "show the flag" is as much a waste of time as the repeated, essentially useless, Monday morning meeting. The right question is always, "Is this trip necessary?" If the answer comes back, "No, not really," then the trip should not be made. That you hit the field installations four times last year and the same number of times the year before has very little to do with whether or not you should do the same this year or next. Do people expect you to do so, and look forward to your coming? Perhaps. Is satisfying their expectation enough reason to make the trip and spend many thousands of dollars in out-of-pocket expenses and wasted time? Perhaps not.

Similarly, there is no very good reason to expect appearances at trade meetings and conventions to be pro forma. Oh, someone from your company has always had an exhibit at that meeting? So what? Have you taken a "zero-based" look at the necessity of exhibiting at the meeting this year? Have you costed it out, and tried to make a reasonable cost-benefits estimate? It may be that the money is in the budget, and you do not want to lose that budget item; but what a pathetic reason that would be to waste tens of thousands of dollars.

Selectivity then very reasonably extends to the details in travel plans. All too often, a trip becomes far more complex than it needs to be, as stops are added, and far more difficult than it should be for maximum effectiveness, as short-interval scheduling adds on stop after stop, and arranges meeting after exhausting meeting. There is seldom much benefit to be gained—and much harm can result—from a brief airport meeting after a transcontinental or transoceanic flight; your objectives are scarcely likely to be achieved when you are exhausted and out of phase while those you are meeting with are "up" and ready for you. You can also cause yourself much needless physical stress; even the most experienced travelers sometimes tend to underestimate the impact of flight upon our bodies. It is far better to be carefully selective about travel plans to plan mammoth and often quite unnecessary swings.

Jet lag is dangerous, both physically and to the success of our travel plans. Most of us have come to understand—intellectually, at least—the physical aspect of jet lag in recent years, but very few working managers really act upon that knowledge. Most managers are still capable of very foolishly working all day at the office, jumping aboard a flight into a time zone several hours west, coming off the plane into the eagerly waiting arms of their local associates, and going off to be wined, dined, and persuaded into the wee hours of the morning. Then, after having stayed up all night "working," they compound their error by dropping into bed for only a couple of hours of sleep before starting to work again, perhaps handling delicate and demanding matters.

Some personal and work problems accompany that kind of pattern. First, it is extraordinarily hard on the body. To work all day and all night, spending many hours in transit while doing so, places enormous short-term strain on some pretty important and sometimes fragile organs, including heart and nervous system. To wake in what, for us, is the middle of the night, because of time zone differences and the way our bodies are attuned, creates enormous additional strains. It is perfectly clear by now that it is exceedingly short-sighted and dangerous to travel in this way. Yet many of us continue to do it, figuring that "the next guy" will be the one who has the heart attack. Well, it may not be the next guy.

And a perfectly obvious set of working problems is

created, too. You stack the deck against yourself when you go to work exhausted. Exhausted managers tend to make bad decisions and to antagonize people they are there to persuade. And exhausted managers fighting jet lag and working full days in a distant time zone stay exhausted.

It is far better for the body and for work objectives to take exhaustion and jet lag into account in planning long-distance trips. If you must travel at night, arrive quietly, go to your lodging, stay up until you are quite tired but relaxed, and go to sleep. You may wake up rather early the next morning, but you will be well on your way to conquering jet lag, will not be exhausted, and will have made neither awkward promises nor unnecessary enemies the night before. If you must meet the night of the day you travel, by all means travel early on that day if you can, so that you may arrive, acclimate, and perhaps fit in a nap before you have to go to work in what, for you, is the middle of the night.

The converse is also true. If you are flying from west to east any considerable distance, your problem will arise the next morning. You will not have been able to go to sleep until the middle of the night in your arrival time zone, and should not attempt to schedule anything until the afternoon of the first full day in the new zone; otherwise you will find yourself fighting to stay awake all that day, rather than being in top condition for whatever has to be done. If you stay on, bear in mind that you will still be attuned to a different time zone; try not to schedule very early morning appointments until your body has had a few days to acclimate.

If working effectiveness is to be maximized and working opportunities used, considerable care must be paid as well to other timing-related questions. When and how closely to schedule planes and other transport; how closely to schedule meetings on the same day; and whether or not to travel to dinner at that wonderful French restaurant just 40 miles down the coast shortly after a five-hour flight—these are all matters to consider carefully. Bear in mind that it is often easier and better to gently suggest changes of itinerary to eager hosts than to flatly say "no," but it is also possible to say "no."

Careful selectivity should be worked into the fabric of every business traveling day. You need not attend every cocktail party, or stay until the end of any of them—unless it is your party, of course. You need not accept nightcap invitations, which so often turn into informal but long and draining meetings. You need not schedule end-to-end meetings, or attend every possible meeting, when others can handle some as well as you, or when you are merely observing rather than actively participating. You are traveling for business purposes, but should not let those purposes fill your days completely, unless you want them to, any more than you do in familiar work environments.

Travelers' Tools

Proper physical preparation is far more important when traveling than when working at your office or home. Small working tools that can be taken for granted in a familiar environment can become vital omissions on the road.

Some basic working tools are apparent and part of the working equipment of almost all managers who travel; but some equally basic tools are often overlooked. On the road, a working manager should have the following:

• A properly flexible, small wardrobe, as washable as possible.

• Adequate writing instruments, and paper to write on. If you normally use a typewriter in the office, then by all means take along a small electric portable, with paper and carbon sets, so that you can send your originals back to the office and keep the carbons as safety copies. Or if you are going to be somewhere for more than a few days, you may want to rent a full-scale office machine through the hotel; many hotels provide such services.

• A small calculator, with a paper tape. Some may prefer the kind of hand-held calculator that is easily carried in pocket or bag, and without the tape attachment, but serious work is much easier with the tape, which can be removed and attached to the work done.

• A cassette recorder, for dictating notes and communications. Some of the very small models are quite attractive, but will take only 15- or 30-minute tapes. On balance, it is desirable to carry the smallest sturdy recorder you can find that will take 60- or at most 90-minute tapes. Beware tapes taking over 60 minutes of material, that is, more than 30 minutes a side; these tapes are more fragile and have much less chance of standing up to the rigors of travel. Caution—do not take your tapes through airport metal-detectors, which can scramble the information you record on magnetic tapes; instead, take them out of your carrying case and have the attendant pass them around to you. Note that many companies have dictating equipment in their offices that can be used by remote entry over telephone lines. Some of your communications from the road can be sent directly in that fashion, if your company is so equipped.

• A small high-intensity lamp and bulb, so that you can convert almost any dimly lit hotel room into a workplace. Many otherwise completely acceptable rooms are designed as bedrooms rather than as offices and are therefore inadequately lighted for working purposes. Bear in mind that without adequate light you cannot work effectively; also that your eyes age faster than most of your other parts, and need much care.

• Two three-socket conversion plugs, so that you can convert a single socket into three sockets, and thereby accommodate the equipment you are carrying. If you are going abroad, to where electrical systems are different, then you also need appropriate conversion units.

• A heavy 12-foot extension cord, which should be long enough to reach from an available plug to that part of the room where you are using your equipment.

• An extra pair of reading glasses as emergency spares, if you use them. These should be obvious, but are often omitted.

• Your office calendar, which should always travel with you, a copy of relevant portions or of the whole calendar being left with your assistant.

• A small quantity of precisely the same office tools and

supplies you normally use—a small stapler, a staple remover, paper clips, rubber bands, small scissors, and the like.

It will help a great deal to outline your needs to hotel staff wherever you are going. It is often as simple as specifying "a room suitable for working in, with table, chair, and good light." Managers who do not do that risk arriving at hotels and motels that might have been able to accommodate modest working needs if they had been informed earlier, but are now fully booked and cannot. On the other hand, a hotel may ignore your careful specifications; if so, it is still sometimes possible to get a proper working place on arrival, if you ask, rather than taking the luck of the draw in a randomly assigned room. Hotel staff can and should be pushed as necessary in these areas; most will try to be helpful without pushing, but some will not, and you cannot know which is which until you try. By all means, force the situation a bit if you must; it will be worth it in terms of being able to take better advantage of work opportunities on the road.

Using Travel Time

Various kinds of work, beyond the specific purposes of your trip, can be accomplished while traveling, although they vary with the kind of trip. Trips differ, and what you can accomplish on a trip in which you "appear" at a sales meeting may be far more than you can accomplish at the kind of trade fair in which you spend every available minute talking business with potential customers.

You will handle vital "office" work, certainly. You will not want to have all your mail and messages sent along, any more than you want it all on your desk, unscreened, but you will want the key items. Which items are to be sent can easily be decided, with a first screening by your assistant and a second screening of doubtful items by you over the telephone when you call your office. And that should be daily, no matter how well things seem to be going. You cannot expect anyone else to be able to make your judgments for you, and assessing which matters are vital and to be handled quickly should be your own personal concern at all times. That should be true unless you have made a conscious decision to cut yourself off for some period while holidaying, of course; but even then, the period should not be too long.

Reading for information and insight is also prime work to do while traveling. You do not need your periodicals sent along; they can be scanned on return. But the road can be a real opportunity for reflective reading of some of the longer-range and deeper works you might otherwise have difficulty finding sufficient time for. The same holds for some of the longer reports and memos that we all too often put aside. Better take along some light reading, too, if only as a kind of security blanket; the world can be a lonely place in that airport motel at 4:00 A.M. far away from home.

Travel time is good for reflective thinking, as well as reflective reading. Physical distance and change of environment often help make the opaque clear. Making traveling time available for thinking and planning can be surprisingly fruitful from this point of view. Some of the most interesting and difficult aspects of life and work can come into focus while traveling, and in the most unlikely circumstances. Planning for that kind of relaxed time in large enough quantities can maximize the possibility that such thinking will happen often, and can make business travel far more attractive from a working point of view.

Successful management of time and work makes it possible to identify and reach for opportunities, rather than be overwhelmed by a flood of petty tasks, trivial matters, and bureaucratic responses to the new problems posed by difficult times. Professional managers are, by training and inclination, some of the most astute practical problem-solvers in the world; and for them, learning how to handle their own time and work most productively is always a first—and very much a continuing—order of personal business.

CHAPTER 5

EFFECTIVE SPEAKING

Much of our communication takes place informally: in an impromptu telephone call, in a casual meeting in a hallway, in a staff conference, in a job interview, in a hastily scribbled note, in an off-the-cuff media interview, in a discussion over lunch. In these and other such informal situations, "tricks" and "tips" on effective communication have little or no place. The essence of the matter is that—whatever image we try, in the short run, to show to others—in the long run, we communicate what we are.

That is particularly true for managers, whose main verbal and nonverbal communications are with co-workers, one to one or in small groups, rather than with strangers. The stranger may be fooled occasionally—although most perceptive, experienced people are rather hard to fool—but people close to us soon understand very well who and what we are. They see us close up, warts and all. In that sense, "effective communication" seems more a fact than an aim for managers; in a mixture of verbal and nonverbal ways, which add up to a great deal more than the sum of their parts, we inescapably communicate what we are to others. Indeed, this inevitable communication is a continuing disaster for the arrogant, cruel, nasty, and hopelessly incompetent among us. For the fact is that, as managers, what we are will be unchanged by any cosmetic work on speech, body language, appearance, or close attention to manipulative techniques. That said, various techniques in writing and speaking can help us all do more effectively what managers do—exchange ideas with, inform, organize, persuade, and lead others in action.

INFORMAL SPEAKING

Most important of all for managers is informal communication with individuals and small groups, whether strangers or associates. In all our face-to-face dealings with peers, superiors, subordinates, customers, and vendors, whether at the long-drawn-out, intracorporate meetings that are so much of the stuff of every manager's working life, or at a wide variety of seminars, professional meetings, trade shows, sales meetings, and board meetings—we must recognize that *how* we speak communicates as much as *what* we say. We communicate verbally and nonverbally, with tone, body, and attitudes; often we have substantial "conversations" with others before anyone says a word. Communication is a blending of all the verbal and nonverbal factors into a personal style that is different for each of us, that develops and changes as we do, and that sums up the whole face we present to the world. That places considerable importance upon mastering some very basic, rather simple understandings and techniques of both verbal and nonverbal communication.

In communication, content and form are intertwined, but content precedes form. Without something relevant to say, the best speaker in the world has little to communicate. Although we function in a world full of manipulative techniques and manipulators, some old, familiar injunctions still apply. They are: *listen and learn; think before you speak; if you don't know, ask questions;* and *overprepare.* All have to do with understandings that precede and intertwine with the ability to communicate effectively; none involve direct verbal expression.

Listening and Thinking

Effective listening is work when you are not used to it; it can also become an extraordinarily useful habit. For concentrated listening, above all else, lets us see into the day-to-day problems that are much of the meat of the working manager's job. The subordinate who comes to you with a substantial and complex people-handling problem that has built up over a period of months may indeed need to fire someone, as is being proposed. But hard, careful, responsive, sympathetic listening may elicit information your subordinate did not even realize was significant, or illuminate problems that cut two ways, rather than one. That kind of listening more often than not turns up hidden signals and enables you to ask the right questions and resolve the seemingly unresolvable. It always helps to remember that nonverbal communication is a two-way affair, and that face-to-face listening, whether one to one or in a group, enables you to see, not just hear or read. Face to face, you are usually able to learn a good deal more than you otherwise might. The person who might send you a measured, quite rational memo or sustain a fairly calm telephone conversation may face-to-face reveal considerable tension with set of body, folded arms, nervous fingers, facial muscle tic, or any of the score of other subtle and not-so-subtle physical indicators that you might miss entirely if communication were by memo or telephone. Similarly, careful listening and watching during a meeting are indispensable if you are to properly perceive the real forces at work in the meeting room. That, by the way, is why telephone conferencing has some hidden drawbacks in the area of effective communication, and why the success or failure of a television conference may depend largely on how well all the participants in the conference can literally see each other and gauge each other's actions and reactions.

Responsive listening often calls for more than silent interest and nonverbal encouragement; astute questioning is also needed. Such questioning need not be abrasive and repressive; if done well it can be supportive, while eliciting necessary information and helping provide the basis for thoughtful response. Silent encouragement is valuable, but it is verbal response that starts dialogue.

Sometimes we are the initiators of what we hope will be thoughtful and useful dialogue. Then it is essential to think before we speak. We expect to prepare ourselves when we are delivering a report or speech, but the need is no less great in the one-to-one or small-group discussions that fill a manager's life. Responsive listening and command of our work setting—a command best achieved in the long-term planning time so essential to the professional manager—provide the basic preparation. Beyond that, in all informal communications, we must take the time to form our thoughts before speaking. The habits of speaking before you have quite collected your thoughts, of filling a silence with words, and of responding too quickly in conversations are the enemies of effective speech and communication. For muddy thoughts, no matter how beautifully delivered, will still be perceived as muddy.

Those who speak before they have thought things through also tend to develop some quite significant speech flaws. They tend to talk too fast, to pitch their voices higher and speak louder than is desirable, and to compound those errors with aggressive body language. They often seem to "crowd," to "push," to arrogantly attempt to force their views on others. All these habits are exceedingly counterproductive; all are easily repaired by the development of new reflexes, as long as it is only a surface set of bad habits that is being addressed, rather than a basic personality problem.

All you really need to do to break the habit is to listen hard and responsively, and think before you speak, rather than pushing in with a half-baked response. The listening process will cause you to take a mental deep breath before responding, and will often save you from saying the wrong thing—or even the right thing too soon. If you are starting the conversation, the same kind of thoughtful pause before plunging in will bring you only respect rather than impatience on the part of others. Thoughtful people are highly prized; it is a style that predisposes others to listen to what you have to say.

Relaxation

Relaxation helps speech and communication a great deal. It can help both your thought processes and your speaking and nonverbal communication styles. A voice and stance that communicate ease and relaxation also communicate self-confidence and personal warmth. This is a personal style that puts others at ease, avoids damaging interpersonal tension, and best elicits useful dialogue. Relaxation does good physical things for your speech, too. A relaxed voice is deeper and more resonant, and the words are much more clearly and agreeably spoken. There is more opportunity for variety of tone, pitch, and volume, because breath, tongue, lips, and jaws are free and natural, rather than stiffly controlled.

For example, one of the most common tension-associated problems is that of the "stiff upper lip." Try talking with your upper lip held as stiff as you can. Difficult; you come out sounding like Humphrey Bogart playing one of his early gangster roles. To achieve more mobile, effective speech, you would try to relax a stiff upper lip.

Thoughtful, relaxed speech helps achieve such clarity; so does attention to such matters as poor articulation and unnecessarily impenetrable regional or ethnic accents. Others respect you considerably less when you habitually run words together or mispronounce them while speaking fast and carelessly; but the error, while damaging, is quite avoidable. It simply takes practice, with those close to you or alone before a mirror, teaching yourself to speak relatively slowly, carefully, and in language that will be clear to those you work with. You may at first feel that you are speaking far too slowly and awkwardly, but you will soon realize that you are spending very little more time than before to say the words, and that you are speaking far more effectively. Much the same holds true if you have failed to trim a regional or ethnic accent at least enough so that others can understand you easily. You may not be respected less, but you are certainly making it unnecessarily hard to work with others, by setting up a barrier between you and them.

Do not try to expunge a regional or ethnic accent completely. You want to be understood by those you work with, but you need not change the communicating patterns of a lifetime. Indeed, when you try to change too much too fast, you run the risk of making yourself sound affected and quite false—which is far more damaging than even a relatively thick accent can ever be. Variant patterns change soon enough, anyway, as we live and work with new groups of people, and our speech "rubs off" on each other, so that we approach a group norm.

A far more considerable hazard for all of us is how we sound, especially in the area of pitch. A voice that is pitched high, coming out of a tight, tense throat, often offends the ear. It can be perceived as a grating, shrill, and unpleasant whine; in short, it is anathema to others and quite damaging for its unfortunate possessor. It is fixable, though, with a little help from your friends—and it should be fixed. Slowing down will usually help, as will relaxing that tense throat, sometimes bringing the voice down as much as a whole octave. If you have a severe problem with the sound of your voice, you may want to consult a professional speech therapist; it would be well worth the special effort to rid yourself of speech habits that might be a bar to a successful career in management.

Speaking too loudly also presents a hazard. Relaxation and slowing down usually help in this area, too, unless the problem is the result of partial deafness. Then it is time to consult a specialist. If a friend or colleague suggests that you may have a hearing problem, do not resist getting it. It can greatly help you to hear, understand, and communicate, and can make life a great deal easier for you and those around you.

Problems of pitch, volume, accent, and pronunciation are easily repaired, if basic attitudes are right, and if repair efforts are consistently pursued. So, too, can a whole series of small habits that are best described as verbal and nonverbal "fidgets" be remedied. These include filling in pauses with "ah," "er," "like," or "y'know"; repeatedly clearing your throat before speaking; head scratching; nose rubbing; chin scraping; repeatedly folding and unfolding hands and legs; repeated chair shifting or briefcase handling; finger tapping; and playing in a distracting way with pen, pencil, and other materials. All indicate a certain amount of tension, and all are helped greatly by training yourself to relax and by concentrated responsive listening. Note, though, that once a habit is in place it usually takes a concerted, sometimes long-term effort to dislodge it. That best involves the help of those close to you. Mirror practice can help only a little; since such habits are caused by tension in interpersonal situations, they may not show up when you are all alone before your mirror.

All this does not, however, mean that you should avoid "talking with your hands"—or for that matter with the rest of your body. Just control it. Do indeed talk with your hands, if that is part of your natural style, and with your shoulders, the angle of your head, the tension or relaxation of your whole body, just as you talk with lips, tongue, and the air that flows from your diaphragm to be shaped into words. Talking is far more than speech.

Many of us are afraid of our bodies, and of using them to achieve full communication. We defend ourselves with stiff-ness, and tell ourselves that we are defending our own privacy, sticking to business, and avoiding personalities. Not so. The only personalities we are avoiding are our own. And what we manage to do is to project stiffness, tightness, tension, and coldness, and to build barriers between ourselves and others. We certainly do use body language every day in face-to-face and small-group situations; the only question is whether we use it well or ill.

Telephone Talk

The telephone poses some special and often rather difficult communications problems, for it depends wholly on what the voice can achieve and blocks nonverbal communication completely. Since most managers spend a great deal of time on the telephone, that places a premium on purely verbal matters as roundness of tone, low and pleasant-sounding pitch, moderation of volume, relatively slow delivery, careful pronunciation, and control of regional and ethnic accents.

On the telephone, you must first of all be understood, clearly and completely, and there is no way to check nonverbal response to see if you are being understood, much less being persuasive.

Telephone conversations must therefore go slower—often much slower—than you would like if they are to become effective communications. Even when they are conducted very carefully, you still cannot be as sure as you can be face to face that understanding—and, if desired, persuasion—are actually taking place. It is not at all unusual for agreements reached over the telephone to become, in practice, partial or even total disagreements, with both parties to the conversation thinking the other at least rather stupid and at worst unforgivably dishonest. That is one reason—though only one—why managers travel so much, and engage in face-to-face, one-to-one, and small-group meetings on matters that might seem easily resolvable by telephone.

As we discuss in Chapter 4, the keys to effective telephone talk are those matters of voice and attitude; the proper choice of communications medium, as when a written or face-to-face communication will work better than the telephone; and the provision of adequate time, preferably of your own choosing, for such telephone conversations. Stack your calls as much as possible, and return them when it is best for you. Get as much help as possible on the mechanics of all calls and the direct handling of low-priority calls from your assistant, and take the time to train your assistant well in this area. Allow the time you need—as best you can—for handling calls that will take time. In sum, treat telephone communications skills with as much care as you treat written and face-to-face communications.

As important as informal communications are in the manager's life, formal public speaking and writing skills are just as vital. In these areas, there are useful techniques and guidelines affecting the overall impression made by a speech or a report.

PUBLIC SPEAKING

Public and semipublic speaking before large groups requires special attention. For the larger group is not merely an extension of the small group, any more than the small group is an extension of the one-to-one situation. The personal interactions that characterize a small group are mostly absent in a large group; so are the opportunities for close and revealing dialogue and persuasion. For the large group, formal preparation and much practice are essential, accompanied by well-developed voice and presentation skills.

When you address a large group, you are working on a stage or public platform with a live audience, and need some of the skills and attitudes of the politician or actor. If you are working without amplification you need to be able to speak clearly and loudly enough to reach the last row or the farthest portion of a room—but not too loudly. That takes practice, if at all possible in the room where you will be speaking. Sound behaves differently in each space; no matter how much alike two spaces look, what works well in one will work ill in another. If you are working directly with a microphone or any other kind of public address system, be aware that each of these behaves differently, too. Each needs adjustment to your volume, pitch, and style, which is best achieved during a brief practice session, rather than during the crucial first two minutes of your speech or presentation. A main thesis inaudibly presented or presented over a high whine in the public address system can and often does ruin what might have been an extremely effective speech or presentation.

Preparation extends to any other vehicles you use as

speech or presentation aids. The speaker who uses a flip chart as an essential aid had best be sure that it will be seen from every part of the room or hall. The speaker who uses a projection device, such as viewgraph or soundfilm, had best be sure that the machinery is in good working order, that there is something adequate to project upon, that proper electrical outlets are available, and that he or she will not have to turn entirely away from the audience to work whatever devices are being used. All this requires preparation and practice, if possible directly on-site.

Most of all, preparation applies to you and your speech. Whether you write it entirely yourself or have the help of a speechwriter or promotion department, it must be fully prepared—that is, written out entirely, timed, fully practiced, and memorized or largely memorized. That is especially true if you are inexperienced or out of practice at public speaking. A very experienced speaker can sometimes work solely from notes organized into an outline, but even then almost never as well as from a fully prepared speech. A novice who attempts to work without full preparation will, in most instances, fall flat on his or her face.

Modern technology can greatly assist such preparation. A speech that is written, practiced again and again live before a video camera, and then critically viewed whole is a speech that can be refined very effectively. What seems to work on paper often does not work live. What seems short and pointed on paper—perhaps too short—can turn out to be too long live, for we speak slower than we read, and at various rates of speed. A speech that takes 20 minutes to read may take twice as long to deliver well, although a poor and rapid-fire speaker may deliver it far more quickly. Delivering the speech again and again, live and on camera, makes it possible to refine both the speech and its delivery; it can help you develop and deliver an excellent speech. And, if no video setup is available, a tape recorder and mirror will serve almost as well. The keys are the live delivery, practice, and memorization or near-memorization of both verbal and nonverbal elements, and your ability to fuse them into a single excellent speech or presentation.

You should make every attempt to gear a speech to the audience and local conditions. It would be a good idea to develop and refine one or more basic speeches that you will use for years, in many locations and for many purposes, adapting and revising them as needed. As a career matures, for example, a company officer may speak a dozen times a year, or more, to community and institutional groups of all kinds, presenting the company's face in these instances to its several publics. Proper preparation will elicit information that enables the speaker to adapt an icebreaking joke or to comment on local conditions; in this he or she operates much as a standup comedian or politician does. Proper audience assessment will enable the speaker to stress those matters of current significance for the particular audience. Proper assessment of audience and occasion will dictate the speaker's approach to such matters as timing and style of delivery. The heavyweight half-hour speech that went over so well keynoting the Elks convention cannot be used when you have ten minutes at the state fair; yet the ten-minute speech may be an adaptation of the same basic speech.

Preparation extends to the seemingly impromptu portions of the speech-making process. Just as a sales professional prepares to handle anticipated stalls and objections on the way to a successful close, so an experienced speaker plans to handle questions and answers after delivery of the prepared speech or presentation. No, you cannot anticipate them all; but you will probably be able to anticipate and prepare for most of the main questions and disagreements that can come up. That is especially so if you have adequate research and writing help, but it can be so even if you do it all yourself, for then you are likely to be working in a thoroughly familiar content area. Here, too, live practice is the best possible approach; what looks good on paper must be refined and practiced live to work well before an audience.

Note that working before a live audience is very different from working on television or radio. There, even when you are working with a live studio audience, you are generally either working one to one with an interviewer, delivering a speech essentially alone on a relatively small screen, or speaking directly to individuals or small groups of viewers or listeners. You are being heard and perhaps seen close up, warts, tics, fidgets, and all, just as in an office situation; as a result, you need to work in the small just as you do person to person. In radio and television, your speech should not appear to address a multitude; to communicate effectively, you should speak softly and persuasively, imagining yourself face to face with an individual.

Whatever the type of speaking, accept nervousness as normal, at least at the start. Most of us, even the most experienced of us, have "butterflies in our stomachs" before we get up to speak, dance, play, or otherwise perform. And for most of us, that is as true the thousandth time as it was the first time, whether we choose to characterize it as stage fright or creative tension. It is better to think of it as creative tension, though; that way it may disappear reassuringly quickly once you have gone into action. Folklore has it that the performer's nervous tension is subsumed in the action and disappears during the first few moments. Yes, that is true for some people from the start. For others, it takes a little time and experience for that to occur; for some, nervous tension is never lost. Do not be surprised and disheartened if that kind of tension stays with you through many years of successful speaking. It need not affect the quality of your speaking, and in some ways may help you stay a fresh and lively speaker throughout a long career.

CHAPTER 6

EFFECTIVE WRITING

Writing takes as much preparation as public speaking —perhaps more. What you set forth on a piece of paper tells others much about you and shapes their opinion of you. Everyday speech may hide the fact that your spelling is poor or that you tend to digress, but written words hide nothing. Nor can they be immediately modified, as can spoken words, if a reaction to them is unfavorable. Written words stand and fall on their own.

A good portion of business writing, perhaps the majority of it, revolves around routine items, the nuts and bolts of your job. Most letters and memos will not win any awards; people generally will not even take exceptional notice of them. Yet such routine items, when they are poorly written, are capable of creating misunderstandings and negatively affecting the way decisions are made.

Good writing skills are a vital asset for the career-minded professional. The ability to write well can help you gain notice and persuade others to follow your suggested courses of action. Even as electronic communications become more prevalent in business, writing skills will remain important. Messages may be transmitted electronically by computer and satellite, but they still appear printed on paper or displayed on a video terminal.

There has always been a certain mystique surrounding

the writing craft. Films portray the newspaper reporter who rushes into the city room and pounds out a snappy front-page story, or the novelist who composes gripping best sellers with ease. One could easily conclude that being a good writer requires innate talent. Of course, talent does play an important role for professional writers, just as it does for other professionals in their own fields. But good business writing is a skill that can be learned. With the proper knowledge and practice, anyone can write in an effective, polished style.

Good writing, whether it is a news story, a novel, or a report for the company president, does not just "happen." It is a product of creative conception, organization, planning, drafting, revising, and proofreading. The journalist has learned to write stories following a certain organizational framework. The novelist has conceived the plot, characters, and many of the actions and events that will take place. Even with a beginning outline, both journalist and novelist modify their stories with revisions. As they write, they get ideas that will improve their work. They rewrite, edit, and refine; they know how to use words effectively; and they must occasionally overcome writer's block.

The same holds true for the business writer. Remember, writing is one of your most important business tools. How you communicate will influence how your superiors and other professionals regard you. A well-organized, clearly written document creates a positive impression.

Before you begin writing, take time to prepare yourself. You will get going faster, make fewer false starts, and avoid a lot of rewriting if you do so.

First, determine the purpose of your document. If it is a report, memo, or proposal requested by a superior, make certain you get specific guidelines as to its objectives and contents. Are you being asked simply to provide a summary of facts and status about a matter, or are you also being asked for your opinions and recommendations? If you do not get guidelines, you may waste a great deal of time drafting a document that will be greeted by, "Well, this isn't quite what

I had in mind." Find out beforehand the expectations of whoever assigned the task.

If you are initiating the communication, ask yourself why the reader needs to know what you have to say and what action may need to be taken as a result. If your information is not essential, do not write it. Do not be tempted to fire off an unsolicited status report on a flag-waving memo on how the branch office will get a morale boost from the new product that was just announced. Managers are deluged daily with information and paperwork, much of it unnecessary; their time—and yours—is at a premium. A report or memo that is self-serving for the sender will not be appreciated, often not even read.

Next, consider who will read your documents. Your department head, the company's senior officers, your peers, customers, the public, the press? Is the vice president of marketing likely to pass it on to the vice president of finance? What is your readers' level of understanding about your subject?

Effective writing is tailored to the audience it addresses. If you were reporting the results of a research project, you would write differently for scientists than you would for market executives. But regardless of the audience, it is usually a good idea to keep your writing free of jargon and shop-talk terms. A report or proposal that cannot be understood does not accomplish the writer's purpose and wastes everyone's time. When you are uncertain about the audience, aim for a general lay level. There are times, however, when the shorthand of shop talk is appropriate. Reserve shop talk for internal memos when you are absolutely sure of your audience and its understanding of the subject.

The purpose and audience of your communication will guide you in setting the tone. How do you wish to come across to your readers? Are you denying a request or making a pitch? Do you want to sound authoritative, friendly, or sympathetic?

Consider your relationship to the reader—is it formal or

informal?—as well as any biases the reader may have toward you or your subject. Choose words that will communicate the right attitude. It is not always easy, especially if the subject is a delicate one. Since you cannot see the reader, you cannot judge any reaction to your words by watching facial expressions, and change your tone accordingly. Sometimes factors beyond your control or knowledge, such as political or personal sensitivities, or differing interpretations of certain words, will make a reader "hear" the wrong tone.

Your best approach is to try to place yourself in the reader's position and anticipate how that person is likely to react to what you say in print. For example, a customer with a complaint may want empathy and assurance that a problem is being resolved. Notice the difference in tone between the two letters in Figure 1. Both are perfectly "correct," but the first is wooden and brusque, while the second communicates understanding and personal attention. The recipient of the second letter is much more likely to place repeat business with this company.

FIGURE 1

Dear Mr. Raymond:

The wide-angle lens #A58, which you ordered from our catalog, has been shipped to you by Parcel Post.

The delay in filling your order was due to a clerical oversight. We customarily process orders within one week of receiving them.

I hope you have not been inconvenienced. Thank you for doing business with us, and please consider us again for your future optical needs.

Dear Mr. Raymond:

Pursuant to your letter of June 30, we have shipped you one wide-angle lens #A58, which you ordered from our catalog. We are sorry for the delay, and thank you for bringing it to our attention.

Above all, remember that writing is communication between human beings. Too many managers think business writing must be formal, dry, and riddled with ornate prose. They turn into robots the instant they pick up a pencil or begin dictation, churning out stiff, lifeless letters and boring reports.

Where it is appropriate, stay in touch with your audience through the use of personal pronouns such as *I, you,* and *we.* Imagine you are having a conversation with the reader. Face to face you would never say, "ABC company wishes to extend its appreciation for the volunteer services you provided in the community charity drive." Instead, you would say something more like, "Thank you for volunteering to help us in our community charity drive." The latter has a much warmer, more human tone. Set the tone that will help you accomplish your purpose.

It is also important to be aware of timing. Find out precisely when your finished report, memo, or proposal is due. If you are setting your own deadline, consider whether purpose or content hinges on a time factor. Then you should plan your writing schedule to meet the deadline with time to spare. Be sure to build time into your schedule to conduct necessary research or obtain information from other sources. Do not count on wrapping up your report at the last minute, because—as in Murphy's Law—something is bound to go wrong. An emergency will sidetrack your attention or a co-worker who is helping you will get sick.

You also will need time for revising and editing. Few good writers ever stop with their first, or even second, draft. Even one-page letters and memos need a once-over for corrections and polish.

Writers' Tools

Your writing environment is also extremely important. Wherever you write, whether in office, home, airplane, or hotel room, make your working area as comfortable as possible. Have all your research, notes, and reference materials at hand. It is annoying, as well as counterproductive, to stop writing to search for a piece of information. Most offices are reasonably well set up for writing work, but managers who write elsewhere must carefully create the proper environment. Otherwise the task is not as productive as it could be, and far more frustrating than it should be.

At home, do your writing away from main family activity areas, especially where a television set or radio is on. If you have not yet set up an office at home, at least shut yourself in a bedroom or study and request that you not be disturbed. Writing at the kitchen or dining room table or in a living-room easy chair invites interruption. It is best to work at a desk or table with a chair of the right height for your working surface. A chair that is too low or too high causes muscle strain. Metal folding chairs are unsuitable for long periods of writing work. If you do a lot of work at home—and professional managers should expect to—it would be wise to invest in a good office chair; the added comfort will be well worth it. Otherwise, try your kitchen or dining-room chairs, adding a cushion if necessary. Above all, you need adequate light to avoid straining your eyes. Overhead lights are not enough. Compact, high-intensity desk lamps are inexpensive, and some models have clip-on features for attachment to furniture.

The same comfort considerations should be given to your hotel accommodations. Ask for a room with a desk or table and chair and try them out as soon as you check in. If the furniture does not feel comfortable or the lighting is not good, request another room. You will get far more accomplished with less fatigue in an adequate work area.

You can also make productive use of flying time by carrying on writing work. The small meal trays are not well suited as writing surfaces, however, because they usually force you to lean forward to write. Use an attaché case in your lap as a writing surface; or if you carry a soft portfolio, include in it a clipboard or hard notebook binder. If you plan to work throughout a long flight, minimize mental and muscle fatigue by taking an occasional walk down the aisle.

Effective writing also requires good writing habits. That means disciplining yourself to write, whether or not you "feel" like it and in spite of minor distractions. If professional writers wrote only when they "felt" like it, newspapers, magazines, and books would never get off the presses.

Unless you are thoroughly comfortable with writing, you may want to do it when you are least likely to be interrupted. Many prefer to write before and after office hours. As a manager, you cannot always shut yourself away to write, however, and interruptions are certain to happen. Do not let them discourage you. To pick up your train of thought again, concentrate for a few minutes on the subject, consult your notes, if any, and reread some of what you have already written.

Do not try to write too much at one time. Set daily or weekly goals for research and writing. If you are involved in a lengthy project, take frequent breaks. Marathon sessions create fatigue, which causes muddy thought, sloppy writing, and sometimes writer's block.

Even under the best of circumstances, however, writer's block may occur, as it does to almost all writers. If that impasse occurs, do not be alarmed by it. Sometimes writer's block is simply a signal that you are overdue for a break. Sometimes it indicates an unsolved problem in material. Whatever its cause, it should not produce great anxiety.

Writers deal with such a block in a variety of ways. For some people, walking around for a few minutes, perhaps getting a glass of water or cup of coffee, clears their heads enough so the block disappears. For others, getting up and walking away from the writing only makes matters worse; when they return they still feel the block, but feel they have wasted time and created tension. If you are one of those writers, the best solution is to stay at work. Write anything, just to get the process going again. It does not matter if the result is not exactly what you want; you can always go back and revise or even replace it. Your aim is to break through that block. Once you do that, your writing will begin flowing again. Indeed, the process of "just writing" often clarifies unresolved problems that may have caused the block.

The best way to avoid writer's block is to organize your thoughts before you begin to write. You will already have

determined the purpose, audience, and tone of your communication. Now, for anything more than a simple letter, you
should plan its contents and the order of presentation. The
method you use depends only on the scope of your writing
project and what works best for you. Some managers prefer
to jot down a rough outline, while others need a more
detailed one. Still others like to work with three-by-five-inch
index cards, moving them around until they find the right
order. Experiment until you find a technique you are comfortable with.

A rough outline for a report might look something like
this:

PROPOSAL FOR NEW HOSPITAL WING

I. Need
- Existing capacity
- Occupancy rates
- Other local hospitals
- Population projections

II. Specifications
- Location
- Square footage
- Additional capacity

III. Cost
- Financing
- Debt amortization

IV. Construction
- Bids
- Completion time

V. Staff requirements
- Number of additional personnel
- Estimated cost in salaries and benefits

VI. Recommendations

Once you have a draft outline, you can rearrange and
change your headings and emphasis to fit your audience and
purpose. If, for example, the biggest issue facing the hospital
board is not answering community need, but cost and financing alternatives, then construction and finance costs, as well

as the increase in payroll costs, should be moved to the beginning of your report and developed in adequate detail. Whatever method of organization you choose, remember that it is only a beginning framework; the finished product will be quite different from your first outline.

In lengthy documents, such as reports and proposals, decide at the outset how you want to develop your ideas. Look at each section heading in your rough outline. What facts and assumptions lead you to draw your conclusions?

You may organize your material in any of several ways. In most cases, you will want to present the most important material first, putting conclusions near the beginning and supporting evidence later. The presentation is, in effect, the result of a culling process; information researched but discarded is not included because it has no bearing on the final results.

In some cases, however, you want to take the readers through every step, as information is sought and verified or discarded, as in some scientific research reports. Then a *chronological* presentation of information is better, leading the readers from idea or hypothesis through all tests and analyses to the end results and conclusions. In most business writing, readers will not want to be burdened with all the details involved in your research. They will simply want to know the findings, conclusions, recommendations, and substantive facts.

As you begin your first draft, do not be overly concerned with making every sentence perfect; your progress will be smoother and speedier if you save the fine-tuning for later. The various types of writing require different approaches, however.

WRITING EFFECTIVE LETTERS

A good business letter, whether it accepts, rejects, tells, or sells, has warmth and a human touch. It is direct, polite, and sincere, and tells the recipient what he or she needs to know. Many business letters are form letters, processed by compu-

ter or word processor, telling the same thing to each recipient. But even form letters churned out by the hundreds or
thousands need not be mechanical and cold. If you are
responsible for drafting a form letter, give it a little personal
touch. Even the Internal Revenue Service, that cold, impersonal enforcer of income tax laws, sends out polite, consider-
ately worded form letters. Above all, letters should have a
pleasant tone, even if you want to complain about something.
Angry letters do not accomplish nearly as much as firm, well-
reasoned ones.

Before you write a letter, think first what you would say
to the recipient if you were communicating in person. Would
you ever really say, "I am sending forthwith . . ." or "re your
letter of August 18 . . ."? We hope not. Certainly you should
avoid such cumbersome, overly formal phrases in your writing. A pleasant tone is not conveyed by awkward, stilted
phrases.

The use of personal pronouns, such as *I, we,* and *you,*
helps set a pleasant tone in letters. Avoid using harsh negatives and commands. Instead of saying, "We cannot fill your
order," say, "We are unable to fill your order." Do not tell the
recipient that he or she "must" or "has to" do something.
Instead of, "You must sign the enclosed form letter before we
can issue the title," say, "We need your signature on the
enclosed form before we can issue the title." For an informal
tone, use contractions, which are more conversational.

Letters should come right to the point. Give the pertinent information and sign off, not abruptly, but without
digression or padding. One exception to that rule is a letter
replying to a complaint, in which you are trying to soothe
someone. Another is a rejection letter, in which you may not
want to come to the point quickly, but lead up to your "sorry,
no thanks" with some rationale, letting your reader down
easily.

Whatever their subjects or purposes, all letters have in
common a salutation and a closing. Each must be chosen to
suit the tone you have adopted—formal or informal—and the
relationship between you and your reader.

The most common salutation is *Dear* _____ followed by a comma (informal) or a colon (formal, and most commonly used for business purposes).

Dear Mary,
Dear Mr. Jones,
Dear Ms. Randall:

Very formal salutations are *Dear Sir* and *Dear Madam;* reserve those for persons of very high rank or eminence. You may wish to use *Dear Sir or Madam, Dear Sirs or Mesdames,* or *Dear Ladies and Gentlemen,* when you are uncertain who will receive your letter. While none of these choices is terribly attractive, they are preferable to *To Whom It May Concern,* which has a legalistic, antiquated sound to it. In this type of a situation, the best alternative would be to use a neutral label, such as *Dear Advertiser* or *Dear Manager,* if possible.

What if you are uncertain of the gender of the recipient? Say you are writing a formal letter to a Leslie Smith, but you do not know if the person is male or female. Do not use Sir/Madam or Dear Mr./Ms. Smith. Above all, don't guess. Instead, write out the full name: *Dear Leslie Smith.* It may sound a little cumbersome, but it is far better than risking an insulting error.

If you do not know the marital status of a woman, use *Ms.* The neutral title has lost its feminist image and is now widely used and accepted. Many businesswomen prefer it, regardless of marital status.

Closings are simpler. The choice is simply between informal and formal. The best all-purpose closings are *Sincerely* and *Sincerely yours.* Some good informal closings include:

Cordially,
Best regards,
Regards,
Warmly,

Formal closings include:

Respectfully,
Yours truly,
Very cordially yours,
Respectfully yours,
Very truly yours,
Very sincerely yours,

Avoid being cute or clever in closings; in general, avoid extremes, like the too-casual *Yours* or the somewhat groveling *Respectfully submitted.*

In general, letters should come right to the point. Give or ask for the pertinent information, and sign off, not abruptly, but without digression or idle chitchat. One common type of letter requests information, products, or favors.

Here is a good example:

Dear Mr. Blackwell:

As program manager for energy conservation for my company, I am researching the effectiveness of solar heating. I understand Premiere Manufacturing installed a solar heating system about a year ago.

I would appreciate receiving information on your system and its effectiveness. Specifically, I would like to know:

what factors influenced Premiere to select solar heat;

what kind of equipment was installed;

what were the results in terms of energy saved.

I would also appreciate the names of any other companies you know of who use solar heat.

Thank you very much.

Sincerely,

The first paragraph briefly explains to the reader who the writer is and why he or she is writing. The second paragraph defines and limits what is being sought. It is best to be specific; do not ask someone to "tell me everything you know" or "send me everything you have." If you do, you may not receive an answer—your reader may be daunted by the unlimited task. The third paragraph includes a secondary request for optional information, and the last paragraph winds the letter up with a *thank you*.

Occasionally you may be called upon to answer a letter for another person. Tell the reader so in the first paragraph; then answer in your own words.

> Dear Miss Wood:
>
> Mr. Cranston asked me to respond to your letter. I am enclosing . . .

Here's another example:

> Thank you for your recent letter to Judith Temple regarding . . . Our new supply of widgets is due . . .

Avoid such wordings as, "Ms. Burton told me to tell you," or, "Ms. Burton says."

Even formal letters deserve a personal touch. Too many informing letters begin with a mechanical, "This is to inform you that . . ." Note the difference that the use of personal pronouns makes:

> Dear Clayton,
>
> I am delighted to report that you have been elected to the board of directors of Thurber Mineral and Mining Co. As board chairman I wish to extend you a hearty welcome, and I look forward to working with you.

The same holds true for letters of acknowledgment, which should be sent whenever a long delay is anticipated in responding to a sender's request. Here is a form letter of acknowledgment sent by the Internal Revenue Service. Although the salutation *Dear Taxpayer* is anonymous, the letter is direct and courteous.

Dear Taxpayer,

Thank you for the item identified above. We are looking into the matter you brought up and should have the answer to you shortly.

If you write again before hearing from us, please attach the copy of this letter to your correspondence. This will enable us to associate your inquiry with the specific tax account involved.

Thank you for your cooperation.

Sincerely yours,

A letter of transmittal or a cover letter is usually included with a report or proposal you are submitting to someone for their consideration. The letter should state what is being sent, briefly summarize it, and name those who contributed to it, as in this example:

Dear Ms. Carson:

Enclosed is a copy of the Geology Department's report, "Oil Prospects in the Baltimore Canyon."

The report recommends the closing of Wells 13, 3, and 7 in the North Atlantic, which are yielding less than xx barrels per day. The report also recommends new drilling in five locations in the canyon.

The report was compiled by the Survey Committee, of which I am the chairman. Other members include Bob Jones, Gail Smith, and Ted Larson.

I hope the report meets with your approval.

One type of letter that requires special attention is the complaint. We usually want to write complaint letters while we are still angry or upset about a situation; it is natural to transmit that emotion to the words on paper. You may feel better after blowing off steam—but do not mail the letter. Throw it in the trash instead and write another, cooler letter. No one likes to deal with a hot head. The irate letter in Figure 2a, for example, should never go into the mail.

FIGURE 2

a.

Dear Mr. Wise:

I am most upset about the way you printed our latest issue of Bird News. Not only was the color off, but the printing was crooked on four pages in the middle!

Our subscribers pay $36 a year for this magazine, and printing such as this is absolutely unacceptable.

I demand an explanation. This had better not happen again!

b.

Dear Mr. Wise:

Super Press has printed Bird News for the last 10 years, and you have always done a good job for us. This last issue, however, contains several very visible errors.

On the middle four pages, the color is off and the type is noticeably crooked.

Did all copies go out this way, or were these errors confined to a few copies? If the number is significant, perhaps we can agree on an adjustment to the bill.

Wouldn't you have felt foolish if you had found out that the error described in Figure 2a was confined to a handful of copies, and that you had received one of the few faulty copies by accident? A more courteous approach and certainly one that is better suited to long-term working relationships would be worded something like the second letter in the figure.

Mistakes, however, do happen. If you are on the receiving end of a valid complaint, own up to it with a polite apology.

Dear Mr. Southwell:

Since we received your letter about the improper printing of the last issue of *Bird News,* our vice president of production has met with our press foreman to determine what the problem was.

Apparently, a press person loaded the paper feeder incorrectly. The error was spotted, and the bad copies were pulled out of production. Evidently a few slipped through—we think it could not have been more than 30 copies.

This was a human error, and all personnel have been alerted to be much more careful in the future. We apologize for the mistake and wish to assure you that all precautions will be taken in the future to deliver a product of which we can all be proud.

If the complainer is in error, or if you cannot comply with his or her request, be polite but firm.

Dear Mr. Calder:

We have double-checked our records and find that our last billing was correct. Your last payment was received on March 17, and your account shows that $54.29 is still owed us.

Perhaps your payment envelope was misplaced or lost in the mail. If so, you may still avoid a finance charge by remitting the above amount by the next billing date.

Rejection letters are the most difficult letters to write. No one likes to be rejected; neither does anyone relish the job of rejecting. Letters spare the face-to-face discomfort involved, but you should be especially sensitive to your readers when writing rejection letters. Even so, you should be firm and clear. You would not want, for example, to give unsuitable job candidates false hopes for future consideration. Better that they cross your company off their lists and spend their job search time more productively elsewhere—and better that you be spared the unpleasant task of repeated rejections. Whatever you do, avoid rejection letters that are obvious form letters (printed or photocopied with the individual's name typed in); they are totally unprofessional.

Whatever type of letters you routinely have to write, you will benefit from developing your own standard "form" letters. Examine your own files for a certain period, isolate the various types of letters, and analyze the contents, retaining what you think on reflection worked well, and replacing what did not. At best, you will discover that some letters you have been writing could easily be handled by your assistant, with your forms as guidelines. At worst, you will save yourself a good deal of rethinking for those parts of your letters that are relatively routine. A caution, however—avoid form letters when you are dealing with a single person or company over a long period of time. They would surely be insulted by them.

WRITING EFFECTIVE REPORTS

A great volume of information is exchanged daily in business, science, and government in the form of reports, yet too often the contents are inscrutable. Conclusions and recommendations are unclear or buried; text is foggy, with rambling digressions; the material jumps around in a haphazard fashion, making it difficult to follow a train of thought or logic. Trying to decipher such reports is an annoying task for a busy manager. Many such reports are set aside; some are ignored altogether.

A successful report is well planned, from contents to paper to binding. It not only captures a reader's attention; it commands it. If a report merely "looks interesting," it may not get read.

Preparation of a large report requires careful analysis of all factors relating to a situation or problem, careful research, and thorough, objective reporting. It requires a sensitivity to the internal politics at work in any professional environment, as well as an awareness of the relationships between your readers and your topic, especially if they will be affected by your recommendations. And it involves an artful tailoring of your presentation to your audience. Not that you should try to color facts or hide information that does not support your viewpoint—that is generally self-defeating, in the long run. But no two reports are structured the same, just as no two sales calls on prospective customers are the same; you will structure your communication to fit your point of view. Your persuasiveness depends not only on the contents of your report, but on its style and packaging as well.

A frequent mistake people make when they attempt a persuasive report is banking on the facts to do the persuading. They pay scant attention to their tone of "voice" and their packaging of the material. No need to worry, they think; the facts are irrefutable and speak for themselves. Granted, you do not have much of an argument without solid evidence to back you up, but information alone will not persuade or change attitudes. Decisions, large and small, are made every day that disregard fact and reason. Why? Because nothing convinced the decision-makers to act differently. People cling stubbornly to biases and preconceived notions; they remain entrenched in habits and ignore advice they think will affect them adversely. They reject anything that offends them—including a report that lacks credibility, is difficult to understand, or sounds condescending. Some factors will always be beyond your control; for example, you cannot control the events in a reader's life that affect overall mood and receptivity. You can, however, tip the balance in your favor by constructing the most persuasive case you can—and you should do this even if you think you have an easy selling job.

First, analyze the subject of your report. What are all the factors you must consider about your subject? Outline the different ways to approach it. If your subject is a problem, define it and its causes. You may wish to use flowcharts and diagrams to help you better understand the problem and its causes and effects. If there are several possible solutions or lines of investigation, examine each one carefully. Once you have prepared in this way, it is time to set up a procedure for research and investigation. Determine sources of information; you will discard some and discover new ones as you go along. It is important that your sources be credible with your readers, otherwise your report may be easily and quickly dismissed. Naturally, your deadline will influence the extent of your research and the depth, perhaps even the scope, of your report. You cannot do the same kind of job in several days that you can do in several weeks. Even with a short deadline, however, you can put together a convincing document.

Pay particular attention to analyzing your readers. What are their ages, positions, experience, attitudes? Do they have any known prejudices for or against your subject? What are their personalities? An important reader, for example, might be a stickler for details and be dissatisfied if they are not provided. Convincing this reader will require attention to figures and precise explanations. Or perhaps you know that another reader is sensitive about his or her position of authority and prefers to keep a formal distance from subordinates. The tone of your writing, then, should not be too informal or familiar. Do you think your recommendations will be received favorably, or do you have an uphill battle? What obstacles do you think you will have to overcome? Remember, your readers' points of view may be vastly different than your own. Every person who sees your report is going to ask, "How is this going to affect *me*?" Keep your readers in mind at all times during your writing.

You will also want to assess your readers' views of your credibility. In many situations you will automatically have a certain amount of credibility and authority with your audience due to your position, experience, knowledge of the subject, or professional standing. You can acquire additional credibility through the research, facts, opinions, and recommendations you present in your report and the manner in which you present them. Cite sources of authority your readers are likely to respect, and cite them by name; nonspecific references such as "authorities say" or "according to one analyst" are less persuasive. If your readers perceive you to have any biases toward your subject, carefully bal-

ance your material to avoid appearing one-sided or prejudiced. You will be much more credible if you examine all
facets of the issue or problem without bias.

Once you have analyzed your topic and your readers,
select the tone that will best suit your work. The tone of your
writing reveals your attitude toward your readers and your
subject. A good report can be undone with the wrong tone.
Generally, most people do not appreciate being lectured, nor
are they convinced by a timid style that lacks conviction. To
be most persuasive, write with a friendly, sincere, and objective voice; strive for a middle ground between informality
and formality.

Watch your use of imperatives, such as *must, should,
have to,* and *ought to,* because they carry negative connotations. Too many imperatives can make readers feel something is being forced upon them. You can still, however,
write with authority. Your readers are, after all, looking to
your report as a source of information and guidance to use in
making decisions. You will be more persuasive if you use a
personal voice from time to time. Write, "I believe that . . ."
rather than the nebulous, "It is believed that . . ." or, "I
conclude . . ." rather than, "It can be concluded . . ."
Compare the following examples. Note that the paragraphs
with the personal voice have a more authoritative ring:

> ***Impersonal:*** *It is suspected* that once inflation is initi-
> ated and persists for a time, expectations
> arise that it will continue. These expecta-
> tions then become a force for inflation's
> continuation or acceleration. Unless pos-
> itive action is taken to dampen these
> expectations, inflation will persist or
> worsen.

> ***Personal:*** Based on these historical patterns, *I be-
> lieve* that once inflation is initiated and
> persists for a time, expectations arise
> that it will continue. These expectations

then become a force for inflation's con-
tinuation or acceleration. Unless positive
action is taken to dampen these expectations, inflation will persist or worsen.

Impersonal: *It is believed* that American businesses
will have to cope with a high rate of
inflation well into the future. *It is sur-
mised* that the most successful companies will be those who change their
policies and resources to manage an inflationary environment.

Personal: *I believe* that American businesses will
have to cope with a high rate of inflation
well into the future. The most successful
companies, *in my opinion,* will be those
who change their policies and resources
to manage an inflationary environment.

Some managers seize a report assignment as an opportunity to show off their expertise or their command of the
language. Such reports are more likely to alienate than to
persuade. Readers are forced to wade through windy ora-
tion, abstract concepts, or material that is irrelevant to the
subject but supposedly demonstrates their knowledge.
Think of your readers as busy people, like yourself, who
want the facts—straight, simple, and unadorned.

In most cases, you will want to put your conclusions and
recommendations at the beginning of your report. Readers
remember most what they see first and last, and most will
want to know immediately what you are recommending and
how they will be affected. On the other hand, if you expect
your audience to be sharply skeptical of or downright hostile
to your recommendations, you may wish to place your conclusions and recommendations last, building a chain of concrete facts that lead to an irrefutable conclusion. If that is the
case, try hard to hook your reader in the first paragraph, so

he or she will follow your logical progression rather than
flipping impatiently to the back of your report.

In any case, present your strongest points first. Do not
count on a marginally interested reader staying with you all
the way to the brilliant strong points you tucked into the
middle or back of your report.

Above all, keep your report simple. Delete all material
that does not illuminate the subject for your reader, no
matter how much you would like to include it. Be ruthless.
Write to conserve your readers' time and maintain their
attention. Abide by the old axiom, "When in doubt, leave it
out." Background sections are appropriate dumping grounds
for extraneous information. Remapping the world and rein-
venting the wheel in the main body of your work will only
bore your audience. Gauge your detail by your readers'
familiarity with your subject.

Similarly, keep your language lean and spare. Many
writers think they will appear more intelligent and profound
if they use big words and long, complicated sentences. Instead, they usually obscure their message. Make reading
easy for your audience by sticking to simple sentences and
short, familiar words. The author of the following sentence
made an important but simple observation. Its impact, however, is diluted by the verbiage:

> Inflation can create an astigmatism for managers and
> investors, but when we have ground and fitted the cor-
> rective lenses and put them on for the first time, we see
> the answer to dealing with inflation: good management.

That 37-word sentence has more punch when pared
down to its 15-word essence:

> The answer to dealing with inflation is so simple it is
> often overlooked: good management.

You should gauge your level of detail and substantiation
according to your audience, your purpose, and—perhaps

most of all—your personal expertise and credentials. If you are a recognized authority in the area of the report, you may make substantial generalizations without citing specifics to back them up, as in the following paragraph:

> This decade is the first in the nation's history in which most workers earn their livings in the office. As part of their daily tasks, these white-collar professionals are called upon to manage an increasing flood of information. American offices each day generate 100 million letters, 900 million computer printouts, and 365 million photocopies.

In most cases, however, you will want and need to cite sources and authorities for your information, so your readers need not wonder if you pulled your generalizations out of thin air. The italicized sections below indicate how such attributions can be neatly handled:

> This decade is the first in the nation's history in which most workers—55%—earn their livings in the office. *Demographic information from the U.S. Bureau of Labor Statistics shows* that the halfway point in white-collar versus blue-collar jobs was passed five years ago.

> These growing numbers of white-collar professionals are called upon daily to manage an increasing flood of information. American offices each day generate 100 million letters, 900 million computer printouts, and 365 million photocopies, *according to a study done this year by the Young & Harvey consulting firm.*

Not every specific must be attributed to a source, of course. Your judgment of the audience's level of knowledge and receptivity will determine how much or how little detail is to be put in. Even if you do not cite sources, specific data often make your points more clearly and sharply. For example, here is a generalization that could be strengthened by specifics:

Cable television has finally become a mass medium. There are enough cable subscribers across the nation to interest major advertisers in underwriting programming costs.

or

Cable television has finally become a mass medium. *More than 27% of the nation's 80 million TV households are hooked up to a cable system.* That penetration is high enough to interest major advertisers in underwriting programming costs.

Quotations can also be used to add interest and validation to your material, but use them judiciously. Frequent or long quotations lose their effectiveness and become tedious.

In addition to validating and substantiating your general statements, it is helpful and persuasive to *tell the readers why*—to explain the significance of your material to your audience. Readers should not have to guess why you took a certain approach to a problem or what you were looking for, nor should they have to unravel your report as though it were a mystery novel. It is far easier to persuade your readers if they are not befuddled. Explain why you took a particular approach and why an observation or fact is significant.

Similarly, new ideas and unfamiliar concepts will be easier for your readers to grasp and accept if you do some preparation before you present them. Move from the simple to the complex, the familiar to the unfamiliar, the noncontroversial to the controversial. Elaborate on the unusual. Anticipate the objections that your readers will raise and deal with them before doubt is allowed to build. If you fail to answer those objections, your conclusions and recommendations may be discounted, and you may not have a chance for rebuttal.

If you must present bad news, do so tactfully. In ancient times, messengers who carried bad tidings were often killed. Although people no longer execute messengers, no one likes receiving bad news. If you are recommending the divestiture of a division, the termination of a project, budget cuts, or layoffs, be considerate of the egos and personalities involved. It is natural for those who have something at stake to react defensively.

Present the situation in as positive a light as possible. Were the external factors beyond someone's control? If so, point them out. Do not try to coddle your readers, however; such attempts may be transparent and only alienate them. Also, be careful to avoid laying blame directly. Whatever the case, there is no need to be brutal.

Maintain an objective stance throughout your report. Presenting both sides of an argument puts the pros and cons into perspective, and is especially important if your readers are skeptical or hostile. They will have a much harder time disagreeing with your recommendations if you show a thorough examination of both sides of an issue.

This means that you should report all conclusions. Frequently, not all the conclusions you reach will support your recommendations. Report them all anyway, lest a sharp-eyed reader concludes you have omitted something out of prejudice or negligence. Reporting all conclusions will emphasize your objectivity and thoroughness. Sandwich negative conclusions between your positive ones to begin and end in a position of strength.

STRUCTURING REPORTS

Most reports are broken down into the same parts: title, summary, table of contents, conclusions, recommendations, introduction, body, appendixes, bibliography—generally in that order. Some reports may also have a foreword, preface, and acknowledgments. Several of these parts are optional, and their order varies, depending on the type of report, the audience, and "political" considerations. It is usually advisable, for example, to place conclusions and recommendations up front after the summary, which saves readers time. If you wish to include foreword, preface, and acknowledgments, for example, one standard organization would look like this:

> Title
> Foreword
> Preface
> Acknowledgments
> Summary
> Table of contents
> Conclusions
> Recommendations
> Introduction
> Body
> Appendix
> Bibliography

Titles should be specific and tell the reader what type of report they are receiving. They also should indicate whether the report recommends, evaluates, analyzes, informs, or instructs; otherwise, the reader is left to guess by thumbing through pages. For example, a title that reads simply "The Donaldson Cooling Process for Combining Polymers" gives no clue to the purpose of the report. But "An Evaluation of the Donaldson Cooling Process for Combining Polymers" does. Similarly, an instructional report may be titled "Procedures for Improving Administrative Productivity," while the title of a recommending report may be "A Proposal to Relocate Smith Industries Corporate Headquarters to Dallas, Texas." Reports are abstracted and filed according to their titles, so it is very important that they accurately reflect the contents. While they should be specific and descriptive, they should also be as brief as possible. A title is placed on a separate cover page, along with your name as author, or the name of the responsible group, committee, or company.

Forewords and prefaces are optional elements in reports. Usually one or the other is selected; occasionally both. Forewords are written by someone other than the author of the report, while prefaces are written by the author. They are brief sections of one or a few paragraphs, describing the purpose of and need for the report, and, in very general terms, its contents.

If persons other than the authors made significant contributions to a report, the author may choose to recognize them in a separate acknowledgment section containing brief statements expressing thanks or appreciation.

The summary is one of the last elements of a report to be written. It should be concise—200 words or so—and should tell the reader the scope of the report, the important findings, and the conclusions and recommendations, if any. Save details for other sections; the summary is intended to contain the most important information in a nutshell.

How you present your conclusions depends on how you perceive your audience's reaction to them. Decide which order is most effective for presenting your conclusions: most important first; most important last; negative first; or negative last. Follow each conclusion with a supporting statement or two, but keep this section brief. The body of your report is the place to develop and build a case.

Not all reports require recommendations. Do not offer any unless they are part of your charge. Handle them in the same way you handle the section on conclusions. Decide on an order of presentation, with supporting statements following each recommendation. Again, the body of your report will provide the details.

Wait to draw up the table of contents until after the report is finished. Then list all sections of the report, including all headings and subheadings except the most minor ones. Make a separate list of the illustrations in order by page or illustration number, giving caption or title.

Use the introduction to grab the reader's attention and stimulate interest in the rest of the report. Think of it as a beginning to any good news story or article. Introductions should incorporate the basic five W's: who, what, where, when, and why. Do not load your introduction with background material. You will only bog down your reader at a crucial point. Establish your foundation, generate interest, and then move into the body of your report.

Finally comes the body of the report itself. Fairly short reports will have few of the other sections mentioned, and the body of the report itself may be one unbroken section. But if your report is lengthy, the body should be divided into main sections or chapters, each of which—if the length of the report warrants it—is composed of subsections. Place nonessential, supplementary information in appendixes in the back. Introduce these sections with headings and subheadings; they break up text and they help readers stay on track. Headings and subheadings should be descriptive. Instead of "Factors" say "Factors Influencing Buyer Resistance." You may choose from among several styles of headings and subheadings, employing a hierarchy of variations in placement, capitalizing, underlining, or numbering. Whatever style you choose, follow it consistently throughout your report. That is, do not capitalize main headings in one chapter and underline them in another.

Here is an example of a common way of using headings:

CHAPTER OR SECTION TITLE

Main Heading

Subheading.
Text is indented on the following line.

Minor heading. Text follows immediately on the same line.

In this example, the chapter or section title will be centered, all in capital letters. All main headings will be centered, with the initial letter of important words capitalized. Subheads also have initial letters capitalized, are italicized or underlined, and are placed flush with the left margin; text follows on the next line. Minor or "sub-sub" headings are similar, although usually shorter and followed by text on the same line.

Numbers and decimals also may be used with headings. The method shown below is common in scientific and technical reports and proposals:

1. CHAPTER OR SECTION TITLE

1.1 *Heading.*   Followed by text.

1.2 *Heading.*   Followed by text.

For special emphasis you may also use lists of points, highlighted with bullets or by underlining text.

Lists are helpful in drawing the reader's attention to points that otherwise might be lost in a gray section of type, and in neatly summarizing information. They are eye-catching if pages are being scanned and make it easier for readers to remember your material.

The following paragraph is perfectly clear and readable:

> Present qualifications for homeowners' mortgages include: a $2,000 minimum savings account established at one of our branches; a 30% down payment; and a monthly mortgage payment 25% or less of the gross monthly income.

But the information stands out better when presented in list form:

> Present requirements for homeowners' mortgages include:
>
> • A $2,000 minimum savings account established at one of our branches
> • A 30% down payment
> • A monthly mortgage payment 25% or less of the gross monthly income

Numbers can also be used in lists, especially where order is important:

The directors of the board outlined three broad marketing objectives for the next 12 months:

1. To draw more customers into the company's
   stores
2. To convert occasional customers into steady customers
3. To hold present customers against competition

Supplementary information, such as background studies and cases referred to in the body of your report, is placed
in an appendix at the end. You may have no appendix, or
one, or several, depending on the volume of material. You
should organize appendixes by subject and assign titles to
them.

A bibliography at the end of your report cites your
research and information sources; it may also be titled something like "Further Reading," "Sources," or "References."
List books, articles, studies, and reports alphabetically by
author. If no author is specified, alphabetize either by title or
by name of originator, such as a laboratory or company. If
your bibliography is extensive, you may wish to separate
references into categories and alphabetize each one. The
following examples give one standard form for bibliographi-
cal entries. Note that subsequent lines of each entry are
indented.

Eames, Alfred, *The Flight of Man*. New York: Carter
Press, 19xx.

Hack, Ralph, "Wings Over the Earth," *Science News*,
July 19xx, pp. 33–37.

Milton Research Corp., *Industrial Pollution in the
Wide River*, Technical Bulletin No. 3328 (Washington, D.C.: U.S. Dept. of the Interior, 19xx), p. 46.

When you directly quote or refer to published material
in the body of your report, you should footnote it. To do so,
insert either an asterisk or a number, raised a half-line above
the text, to signal the existence of a footnote. If you use only

one or a few footnotes in your report, asterisks are fine to use, and a footnote should simply be placed at the bottom of the appropriate page, separated from the body of the text by a half-line. If you have many footnotes, it is preferable to number them in order; then footnotes should be either at the bottom of the appropriate page, or grouped together at the end of a section or at the end of the report. The example below gives a standard form of footnote.

[1]Jackson, Anthony, *Winning Ways*. Chicago: Tremble Books, 19xx, p. 81.

You should provide the same source information as in a bibliography. Always include page numbers for specific references, even with books.

If you are using illustrations with your report, place each one as close to its text reference as possible. Select visuals with care and use only those that help the reader understand your text, a trend, or "big picture." Visuals sprinkled throughout the report should be simple; save the complex ones for an appendix.

Visuals are customarily labeled figures, exhibits, or illustrations. Assign them Arabic numbers, Roman numerals, or letters of the alphabet, as in "Figure 3," "Exhibit IV," or "Exhibit A." Always refer to your visuals in your text, as in these examples:

As we can see in Figure 7, companies with high-quality products generally have a higher return on investment than companies with low-quality products.

Companies with high-quality products generally have a higher return on investment than companies with low-quality products (see Appendix, Figure 7).

. . . is shown in Exhibit X.

Figure 1 indicates . . .

Choices

Your budget, the significance of your report, and its circulation will influence how it is printed or photocopied and bound. Select a good-quality cotton rag bond paper, at least 20-lb. weight, white or buff in color. Steer clear of brightly colored paper and colored ink, which make reading harder. Whether the report is stitched, bound, or simply placed in a folder or notebook, it should be easy to open and stay relatively flat. Caution—some plasticized notebooks resist staying open and are awkward to handle.

Illustrations deserve some special attention. They are most useful tools for explaining and interpreting data, trends, and comparisons, and you should consider ways to use them in your writing. Visuals include charts, tables, drawings, diagrams, and occasionally photographs. They help readers to better understand facts, figures, and relationships. They also enhance the attractiveness of your manuscript by breaking up blocks of text and catching the reader's eye. Many readers skim through written materials looking at the illustrations; a good illustration can cause a reader to stop and read the text, perhaps the entire piece. Visuals should not be used indiscriminately, however, as too many can be distracting. Use them to help make complex information simple, and to avoid lengthy written explanations.

You need not have the services of an art department to create interesting and helpful visuals. Illustrations are best when they are simple, and you can do a lot with pencil or pen, a ruler, and a compass. Diagrams and drawings should not be amateurishly executed, however; if yours are complex, consider using a graphic artist for the job.

You will probably get ideas for visuals as you organize your material, before you begin writing. Do roughs of your ideas. After your text has been drafted, see where visuals fit in the best. You may not need or want all of your original ideas; do not hesitate to discard whatever is not appropriate.

Where possible, present the visual—whether horizontal or vertical—so that it lies on the page in normal reading position, rather than being placed so that the reader must turn the page to read it. Make illustrations as small as possible while still being readable, understandable, and fair in scale. Distortions of scale make data misleading. For example, a compressed horizontal scale can make a medio-cre increase appear dramatic, while an elongated vertical scale can flatten out a sharp increase.

In general, place visuals as close as possible to their reference in the text. Always refer to an illustration's page number, even if it is on the same page as the reference. It is best not to say "see chart below" or "see graph on next page," because revisions or printing could change the position of the visual. In memos, you may prefer to place all illustrations at the end.

Each illustration should be labeled, such as Exhibit A or Figure 1, and be captioned. Explanatory or narrative captions communicate most effectively. For example, instead of captioning a chart "Increase in Sales," use "Sales increased 50% in 19xx." If an illustration requires a detailed explanation in order to be interpreted, discard it or try to simplify it. The best visuals are those that are virtually self-explanatory and illustrate a single point. When making comparisons, limit elements to three per illustration.

In general, tables are good to show quantities and growth or decline, while charts are effective at showing relationships. There are four general kinds of charts: pie charts show pieces of a whole; bar charts indicate comparisons; line charts show trends and changes over time; and dot charts show changes in variables. Your best course is to keep a file containing copies of illustrations you thought were particularly effective, and, when you are doing a report, look at the file to get ideas for how best to present summary data visually.

EDITING YOUR WRITING

The final editing of your work is just as important as the writing of it. It is your chance to refine your draft into a polished piece of work. Once you complete your draft, set it aside for a while—a day or two, preferably—to let it cool. This is particularly important if you have been working on a long or complicated report, for the longer you are immersed in a project, the more likely you are to overlook inconsistencies and small errors. You will be surprised at what pops out after you have put some distance between you and your writing.

Then take a good, distanced look at your draft. As you read, you should keep in mind some general principles of good writing. Most important, your work should be clear and concise. Your readers should be able to understand you without rereading sentences or paragraphs or jumping back to a reference on a previous page. If that happens, you have failed to communicate. Often that occurs because the piece is overloaded with clutter. You want to tell your readers immediately why you are writing, rather than making them guess or wade through windy introductory remarks. Not all members of your audience will have the time, interest, or patience to sift through long sentences looking for the salient points. This memo, for example, serves the purpose of the writer and not of the readers:

> As you know, the sales promotion and marketing support department has been reorganized. The reorganization came about as the result of a study we undertook to examine the efficiency of the department.
>
> While most of those polled within the company were pleased with the services provided by the department, it became obvious that a number of changes were needed to be of better service to the branch sales staffs.
>
> Therefore, here is a list of new sales promotion and marketing communications services the department will now provide . . .

The reader does not need a recap of the department's study and subsequent reorganization. The important information—the change that will help the sales force do a better job—is buried in the third paragraph. The memo will be much more effective rewritten this way:

Here is a list of the new services provided by the sales promotion and marketing support department. The changes are the result of a recent study of the sales force's promotional needs.

1. The marketing information bulletin will be expanded from 12 to 20 pages . . .

The memo is shorter, more to the point, and successful in communicating necessary information.

Even if you put your most important information first, your writing will not be clear if you drown it in a flood of extra words and awkward sentences. Keep your prose well pruned. Have you used two adjectives where one will do? Have you peppered your writing with empty phrases such as "I might add," "as you know," and "you'll be interested to know that"? Avoid redundancies similar to the following:

He summarized at the conclusion by saying, "I think the move will be good for Bingham."

Properly edited, this example would read:

He summarized: "I think the move will be good for Bingham."

Too much surgery leaves dry, lifeless writing, as unpretty as a tree stripped of foliage. A caution here: the intent should be to excise spongy, excess phrases, not to cut words that supply meaning and liveliness to writing.

The following portion of a report suffers from four clarity problems. The important information is buried at the end; it is riddled with unnecessary words; the sentences are awkwardly constructed; and the information is not presented in a form easy for the reader to grasp.

Trivalent chromium gives a finish which is indistinguishable from the hexavalent sort (to the metal plating nov-

ice, at any rate) but it has proved singularly hard to
develop commercially.

The problem is tied up with the difficulty of achieving a
stable plating solution. Technically, the electrochemistry
of the trivalent chromium is complex, giving rise to slow
electron transfer during the plating process, slow formation of metal complexes, and rapid breakdown of the
newly formed plating complexes. In other words, not a
commercially attractive proposition.

After a revision, the information becomes clearer:

Trivalent chromium would not be a cost-effective metal
finish alternative to hexavalent chromium. The two finishes look nearly the same, but trivalent chromium solution is much harder to stabilize.

Stabilization is difficult because of:

- Slow electron transfer during the plating process
- Slow formation of metal complexes
- Rapid breakdown of complexes formed

The revision tells the reader that a metal finish under
consideration is not advisable and why. The bullets group a
series of related facts and make them easier to read and
remember; numbers could have been used for the same
purpose.

Jargon—nonwords and often meaningless gibberish—is
a bane to clarity and conciseness. In government agencies
and businesses large and small across the nation, executives
are solutioning problems, dollarizing new production processes, getting orientated to situations, and through-putting
suggestions. While some corporate publications have taken
up a "ban the jargon" standard, and many seminars and
books tackle the subject, jargon still thrives.

We are guilty of using jargon when we turn nouns into
verbs, create nonwords, and otherwise mangle the English
language. A favorite in the corporate lexicon is *escalate*.

Used properly, it means, "to increase in extent, scope, or volume." Used as jargon, it means taking an issue to a higher authority, as when someone dislikes a decision and announces, "I'm going to escalate this to the vice president."

Not surprisingly, lawyers are among the worst offenders. Legal mumbo-jumbo renders incomprehensible many contracts, laws, regulations, and applications.

Jargon and obfuscation have long been problems in the bureaucratic ranks of the federal government, so much so that an internal campaign was launched in 1979 to fight them. Members of the Document Design Center, a division of the private, nonprofit American Institute of Research, have been instructing government employees how to write in plain English. Alas, thousands of confusing regulations and application forms still are churned out every year. Ironically, the campaign created new jargon; *good paper* and *bad paper* are now terms to describe the clarity or lack of same in government writing.

Much jargon comes from plain laziness. It is faster to say, "Dollarize this," than to say, "Estimate how much it will cost to do this." Some jargon comes from ignorance. *Solution* is a noun, *solve* a verb. Problems are solved, not solutioned. A quick check with a dictionary would save many a writer the embarrassment of an improperly used or nonexistent word, like the sales executive who reported that sales of a certain product were "denigrating." (He meant *declining*).

Some jargon users sincerely believe that jargon makes them sound impressive. Quite the opposite. A trip to the dictionary here, too, would cure a few jargon ills. At worst, jargon will reduce your writing to gibberish and make you appear uneducated. At best, it is annoying clutter. If some jargon has crept into your draft, excise it. Do you really mean "electronic mail" instead of "electronic document distribution"? Are you offering suggestions instead of inputting them?

An active voice, rather than a passive voice, will contribute to your clarity and conciseness. In an active voice, the subject of a sentence performs an activity or takes action. In a passive voice, the subject receives action. A passive voice, which is used far too often in business communications, weakens sentences and dilutes their meaning. Because it can provide an anonymous cloak, it is a favorite of writers who wish to blunt their words or evade responsibility for a statement.

See how much stronger the following sentences are when written in an active voice:

> *Passive:* Replacement of existing copiers with newer, faster models is being planned for the next fiscal year.
>
> *Active:* We plan to replace all copiers with newer, faster models next fiscal year.
>
> *Passive:* It is recommended that our prices be increased by 10%.
>
> *Active:* I recommend a 10% price increase.

Note that the active voice sentences are shorter, more concise, and more powerful, and have more impact on the reader. If you find that your writing is largely passive, rewrite your sentences in the active voice during editing.

It is also important to establish a smooth pace and pleasant cadence for the written word, just as for the spoken word. Sentences that are short and choppy give the reader an unsettled, stop-and-go feeling. Long sentences that must be reread and deciphered leave the reader feeling exhausted and confused.

Here is a single sentence published in the U.S. Department of Agriculture's October 1981 telephone book. Fill up your lungs and try to get through it in one breath:

> To ensure that the information on all USDA employees on file within O&F is current, it is essential that all employees promptly notify their designated agency contact of all changes to any of the information contained in the alphabetical listing section of the directory, i.e., name, room number, building location, and telephone

number, so the contacts can transmit this information to the AMLS and Telephone Directory Section of the Reproduction and Distribution Division which maintains the data base for this information from which the alphabetical listing section of the USDA Telephone Directory is prepared as well as periodic updates of telephone directory information on USA employees which are transmitted to the GSA Locater Service here in Washington, D.C.

Do you know what this says? There are 135 words in this sentence, counting the abbreviations as single words.

These two possible revisions are more understandable and save the reader considerable time in reading and rereading:

Please submit promptly all changes of name, address, and telephone number to your agency contact in order to keep federal directories up to date. (One sentence, 24 words)

or

Please help keep federal directories up to date. Submit promptly all changes of name, address, and telephone number to your agency contact. (Two sentences, 8 and 14 words, respectively)

For your readers' sakes, keep your sentences of a manageable length. If your sentences *average* 17 to 20 words in length, you are in the ball park. Some sentences will be shorter and some longer, of course. You should vary the lengths to avoid monotony. Calculate the lengths of a few sentences you have written. If they *all* ran longer than 20 words, break several of them into shorter sentences.

Your information should be evenly paced throughout your document, too. Do not drop too much on the reader at once, but do not skip over something too lightly.

Give your material a test by reading it aloud. Do any

parts of it sound jerky, as though you are missing a transition? Can you combine two choppy sentences into a single sentence? Does your material look pleasing to the eye? Is information neatly packaged in manageable paragraphs? If it is a report, have you used headings and subheadings to break up chunks of type?

Most often, editing involves dealing with several types of problems at once. Be ruthless in chopping out unnecessary words and jargon, and in changing sentences from passive into active ones.

Here is an example of passive and muddy sentence construction:

> The findings of your department have been received by me. At this point in time, we should dialogue to improve our interrelationship. We haven't experienced enough productive interfacing to solution this knotty problem. My staff will be continually checking the procedures now being utilized.

The example begins with a passive voice, *have been received,* followed by an unnecessary phrase, *at this point in time.* The noun *dialogue* is used incorrectly as a verb; *interrelationship* is virtually redundant—*relationship* is sufficient. An interface is what enables computers to communicate— humans should not be reduced to this mechanical level. *Solution* is a noun used incorrectly as a verb, while *will be continually checking* is another unnecessarily long construction. Finally, *utilized* is an inflated term; *used* would be better.

Translated and edited, the example might read something like this:

> I've received your department's findings. I don't think we've cooperated enough to solve this problem, and we need to meet soon. Meanwhile, my staff will monitor the procedures now in use.

This 37-word sentence also suffers from a weak, passive voice:

> Recognition that a measurement is needed to show the unions and employees a more realistic financial position for wage bargaining purposes, and to limit dividend expectations, has helped acceptability of the current cost accounting method in America.

The point here is that the current cost accounting method is gaining acceptance in the United States, but that information is buried at the end of the sentence. This sentence is better divided in two:

> Current cost accounting is gaining acceptance among American businesses because it provides a more realistic financial picture. This is advantageous for wage contract negotiations and for limiting dividend expectations of stockholders.

Too often writers pad and inflate in order to make something appear more important; they tiptoe around negatives or unpleasantness with euphemisms. Say what you mean, and say it directly. Do not use big words and euphemisms when simple, direct words will do. Members of Congress really fool no one when they call a tax increase "revenue enhancement," or bombing "air support," nor does a company soften the blow of a layoff by calling it a "workforce consolidation."

See how this example is buried in long words and euphemisms:

> The workforce consolidation is the result of continued advances in technology and improved manufacturing efficiencies. An example of these improvements is the continuing trend toward using automated mechanical devices, which has reduced the need for some traditional manufacturing assembly operators.

What the above example really says is this:

> One reason for the layoffs is the increasing use of robots
> instead of people on the assembly line.

Revised, the word count is cut in half, from 41 words to 20.
Two long, awkward sentences are reduced to one simple and
direct statement.

Take a good, long look at your draft. Is your writing
laced with empty phrases such as "please be advised" or
"attached please find"? Edit them out.

Also check to see that your writing is not sexist in tone,
assuming by its references that the world is all male. More
and more, writers—professional and business alike—are
learning to avoid discriminatory gender references. That is,
masculine pronouns such as *he, him,* and *his* are no longer
used universally to refer to all people. The answer is not
merely to substitute *he or she, him or her,* or *his or hers,*
which become ridiculously cumbersome when repeated.
Nonsexist writing takes a little more thought and effort at the
start, but it gradually becomes second nature. No job should
be sex-stereotyped, no matter how few women or men are
likely to hold it. Do not assume that all managers, presidents,
doctors, or engineers are male. Likewise, do not assume all
nurses, teachers, and clerks are female.

One way to avoid gender pronouns is to use plurals,
which are neutral. Instead of saying, "The lawyer . . . he,"
say "Lawyers . . . they." Or substitute pronouns such as *you*
and *your.* Instead of "The first-line manager is responsible
for his employee's performance," say "First-line managers
are responsible for their employees' performances," or "A
first-line manager is responsible for an employee's performance," or "As a first-line manager, you are responsible for
your employees' performance." In the last two examples, *a*
and *an* and *you* and *your* are substituted for pronouns identifying gender.

Whenever possible, refer to a person by name. Instead
of "Give it to the secretary and she'll take care of it," say

"Give it to Gloria Wilson and she'll take care of it," or "Give it to Tom Jackson and he'll take care of it."

Alternate male and female references, but not in the same example. Thus, you would not say "The manager must evaluate each of his employees once a year. She must write up the evaluation for the employee's personnel jacket."

It is acceptable to use *him or her, his or hers,* and *he or she,* but do so infrequently, because they are clumsy. Similarly, avoid *he/she, his/hers, s/he,* and *(s)he.* In those rare instances when you want to use masculine pronouns to represent everyone, be sure to announce that choice in the beginning of your text. In most cases, though, it is best to try to write around gender.

Find neutral substitutes for words that traditionally have been masculine, such as *chairman, mailman, stockboy, manpower, manhours,* and *salesman.* Here are a few examples of neutral substitutes for these nouns:

chairman	chair
mailman	mail carrier
stockboy	stock clerk
manpower	workforce
manhours	workhours
salesman	sales representative

It is best not to substitute *-person* or *-woman* in masculine words, such as chairperson or chairwoman, although you may have to do so in a pinch.

Along similar lines, avoid describing women by their personal appearance, unless it is essential to what you are saying and you are treating men the same way.

If you said this about a woman: "Senator James, an attractive redhead . . . ," would you say this about a man: "Senator Harris, balding and broad-shouldered . . ."? Personal appearances rarely have anything to do with a person's professional ability or standing, and such descriptions have no place in business writing.

This first general look at your draft should focus on

overall content and structure, checking for clarity, conciseness, smooth transitions, tone, and pace. After that, you should take a closer look, focusing on specifics. See that headings and subheadings are consistent. Be sure that your illustrations are labeled and referred to correctly in the text. See that they are readily understandable by themselves. Verify the completeness and accuracy of your footnotes, references, and appendixes. And, finally, check grammar, punctuation, spelling, and usage.

Editing is a vital part of the writing process. Build time for editing into your schedule, so that you can complete the job in proper style. To make your editing readily comprehensible to anyone who reads or types it, it is a good idea to become familiar with professional proofreader's marks.

Finally, you must proofread your report. It sounds obvious, but it cannot be overemphasized. If possible, give your draft to someone else for a proofreading, preferably someone with an appropriate background, if the subject is technical. The more you work with a document, the easier it is for errors, gaps, and inconsistencies to slip by you. You become so familiar with your material that you may not see that an explanation is inadequate or a transition missing. And embarrassing typos have a way of avoiding detection by the familiar eye until it is too late. You need a cold, objective eye, the earlier the better. In any case, always have a second party proofread your final copy before you send it to the printer.

As a manager, you may regularly edit the work of your subordinates, and occasionally you may edit the work of a peer or superior. No matter whose work it is, you should handle all editing with caution and tact. The urge to change another's writing, to superimpose your own style, is powerful, but an invitation to edit is not an invitation to make wholesale changes. Everyone has pride of authorship, and you should respect a writer's personal style. That does not mean you should let shortcomings in grammar and organization slide by. Correct mistakes, point out holes, but resist the temptation to tinker.

If possible, try to review the writing while it is still in draft form. Your writer will be much more receptive to changes at this early stage than when the document has been finished. To avoid misunderstandings, find out exactly what the writer expects of you as an editor. The person who asks you to "take a look at this" may just want you to check the typos and obvious errors rather than to examine it with a keen critical eye. You will only create bad feelings if you overstep the bounds of the writer's expectations.

Once you get the draft, read it through completely before noting any changes. Look first at substance and organization and then at style. Make sure the writing conforms with your house style as well as general rules of grammar and punctuation. Edit out jargon.

If you mark on the copy, use a regular pencil or dark pen, not a red pencil or pen. Nothing is worse than to receive copy back bleeding red as though it were riddled with errors. Above all, do not ridicule the work by writing such comments in the margins as "awkward" or by appending exclamation points and question marks. If you have comments about the need to clarify or further develop certain points, or suggestions about reorganizing material, it is best to discuss them in person with the writer or to write them on a separate sheet of paper. Always use tact.

One innovation that may make editing easier in the future is word processing. Computer technology in the office will soon become commonplace. Many office professionals, including managers, will use video display terminals (VDTs) to process text and data. Some VDTs are tied into computers that have word processing capabilities. Less expensive and easier to install and operate are stand-alone word processors, which have their own logic and can operate without tying into computers.

Many managers, viewing electronic work stations as tools for support staff only, may resist this trend. If so, they may do themselves a disservice, for computer technology can save valuable time. With a word processor, writing tasks can be done faster and easier. Revising and editing are simple;

you can add, delete, and move words around on the display screen and then have a perfect copy quickly printed out. Subsequent revisions can be made on the screen without your having to redo an entire manuscript; the word processor automatically reformats material to accommodate changes. Documents can be stored indefinitely on magnetic disks. Good printers produce letter-quality printing, using either single-sheet bond paper or continuous form paper.

Some word processors have optional, sophisticated software packages that enable users to do mathematical functions, sort and list alphabetically and numerically, check spelling, and communicate with other word processors to send documents from one terminal to another.

Most word processors are fairly easy to master. Keyboards are like typewriter keyboards with a few extra code buttons. Many software programs have simple commands designed especially for executive users. Some processors may be custom-programmed by the users.

More and more, the writing of letters, memos, reports—all manner of business communications—will be done with VDTs. If your office is not already automated, and plans are not in the works, you may want to explore office automation yourself. The time saved by word processing can translate into money saved and higher productivity.

GIVING DICTATION

In a nonautomated office, much writing is produced by dictation. For many that is a mixed blessing. Many managers would much rather write than dictate, even though dictating saves a lot of time. Some have had a few bad experiences with dictation and cannot overcome their "stage fright" when they pick up a microphone or face a stenographer. Suddenly, they are supposed to effortlessly deliver clear and well-thought-out sentences. Instead, they fumble for the right word and freeze.

Dictation is not like writing. When you write, you may

take whatever time you want to think through a sentence, carefully choose wording, rearrange, and revise. No one is waiting for you and no one sees your false starts. Dictation creates a sense of immediacy, a pressure to keep speaking.

It is sometimes difficult to envision the final written product. The trouble is that most of us do not speak the way we write; our spoken words ramble and we switch tracks in mid-sentence. We hook one sentence onto another with a sequence of *ands* or *buts*. We add emphasis and meaning with tone of voice, facial expressions, body gestures, and volume, all of which are lost on the written page. We punctuate our speech with phrases such as *you know* and *like I said*, which have no place in writing.

The key to effective dictation is to know where you are going. Before you begin dictation, jot down a few notes. Who is the reader? What is the purpose of your communication? What are your key points, and what order should they be in? Do a quick outline, if necessary, and think of phrases that will provide smooth transition between paragraphs or sections. Write down a few phrases or even whole sentences and refer to your notes as you go along. Visualize your audience and your dictation in written form.

As with writing, prevent unnecessary interruptions. Ask for calls to be held and unexpected visitors to return later. Close your door if it will help you concentrate or feel less self-conscious. Then try to relax. Treat dictation as though you were having a face-to-face conversation with your reader. Microphones often intimidate managers giving dictation; they either rush in a nervous babble or drown their words in a mumble. Lift your chin to avoid mumbling, articulate carefully, and speak in a clear, unhurried voice. Do not surrender to fidgety habits that produce distracting noise: paper shuffling, desk thumping, rummaging through the contents of drawers, or fiddling with objects on the desk. Such background noises are particularly obstructive during dictation, because microphones pick up and amplify them.

If you are using a dictating machine, first identify yourself. State the type of communication (letter, memo, bulletin, report), the type of stationery, the number of copies, and when the finished product is needed.

Then proceed into your dictation, following your outline or notes. Resist the temptation to fill pauses with conjunctions such as *and* and *but* that create run-on sentences. State the ends of sentences with "period" and the ends of paragraphs with "paragraph" or "new paragraph." Specify capitalizations and punctuation. A secretary may not know that the name of a project is a proper name, or that your pause means a comma. Spell out proper names, unusual words, and technical terms. Use phonetic spelling to differentiate between letters that sound nearly the same, such as *b* and *d* or *n* and *m*. Similarly, spell out figures, to reduce the chance of error. You would dictate $119,000.40 this way: "Dollar sign, one, one, nine, comma, zero, zero, zero, point four, zero."

When you have finished, always have your dictation played or read back to catch awkward phrasing, errors, or obscured words. Then plan to proofread and perhaps edit the typed copy, no matter how busy you are or how well you think you did. You may not have realized that you digressed or reeled off a cumbersome sentence. And what sounds acceptable in conversation can look shockingly disorganized on paper.

Figure 3a is an example of a dictated memo that takes too many words to get the message across. How could such a rambling, off-the-top-of-the-head memo be avoided? With a few preparatory notes that might look something like this:

Deluxe Inn rates
   $75/night
   one of highest in area
   no corporate rate

Stay at less expensive hotels

Hotel guide
   use it
   lists hotels that are $50–$60/night

A simpler version of the dictated memo is shown in Figure 3b.

Like writing, good, smooth dictation is just a matter of practice, supported by the right kinds of planning and editing.

FIGURE 3

a.

As you may have become aware, the per-night rate charged by the Deluxe Inn in Blanton has now gone to $75 per night and is one of the highest in the area. We have been working with our Blanton office to see if there is any possibility to negotiate special terms. The Deluxe Inn has declined to participate with Corporate Purchasing to provide special rates to our employees.

All managers within the company should have received copies of the company hotel guide. I would appreciate it if you would cover with your staff the fact that this hotel guide is available and they will see in that CQ that the hotel rates of many other hotels in the area are at the $50 to $60 rate per night as opposed to the Deluxe Inn at $75 per night. Please advise them that whenever feasible they should stay at one of the other inns and not at the Deluxe.

Thank you for your cooperation.

b.

The Deluxe Inn in Blanton is now charging $75 per night and is one of the most expensive hotels in the Blanton area. It has declined to give us a corporate rate.

Please instruct your staff to stay at other, less expensive hotels whenever possible when traveling to Blanton. The company hotel guide lists several which charge $50 to $60 per night.

Thank you for your cooperation.

WRITING ARTICLES

In addition to writing in-house material, you may wish to consider writing career-enhancing articles, which will gain you wider visibility. Many trade publications and local newspapers and magazines are very receptive to columns or articles with an expert's by-line.

Consider whether you have something significant to say that would interest others. Can you offer insight into an industry issue currently in the media spotlight? Can you tell how you or your organization solved a difficult problem? Do you have news of research developments? Remember, editors are always looking for stories that grab their readers' attention. "Fresh" is the term they always use. They look for the new and different, as well as new angles on older subjects.

One prime possibility to consider is the opinion piece. Nearly all publications welcome opinions. The simplest form is the signed letter to the editor. Do not dismiss that idea out of hand; letters to the editor are widely read. Much more visible and prestigious, however, is a by-lined column or article. Many newspapers have opinion pages, and some magazines make guest column space available. Such opinion pieces tend to be short—several hundred words long—and usually are tied to current news issues.

Articles tend to be much longer, up into the thousands of words, depending on the magazine or journal. They may also include illustrations and photographs. Articles generally are written from a more objective stance than are opinion pieces, which are more personal.

Whether you are writing an opinion piece or an article, you should do several things before you sit down to write.

Develop an idea. Decide what you want to write about. Do you want to inform, to educate, to comment? What is noteworthy about your idea? Why would someone take time to read your article?

Identify your audience. Whom do you wish to address? Your peers, a general business audience, or the general public? What publications or kinds of publications do you have in mind? Do you intend to use any case studies, anecdotes, or personal experiences?

Do a little research. What has been said about your topic before? Perhaps your angle or idea has already been done. Take a look at some of your target publications. Is your topic approriate for them?

Look for appropriate publications. Look first in your own backyard for publishing opportunities. Most companies have employee newsletters or magazines. Whether someone on the communications staff writes the article or you do, you largely determine the scope and content. If the article is written about you or your department or project, and you are quoted, you will probably have the right of change and approval. Trade journals usually are hungry for stories. You will have a better chance of being published in one of those than you will in a large business or general interest publication. Your local Chamber of Commerce magazine also provides an excellent forum for articles. You may or may not get paid for your article. Many small trade journals offer no pay, just your by-line and a few complimentary copies. But your main reward, apart from seeing your name in print, is the enhancement of your reputation.

Query. Asking whether an editor would be interested in an article before you write it can save you time. For one thing, the answer may be, "Sorry, no thanks." Most publications will consider unsolicited articles, but why risk wasting a lot of time before you know whether or not the idea interests the editor? A query will also save you time if your idea is accepted. You will find out more about the publication's editorial requirements. Sometimes editors will ask you to submit an article on speculation; that is, they will express interest in your idea but will not commit themselves to using it until they see it. Most editors prefer queries by letter. Keep it to one page; outline your idea, explain why it would be of interest to your audience, and state why you are the person to write the article. If you have been published before, cite those credits. Enclose a self-addressed, stamped envelope for the reply. For company in-house publications, just give the editor or department manager a call and explain what you have in mind.

Once you know what you are going to write about and who you are going to write for, get the editorial requirements from the editor. Find out:

- The deadline
- The length (most editors will give you a range of words)
- The specifications for art, if supplied by you, such as photos (black-and-white or color, size of print) and illustrations

The manuscript itself should be clean and double-spaced, with at least one-inch margins on all sides. It is acceptable to mark some corrections and changes on the copy, as long as they are kept to a minimum. Put your name, address, and telephone number in the upper left-hand corner of the first page, and an estimate of the length in words in the upper right-hand corner. Center the title about one-third of the way down on the first page, and then start the body copy. Subsequent pages should be numbered in the right-hand corners. It is also a good idea to "slug" each page, putting your last name or a key word of your title in the upper left-hand corner.

Make a copy of the manuscript—they do sometimes get lost—and mail the original, flat, with some stiffener, in a large envelope. Enclose a self-addressed, stamped envelope if you want to receive a rejected manuscript back. Some publications will accept photocopied manuscripts. If you send a copy, note in the cover letter that it is not a simultaneous submission; that is, that you are not offering the same article to more than one publication at the same time.

Your cover letter should be brief and should remind the editor that he or she is expecting your article. This will prevent your manuscript from landing on the slush pile of unsolicited articles also addressed to the editor. Enclose information for your credit line, such as: "John Jones is director of finance at Big Time Corp. in Newark, N.J."

If you do send an unsolicited article, state in your cover letter what it is about and why the editor should be interested in it, and describe your qualifications.

After the manuscript is sent, be patient. It is not unusual for weeks to go by without hearing anything. Small trade journals that do not pay may not acknowledge anything, even if they intend to use your article. If a number of weeks go by, you might send a short follow-up note asking about your article's status.

Some editors may ask you to make changes in your article or to supply additional information; most will edit the story to fit their publication's needs. In most cases, you can expect to see some changes in your article.

If you send a follow-up note and receive no reply, try calling the editor; or if you choose to withdraw your article from consideration and try elsewhere, send a note stating that to the editor.

If your query or article is rejected, do not be disheartened. Many articles are published after a number of rejections. Try another publication. You may have to change your angle or rearrange your story to fit another's editorial needs, but persistence usually pays off.

CHAPTER 7

APPEARANCES THAT COUNT

For professional managers, personal packaging is important, although not nearly as important as the contents of the package. Putting that a little differently, how we dress and groom ourselves can help or hinder us in terms of early personal acceptance, but it is what we are as individuals and what we accomplish in terms of profit and growth that matter above all. We convey what we are by much more than our dress and grooming, and it is what we are that others really respond to. Most of all we need to look calm, steady, strong, and capable of handling every conceivable thing that might come up; and projecting those qualities depends far more upon such matters as speech, eye contact, carriage, and all the other verbal and nonverbal elements of effective communication than upon dress and grooming.

That said, dress and grooming do still deserve careful attention from all managers. Conservative, classically styled, and fairly expensive clothing, accessories, jewelry, hairstyle, and all the other factors that go into your total "appearance" can help others to accept you as a working professional; conversely, an appearance that is too far from the current behavioral or stylistic norms can jar, and set up unnecessary barriers between you and others. In extreme instances, when grooming and dress are very far from current styles, it is even possible to severely harm career possibilities. These are only matters of current style, of course, and have nothing at all to do with professional skills. Yet they can be important, if current norms are bent too far. The main thing to understand about dress and grooming is not so much that you can do yourself a great deal of good by dressing and looking "well," but that you can do yourself a good deal of harm with a poor appearance. That means keeping up with current standards, looking clean, cool, and alert at all times, and in all climates and conditions; and it means dressing comfortably and classically, and not worrying too much about how you look to others.

Although such matters as how to dress are enormously overrated as career-building factors, it is possible to make situations, and particularly new situations, with new people, far more difficult than they need be, by conveying wrong signals about yourself with manner and dress. Most experienced people have trained themselves to pick up useful clues from a quick first look. Such minor grooming matters as uncombed hair, scuffed shoes, or not-quite-fully-cleaned fingernails can easily be seen as evidences of a general carelessness that may show up in other, more serious ways. The person who seems unwilling to tend to such small matters may not care enough about much more important matters; such a little thing can tip a hiring or buying decision the wrong way. Similarly, the manager who dresses quite inexpensively is all too often seen as someone who may not quite be "making it" economically; that can jar others enough to make them somewhat uneasy about association, as in-company allies, as buyers, as employers, and as co-networkers over a period of years. We want our associates, protégés, friends, and allies to "look good"; it makes us look good, and it makes our company look good.

Similarly, the manager who dresses too trendily or too sexily, or who uses too much cologne, perfume, hair tonic, lipstick, or whatever else is not in this year, tends to jar others. Among management professionals, the least questioned and most accepted image is still basically that created by Gregory Peck in *The Man in the Grey Flannel Suit,* in the period following World War II. However, it is no longer solely a white Anglo-Saxon, Protestant male image, but now encompasses female, Black, Hispanic, Jewish, East Asian, Native American, and a score of national and ethnic images, as well. But all of them share this: they are still conservatively and traditionally dressed and groomed, and in every verbal and nonverbal way convey that they carry upper-middle-class status. No, not upper-class economic status and the social attitudes assumed to go with "old money," which are thought by so many others to be rather nastily condescending. The main American management image continues to be that of the small-town boy—or girl—who made good, and now occupies one of the big houses on the other side of the tracks.

PLANNING A BUSINESS WARDROBE

What constitutes effective business dress varies somewhat regionally and by industry. A southeastern regional office manager may wear a white suit in midsummer quite easily; so may his or her banker. But a banker headquartered on Fifth Avenue or Wall Street in New York City is not very likely to be found wearing that white suit in any season, nor will that banker's clients in the New York area. And when that banker goes to Atlanta on business in midsummer, he will be unwise to don a white suit, although he may leave his dark, pinstriped suit and Ivy League tie behind. A white suit would properly be perceived by local people in Atlanta as phony, while the pinstripe and Ivy League tie would make him seem too alien to be comfortable with; the solution is somewhere in between.

You will find the most conservative business dress on the East Coast, especially in the corridor that runs from Boston to Washington, D.C., as well as at most corporate headquarters, regardless of geographic location. The basic business colors of blue and gray will work well virtually anywhere in the country, but clothing styles loosen up a bit in the Midwest, where more browns and tans are worn by men, and brighter colors by women. Short sleeves and light dresses are common in the South and Southwest. And the West Coast is far more casual than the East Coast, with California being the most relaxed of all. In general, it is best to stay within the conservative range for your region and industry, avoiding sartorial extremes.

Some basic guidelines are helpful when you are planning and upgrading a sound business wardrobe. Perhaps most important is to learn the look and feel of quality. Many people, when they shop, go through the racks until something catches their eye. If it looks all right and the price is acceptable, they buy it. They may check the label for fiber content as a second thought; they may never inspect the finishing and stitching.

If you are shopping for your professional "uniform," you should shop more carefully, with a purpose and plan. Do a little window shopping first. You will find the best quality in better stores; visit them and inspect their merchandise. Read the labels for manufacturers and fiber content, and note prices. This will help you get the best value and quality at the best price, when it comes time to do your actual buying.

Good-quality garments are well finished. Most clothing is machine-stitched, with the exception of the finest suits, which are tailored and stitched by hand. Machine stitching should be small and even. The pieces of a garment should be well joined; that is, collars should lie flat, sleeves should not pucker, and lapels should not pull. Buttonholes should be well finished, without loose threads. Check the inside of the garment for seams that are ample and finished, and that will not begin unraveling with wear and cleaning. Linings should not pull or pucker or droop below hemlines. Buttons, if not bone, should at least be a good-quality plastic or a nontarnishing brasslike metal.

For quality, look for the "real thing"—natural fibers or blends with natural fibers for clothes, and leather for accessories such as wallets, gloves, shoes, belts, and briefcases. In general, avoid garments that are all synthetic and any material that is shiny or semitransparent. Some synthetic fibers have a shininess to them that looks cheap; they also feel rough to the touch. Above all, avoid all polyester knits, especially for outer garments. They are distinctly not upper middle class, and tend to snag, stretch, and bag. The real thing costs more than substitutes and imitations, but it is far better to own a few good-quality outfits than many cheaper ones. The difference in quality speaks for itself.

The best natural fibers are wool and cotton. Wool can be worn year-round, particularly if it is blended with polyester. Wool "breathes" and keeps its color and shape well. It adds richness and texture to a blend. Wool will keep you warmer in the winter and, believe it or not, cooler in the summer than synthetics. Polyesters, rayons, and acrylics, for example, do not breathe well. A lightweight suit that is 45% wool and 55% polyester is cooler during hot months than is an all-polyester suit. When buying wool blend garments, be sure to check the fiber contents label. The minimum for optimum wear, durability, appearance, and texture is 45% wool.

Cotton is comfortable on the skin, breathes well, and is cool in the summer, but it is a fragile fabric that is much better blended with polyester. By itself, cotton shrinks, fades, wrinkles, and wears out quickly. In a blend, you can have the comfort of cotton with the durability of polyester. Some of the best and most expensive men's shirts, however, are all cotton. Buy these only if you are prepared to foot a weekly cleaning bill. Because of the way cotton wrinkles, you will need to send your shirts out for cleaning and pressing in order for them to look crisp.

Silk is a natural fiber that has been enjoying renewed popularity, especially in more fashionable clothing. Silk is especially appropriate, even preferable, for accessories such as ties and scarves. Good silk has a rich, quality look, but the fiber has significant disadvantages in clothing for business purposes: it is expensive, can soil and stain, generally requires dry cleaning, and wrinkles easily. In addition, the rich, lustrous look of silk may give garments—particularly suits—more of an evening wear look than a business look. Many women, however, have made silk dresses and blouses staples for business wear. Silk dresses may be better left for evenings, but silk blouses are certainly acceptable with suits and skirts with blazers, if one is willing to bear the expense of caring for them properly.

Silk, good silk, can be wonderfully soft and comfortable and rich and shiny in appearance. Even though it is a thin fabric, it can absorb up to one-third of its weight in moisture, which makes it very comfortable to wear on hot days. Not all silks are equal, however, and unfortunately, most labels do not tell enough about the quality of the garment. Italian silks tend to be the best; they are generally very soft and quite lustrous, and they are the most expensive. Dyes vary greatly in quality—some are actually water-soluble, a disaster if they ever get wet. Others stain easily, and many will fade when subjected to strong sunlight. Many stores will tell you that you can avoid heavy dry-cleaning costs by washing silk in cold-water detergents meant for woolens, lingerie, and other delicate garments. But that may not be as practical as it sounds. Depending on the quality of the fiber, washed silk may wrinkle considerably and may not iron out well. It is safer to dry-clean brightly colored silks and textured silks, such as crepe and taffeta. If you do opt to hand-wash your silks, take care not to rub or twist the fabric, because the yarns can break and stretch easily. Also, be sure to iron the garments on the wrong side.

Since you can invest a lot of money in silk, it would be worth your while to do some research on the various silk weaves before buying any. There are nearly two dozen of them, all with different qualities and properties. When shopping for silk, remember that good silk is expensive. The popularity of silk has brought many cheap silks to the market, and a cheap silk is just that: cheap. It may not be dyed evenly, it may discolor unevenly, or it may separate or tear easily. If you cannot buy silk, look for silk and polyester blends, or good polyesters that look like silk. If you shop around enough, you will soon be able to recognize polyesters that are good imitators of silk.

Accessories are where many otherwise smart shoppers fall down. They pay top dollar for quality clothes, which they then ruin with cheap accessories. Your entire appearance must convey quality. Do not skimp, thinking you can get by with something pulled out of a bargain basement. Do not buy imitation leather; buy the real thing. Be especially careful with shoes—inexpensive leather shoes look only marginally better than vinyl ones. Any jewelry should be simple, functional, and fashioned from real gold or silver. If you have an inexpensive watch, you may wish to dress it up with a leather band instead of a plastic, fabric, or metal one. Always carry and use a good gold or silver pen, never a cheapie, no matter who else around you may use one.

As you do your window-shopping, note brand names and their various levels of quality and cost. While you will find top brands in better stores, you will also begin to notice the brands that come next in quality and are less expensive. You need not buy the most expensive of everything you need. It is perfectly acceptable—and wise from a budget standpoint—to buy more moderately priced goods, as long as they look high quality. You will find some good-quality, more moderately priced brands in department stores, but avoid discount chains. Discount chains often stock imperfect goods and overruns that have missed the market in their style. The same caution applies to factory and warehouse outlets. Many do sell name-brand goods at marked-down prices, usually with the labels ripped out, but others sell seconds and imperfects that are not marked as such.

A word about name-brand labels: as you become more familiar with the quality of certain brands, you will probably develop a list of favorites that you will trust. Many stores have their own labels, and these are often good bets for quality merchandise at moderate prices. Stores generally are careful when it comes to their own labels, as it is bad advertising to put your name on something that falls apart after one or two cleanings. A discount chain, however, may put its own label on an inexpensive "loss leader" item designed solely to attract traffic to the store. You must discover for yourself which stores are the most reliable.

A designer label once insured good quality. With some designers, that is still true today, but other designer labels have become so diluted through mass manufacturing and merchandising that they really offer no guarantee of quality at all. In fact, the clothing may even be poorly constructed. Such designers license manufacturers to produce their designs, but they cannot possibly monitor quality. They sit back and collect royalties while you pay a premium price for their name—without necessarily getting premium quality. The proliferation of designer labels in department stores, discount houses, and outlets has also reduced their status. Wearing such items is no longer a sure mark of upper-middle-class status and wealth. In fact, in the business world, designer labels can work against you, if the designer's name or initials are plastered all over your garment. Traditional, classic apparel is understated; you should not look like a walking billboard.

A second basic in wardrobe planning is to consider the importance of color. For people in most business situations, dark colors work best, because they convey authority and power. The all-around general business suit color for men and women is dark or navy blue. Charcoal gray and medium gray are good, but dark brown is not universally acceptable. If you have limited funds for your wardrobe, it is best to build it around blues and grays; beige is an acceptable third color.

Women have more latitude to wear bright colors than do men; still, both sexes should take care to avoid trendy, fashion-oriented shades and styles, which make their wearers look frivolous in the conservative eyes of the business establishment. Women should also strike red from their business wardrobes—it is a boldly sexual color. At the other extreme, be careful with black; it is a very severe color and can cause as much negative reaction as a frivolous color, like pink. Some colors, such as gold, pink, lavender, and certain greens, are best avoided in suits altogether.

The quieter your outfit is, the better. Solids work the best, especially for women. Pinstripes function well for men (as long as they are not reminiscent of the "gangster look") but less well for women. Muted plaids and tweeds are acceptable if they are of very good quality; make certain that plaid patterns match where garment pieces are sewn together. Both sexes should avoid fabrics that have busy, dramatic, or distracting patterns, which diminish professional appearance and, consequently, status.

Shirts and blouses should contrast with suits; white and pastels (except pink) are the most acceptable shades for men and women. The pastels should not blend into the color of the suit, for that can create a dull, lifeless look. While women can wear dark shades with light-colored suits—a maroon blouse with a light gray suit, for example—men are best advised to stick to white with light-colored suits.

For important occasions, such as job interviews and board meetings, it is wise to dress especially conservatively. The best colors for job interviews are suits in charcoal or light gray and navy blue, with contrasting shirts or blouses. When job-hunting, women should forego their freedom to wear darker colors in shirts and blouses, and stick with white or pastel blue, the most accepted contrasting colors in the business establishment.

The only kind of clothing for which bright colors are not only acceptable, but expected, is sportswear. You should not go overboard, however, and show up looking like a neon sign at your company's summer executive retreat workshop. Upper-middle-class sportswear colors are white, navy, maroon, and khaki, although many bright plaids are also acceptable. Beware of light blue, which can look cheap, and bright yellow, which can look gaudy.

When selecting colors and putting together outfits, take into consideration your weight and build. Fortunately for

most of us, the dark, "power" colors also tend to be slim-
ming, while brighter colors tend to make people look larger.
A plaid over a paunch can add to the rotundity. Dark colors
on tall, large men and women can make them look too
imposing, almost unapproachable, however. If you fit into
this category, you may want to build your working wardrobe
around lighter shades, such as light gray and beige.

The color of your overcoat is just as important as the
color of your suit or dress. Camel and beige are good all-
around colors in coats, followed by dark gray, navy blue, and
black, which are somewhat more formal and severe. Furs
may be a bit pretentious in the workplace, except for fur
collars on coats, so women should save their fox and mink
coats for evening wear.

When planning your business wardrobe you should
carefully assess your professional environment. Your company, industry, even your geographic locale will influence
your latitude in building your professional wardrobe. If you
work for a conservative company such as IBM, you would be
wise to stick to very traditional dress habits. Whenever you
are in doubt when shopping for clothes, it is safest to go with
the most conservative choices. You may have more freedom
of expression if you are in a trend-oriented industry such as
entertainment, fashion, or advertising, but in most corporate
circles, you cannot be too conservative.

Smaller firms also may be more relaxed in their working
atmosphere, with executives wearing slacks with sports jackets, while at other businesses you may be expected to reflect
some of the latest fashions in your appearance.

Dress customs vary around the country. Drop in at a
mid-Manhattan restaurant during lunch and you will see
mostly dark suits. But in Los Angeles, you will most likely
see brighter colors on both men and women, and even shirts
open at the neck on men.

Look around you and note carefully how your peers and
superiors are dressed, particularly key executives at your
company. You may want to pick out one or two successful
superiors, to analyze their styles of dress and use them as

role models. That does not mean you should copy them—you can make mistakes that way. For example, monogrammed shirts may be seen as fitting for a senior vice-president, but not for a first- or second-line manager. And certain affectations, such as linen handkerchiefs in breast pockets or diamond lapel stickpins, may work wonderfully for one person and look pretentious or silly on another. Use your role models as guides, wear nothing that makes you feel uncomfortable, and add your own distinctive personal touches.

Once you have planned what your business wardrobe *should* be, you should carefully and critically assess your present wardrobe. This is the moment of truth. How does your closet stand up to the test? Divide your clothes into seasons and assess each item—each suit, dress, blazer, pair of slacks, accessory, shirt, blouse, and pair of shoes. Be honest and ruthless, even though it may be painful to see just how much of what you own does not meet critical standards. If you are like most people, you have accumulated your wardrobe in a haphazard fashion, buying this on sale here, that on impulse there, including items which may not fit you quite right, but which were such a terrific deal you could not pass them up. Well, reform time is at hand. No point in lamenting past mistakes—just vow not to repeat them. Give everything in your closet a meticulous examination and be firm in setting aside everything that does not measure up. And that means *everything*. All of those items will eventually disappear from your working wardrobe; how quickly will depend on how much you have to replace, and how much money you can afford to spend over what period of time. What will you do with all your discards? Save what you can to wear around the house, and donate the rest to charity, or, if they are in excellent condition, take them to a thrift resale shop.

As you assess your wardrobe, keep in mind that you will want to build your clothing around one or two main colors. Group those items that go together and then determine what you will need to round things out. Limiting your color schemes will help prevent you from buying something on impulse that you seldom wear because it does not go with many of your other clothes.

What if you feel you must start almost from scratch, but have a tight budget for clothes? In that case, at least eliminate the most unsuitable items from your wardrobe and gradually replace the rest. Work out a timetable with what you feel you can comfortably afford to spend, and start with a few basics that can do double duty for you, such as a dark, solid-color suit that can be worn twice in one week with different shirts and ties or blouses.

Rebuilding Your Wardrobe

Then you are ready to begin reconstructing your wardrobe. You should start by making a list of the things you need and ranking them by priority. Concentrate on the season at hand; if it is summer, focus on your lighter clothing needs. You should also make a list for your fall and winter needs, but you can postpone buying for the next season until it actually arrives. Eventually, when you get your core wardrobe established, you can begin buying for seasons in advance, in order to take advantage of sales. You can get some very good markdowns on clothes at the end of seasons.

But you must be careful, because it is easy to get carried away with sales. Do not buy something that is of mediocre quality or which may go out of style in a season or two just because it is on sale. Do not buy something that is not quite the right color or something you merely *think* will coordinate with clothes hanging in your closet, just because the price is right. The price may be appealing, but chances are the garment will not be quite right, and it will only go unworn—a quite expensive purchase when you consider the small use you get from a particular piece of clothing. A suit marked down $80 is no bargain if you only wear it once or twice a season. You may find that the labels you like to buy seldom go on sale (as is often the case in premium clothing), although you may get lucky and find something you are looking for at a reduced price. The important thing is never to sacrifice quality and practicality for price.

Your general rule of thumb should be to buy the best possible quality you can afford. If you cannot afford a Brooks Brothers suit, buy a less costly brand that comes closest, in your estimation, to the quality you seek. If you cannot afford a good-quality silk blouse, buy one made from a polyester that closely imitates the look and feel of real silk. It is far better to have a smaller wardrobe of high-quality clothes than a large wardrobe of medium-quality or cheap clothes.

When shopping for shirts, ties, and blouses to go with suits or jackets, buy the items together rather than separately. You cannot rely on your memory to tell you accurately the shade of something in your closet; you may get something home and find it does not match at all. If possible, pick out shirts, ties, and blouses at the same time you buy a suit, or take a swatch of suit material with you. Better yet, wear the suit when you go shopping, or take the jacket with you. That way you will be certain to pick out items that complement each other. The same idea applies when shopping for shoes. Do not try on business shoes while dressed in jeans or dungarees; wear an outfit you plan to wear with the shoes. It does make a difference. Remember, you are striving for a well-thought-out, unified, total look.

If you have done enough window-shopping, examining the quality of merchandise offered at various stores, you will probably know which ones you want to patronize. You will probably get the best, most personalized attention at smaller shops which carry top-quality lines, because part of their business is knowing the individual needs of their clientele. Most of these salespersons will not try to pressure you into quick sales; if they see you are serious about your shopping, they will generally take the time to help you assemble well-integrated outfits. Explain what you are looking for and what you can spend. Many of these shops will keep a card on file with your measurements and color and fabric preferences, and experienced sales representatives will keep an eye out for new arrivals that match certain customers' requirements. Many department stores also offer personalized "consultants" to help you with your year-round clothing needs. Some such services are free, while others carry charges; they can be very helpful for busy managers who have little time to shop.

At warehouse and factory outlets, however, you are on your own. Such outlets may have personnel available to direct you to the right racks, even assist you with a fitting, but beyond that, do not look for much advice. If you know what you are looking for, you can sometimes find good bargains at outlets. But you must know your outlets, and be sure they sell store-quality goods and not seconds or irregulars.

When shopping for any type of garment, be sure to try it on and carefully check the fit, because no two manufacturers make the same size the same way. Even two garments of the same size, made by the same manufacturer, may vary slightly. Whether you are purchasing a suit, skirt, blazer, or dress, chances are you will need alterations. Although many women simply wear garments as they come off the racks, it is highly unlikely that clothing will fit well enough without changes. Do not just "make do"; have it altered. Unfortunately, many stores still charge women for alterations that they give men for free. Even so, the extra charge is worth it to get the best possible fit.

When the alterations have been made, buyers should always ask for—and insist on—a second fitting. You should check the fit from all angles in a three-way mirror, walk in it, and sit down. Be exacting in your assessment of the job done, and accept nothing that looks merely passable but not quite right. You are the one who has to live in the suit, not the tailor, and you want to look and feel your best in your clothing.

Unless you have a lot of money to spend at one time, it will probably take you awhile—a year, maybe even two—to acquire what you feel you need. But your investment will pay off handsomely in a well-planned image, and your quality garments should last for several years, with proper care and cleaning. Even so, you will probably want to add a little to it each season.

The general guidelines discussed in this chapter apply to both men and women. But each sex faces some special considerations regarding business dress, so we will look at each separately.

BUSINESS DRESS FOR WOMEN

Unfortunately, managerial dress standards for women are often vague and nebulous. While a company may have clear-cut unwritten guidelines for men, women managers often have few or no female role models in higher positions from whom to take cues. Women have only recently entered management in any significant numbers, and have in the process been confronted with conflicting advice on how to dress.

In the 1970s, when women began moving into the professional job market in earnest, they were admonished by consultants, both male and female, to adhere to conservative, tailored, mannish dress—dark-skirted suits, often with vests, which were cut in a masculine fashion. Many women, however, only looked like imitation men rather than professional businesswomen; mimicking the dress of their male peers sometimes proved more distracting than helpful in establishing a proper business image. Such dress can be very comfortable and effective for some women, however. The key is for women managers to choose such styles only if they feel comfortable with them personally and in their work environment.

Toward the end of the 1970s, the female executive dress pendulum began to swing the other way. Women were told that they had established themselves in professional roles and could loosen up their conservative dress standards and be more "feminine." What that heralded was the reintroduction of fashion in business dress. Women who were lawyers,

securities analysts, and corporate vice-presidents—among
the most conservative positions in the business world as a
whole—were pictured in women's magazines wearing new
"business fashions" of bright colors and high-fashion styles of
skirts, dresses, pants, and even pantalets. But these kinds of
clothes can harm more than help. Fashion is distracting, and
the message it conveys is one of frivolousness. It is hard to
take someone seriously if her attire does not look serious, or
if she looks as if she is ready for an evening date.

Currently fashionable clothes have two additional disadvantages. First, they do not identify the wearer as a businesswoman. The classic, conservative suit identifies a man as a
businessman, and he is treated as such wherever he goes.
The well-dressed businessman is accorded respectful—often
preferential—treatment at restaurants, hotels, and other service establishments. But any woman, regardless of her professional status, can dress herself up in the latest rage. And
when you do not look as if you mean business, you will not
get business—or good service or respect.

Second, fashionable clothes tend to go out of fashion
after a season or two, to be replaced by something else that is
completely different. That, of course, is how fashion designers and manufacturers stay in business. If their clothes
looked the same year after year, women would have no
incentive to replace them every season. It is to the fashion
industry's advantage that clothes for businesswomen carry
seasonal marks. The short-waisted, belted-skirt suit in electric purple that looked so smart one season will definitely be
out the next, and no one would be caught dead wearing it.
Likewise with skirts and dresses that go up and down in
length.

Changing your wardrobe every season is both costly and
foolish. The smart professional woman builds a long-lasting
wardrobe, adding to it each year. The well-constructed,
high-quality man's suit lasts about five years, on the average,
sometimes longer. The same should be sought in women's
business suits and, in fact, in all garments. Clothes should be
selected for their classic timelessness, quality, and durability.

The professional woman who builds such a wardrobe achieves a polished, consistent, upper-middle-class look; she is not surprising her co-workers each season with whatever "look" the fashion designers have decided will rule the day.

While women should not let fashion dictate what they wear to the office, they need not totally ignore it. Many women pay homage to trends through their accessories—scarves, belts, shoes, and handbags. They should not, however, let fashion hold sway in choosing eyeglasses. "Designer eyewear," as it is often called in advertisements, comes in odd shapes and colors, and can be as frivolous-looking and as distracting as high-fashion clothes. A simple plastic frame that complements face and coloring is the best choice. Many businesswomen, particularly those who are petite or very young, find that glasses add to their authority; in fact, some women who do not need vision correction have been known to wear spectacles with plain glass lenses, just for the appearance of gravity and intelligence they impart.

Skirted suits, followed by skirts and blazers, are still the best all-around items of apparel for the managerial woman. A tailored suit or blazer still communicates business and professionalism. Solid colors offer the most flexibility for combinations. Dresses tend to be too fashion-oriented, but they can combine very well with a blazer. A dress with a blazer can solve the problem of going right from the office to an evening social function; a woman can wear the blazer at the office and take it off for the evening. While men can still wear their daytime business suits on into the evening with ease, a woman is better off with a tailored dress. Some women prefer to wear pantsuits, although such styles have, to some extent, become associated with clerical and secretarial help. While many companies find pantsuits perfectly acceptable, others do not. Again, the keys are personal comfort and an assessment of your environment. If pantsuits are frowned on, you may wish to avoid them as potentially distracting; remember that you are striving for a neutral, professional appearance, not one that calls attention to itself. Vests can also backfire for women, by looking either sexy or too masculine, and sweaters and sleeveless or short-sleeved dresses are definitely not managerial. Pantyhose should be neutral, skin-colored shades, not opaque or dark, and certainly not covered with stitched designs.

Women should be sure that jackets do not bunch or roll across the shoulders or pull across the bust. Vents should hang straight and not stick out, and sleeves should end at mid-wrist. Skirts should allow plenty of room around the hips so that zippers do not pucker. Jacket lapels should lie flat. If they do not, a pressing will not help; the lining will need to be readjusted.

When choosing dresses and blouses, stay away from anything semi-sheer or sheer. The best blouses or shirts have a clean, tailored look, which can be dressed up with scarves if desired. A little bit of lace is all right if it is not excessive and frilly. Necklines should be modest, never low. Dressy blouses are certainly appropriate for evening business functions, and can transform a dark tailored suit into evening wear.

Accessories should be selected similarly. Plain, leather, low-heeled pumps are the most practical shoes for women, and are healthier for the feet than high heels. Avoid open-toed shoes and sandals, even during hot weather, because their casualness detracts from a managerial appearance. Your shoes should be at least as dark as your clothes, not lighter. White shoes should be avoided in the summer, unless white also dominates your clothing. Silk scarves and leather belts can add nice touches to an outfit, as long as they do not bear designer names or imprints. Many women tend to go overboard on jewelry, as though more means higher quality or status. However, jewelry—and that includes watches—is most effective when it is sparse and functional, so resist the urge to drape several gold chains around your neck and put a series of bracelets on your arm. Women are better off with a few distinctive pieces of good jewelry than with a multitude of less expensive pieces. It is often effective to have a "signature" piece of jewelry that you wear all the time, such as a tasteful locket, an unusual ring, or a single bracelet (one that does not dangle or clatter). Such a piece can add to your own individual look or style.

Briefcases signal business, and a woman manager should carry one, even if it only contains the morning paper or her lunch. Brown leather is best for women as well as men, although women may wish to avoid extremes of either a distinctively "masculine" attaché or a flimsy "feminine" envelope-type portfolio. With a briefcase, a handbag is unnecessary, although many women purchase a small, flat bag to put inside a briefcase. A handbag carried separately should be simple in design, made of good-quality leather, and just big enough to carry a minimum of personal items. Nothing looks less professional than a luggage-size bag dragging on someone's shoulder. The handbag should match—or at least not jar with—the shoes and the rest of the outfit.

Other aspects of appearance deserve similar attention. Hair should be short to medium in length, in a simple cut that tends to stay in place and requires little fussing. Long hair left to fall around the shoulders may diminish a woman's authority; conversely, hair that is too short can look mannish. Long hair may be pulled up on top of the head, as long as the bun or knot is neat and not odd looking. Hair pulled back from the face this way can give a woman a sterner, more authoritative appearance. Hair that tends to get mussed at the slightest breeze calls for a light hair spray or perhaps another kind of cut. Hairdressers at top salons can cut hair to complement the way it grows, which helps it fall into place naturally. It may be worth spending a little extra money to get a good cut.

While gray hair usually makes men look distinguished, particularly if the gray is premature, it generally only makes women look older. If desired, many rinses on the market can cover up the gray and keep hair looking its natural color. But frizzy permanents and offbeat tinting jobs, such as streaks of different color, are usually out of place in the business environment. Similarly, lacquer-like hair sprays, especially heavily scented ones, should be avoided. So should perfume. They have no place in the business environment.

Likewise, the less makeup the better. Makeup should never be obvious. Men find elaborate eye makeup especially distracting. The last thing a woman manager should want is for someone to be wondering how long it took her to "put on her face" that morning instead of listening to what she has to say.

Polished talons may be in vogue in the fashion magazines, but they are very impractical for business. Long nails prevent people from grasping things properly and can impair handwriting; also one broken nail on a hand of long ones does not look good. Polish requires time-consuming maintenance, and even a few chips give an ill-kempt appearance. It is far better to keep nails filed to a short or medium length with cuticles manicured. Nails may be buffed for a sheen, and a clear polish, which will not show nicks or chips as colors do, is acceptable.

Because there are few reliable guidelines, women managers must experiment and learn through trial and error just what works best for them in a particular job environment. Note that what works well at one company may not at another, not only because of differences in corporate standards, but also because perceptions and impressions created by dress are so subjective. Many men, sadly, are still threatened by the idea of a woman manager; a woman who works with such a man may get far better results by softening her appearance. But whatever the situation, women will be safest in sticking to tailored, classic, conservative styles that have the look of quality workmanship.

BUSINESS DRESS FOR MEN

Men, luckily, do not face the confusion that women do in dressing for corporate success. Since men have always dominated commerce and industry, clothing standards have always been readily apparent and nearly universal; indeed, the business "uniform" has evolved over a considerable period of time. Even within the confines of customary male business dress, however, there is a great deal of latitude, and some men dress to better advantage than do others.

The key is to have a tailored, subdued, well-integrated look. That means colors and patterns should be complementary and not clashing; belt and shoes should match; tie, shirt, collar, and lapels should be neither too narrow nor wide; and nothing should stick out in an obvious or odd way. All parts of the outfit should blend together in a tasteful but not monochromatic or dull way.

Unlike women, men are generally provided with a free fitting, unless they buy suits at an outlet or on sale in a department store. Even if they must pay extra for it, the fitting is vital and should be done carefully and thoroughly. Never let the tailor try to hurry you through one. Places where alterations are most commonly required include:

- *Shoulders.* There should be no bunching or rolling of jacket between shoulder blades.
- *Lapels and Collar.* They should lie flat.
- *Sleeves.* They should hit at the middle of the wrist bone.
- *Jacket Vents.* They should hang straight and not stick out.
- *Trouser Crotch.* It should fit comfortably for sitting, walking, and standing without pinching or bagging. Trouser waists and lengths, of course, usually are fitted. When shopping, be sure to wear a pair of shoes you intend to wear with the suit so the pants can be accurately measured for the proper break over the shoe tops.

Unless you are prepared to care for all-cotton shirts, the best bet for shirts is a cotton and polyester blend, in white, pastel blue, or ecru (a yellowish beige or light gray) with either button-down collars or collars with removable stays. (Stays that are sewn into collars turn the fabric shiny when ironed.) Broadcloth and Oxford weaves are among the most common shirt material, as well as end-on-end, in which white threads are woven among colored threads. Solids are best for business shirts. Shirts that combine more than two colors should be avoided. That is, stripes should be of a single color—preferably dark—against white; likewise, tattersall, which is a kind of check, should also be a single dark color against white. Stripes or tattersalls that combine colors, such as red, blue, and white or black, yellow, and white, should be reserved for sporty, casual wear.

In recent years, fashion has invaded men's shirts. Collar lengths change, from very wide to narrow and rounded, or collars and cuffs may contrast, as with solid white against a striped shirt body. These shirts go in and out of style and should not be part of your business wardrobe unless you are a high-fashion dresser—and are willing to bear the extra cost of replacing them as fashions change. French cuffs are certainly acceptable, however. White shirts with French cuffs have an elegant look, provided they are not diminished with cheap cufflinks.

Think twice before you have monograms added to your shirts, even if the monogramming is free or advertised as a low-cost special, for fashion has taken over this former mark of distinction, too. First, assess whether monograms are appropriate within your company, and for your position. If no one else in your company or in your level of management wears monograms on his shirts, you may only look pretentious, or at least you may stand out for reasons other than your ability. Also, monograms have become fashionable in many circles and can appear on everything from crewneck sweaters to a secretary's blouse. Catalogs and department stores advertise monogramming free or nearly free with a purchase, and thus you may have little to gain by monogramming your shirts. If you do elect to have monograms, they should be small and tasteful, and stitched in uniform size above the left breast pocket or area. Avoid elaborate stitching or initials encased in diamonds or circles.

While putting together your suit ensembles, do not neglect your socks; they always show whenever you sit down. Sock colors should fit in with the color scheme of the rest of

your outfit, of course; never wear brown socks with a blue
suit, or vice versa, for example. And white socks are out for
business wear. Skip the cheap, all-synthetic socks which
have a tendency to pull after several washings. Also avoid
short socks. Make sure your socks are over-the-calf length,
and are the kind that will stay up. Nothing looks worse than
socks fallen down around the ankles, which allow bare flesh
to poke out from under trousers.

   A male manager's most important accessory, which is
really a part of daily business dress, is the tie; like many
accessories, it can make or break an ensemble. Ties should
be selected with great care. Unfortunately, they are often
received as gifts bought with little or no knowledge of what
they might match, or they are picked up by the dozen at sales
and bargain tables. It is time to treat the tie with more
respect.

   Silk is the best material for ties, although thin, shiny silk
will not hold a knot well unless it has a thick enough lining.
Polyester and silk blends are the next best material, followed
by polyester, provided it looks like silk or a silk blend.
Textured or knitted wool is also acceptable, although these
ties look more casual. When a tie is knotted—the half-Wind-
sor knot is the most common knot for business—its tip should
just reach the belt buckle.

   Solid colors or solids with small polka dots are the most
versatile ties, followed by "rep" ties, which usually have
stripes running in a diagonal pattern. Club and Ivy League
ties—those with small emblems, sports symbols, or geomet-
ric shapes—are distinctly upper middle class but also can
convey an Eastern stuffiness or snobbishness. If you are an
Easterner, you may not want to wear such a tie when
traveling to other parts of North America. Paisley is also a
fine choice, as long as the pattern is not large and wild,
although some people regard paisleys as less serious looking.
Save bow ties for sports clothes and tuxedos. Avoid ties that
mix patterns or have borders along the tips. Try to purchase
tie, shirt, and suit or sports jacket together in order to get the
best possible match. Do not put similar patterns right next to

each other; for example, a striped tie against a striped shirt. Solids on solids are fine, however.

Shoes should be of good-quality leather and of simple design, either tie or slip-on, without fancy stitching or a lot of metal doodads. Wing tips are a staple in the business world, but they are a heavy-looking shoe, and a large, imposing man might look better in a more streamlined slip-on. Loafers are too casual, and higher heeled shoes are best avoided as a passing fashion. Half-boots are acceptable in many quarters, but shoes are more traditional. The shoe color should be as dark as your suit, if not darker—never lighter. Black is the safest bet because it goes with everything. Always make sure your belt color matches your shoes; do not wear a brown belt with black shoes, for example. A slim, leather executive wallet that fits in your inner suit breast pocket is better and safer from pickpockets than a hip wallet. Neither should bulge, in any case.

Conservatism is the rule with glasses, too. Steer clear of trendy, oversize designer shapes and wire rims in favor of dark-colored plastic frames. Glasses should not call attention to themselves. The same is true of jewelry, including watches, collar bars, and tie bars. Jewelry has become more and more acceptable for men to wear, but it is best reserved for casual social time. A simple, masculine ring (in addition to a wedding band, if you have one) is fine, but do not risk putting someone off with a bracelet. Watches should be simple. Resist the urge for gadgetry, like those thick diver-style tanks that glow in the dark and tell what time it is anywhere in the world. If you buy a digital watch, keep its functions unobtrusive. Most digital watches can be set to beep on the hour, which can be most offensive and annoying. Meetings invariably suffer a minor disruption when a dozen watches start going off, never in unison. And if you are in a one-on-one situation, a beeping watch gives the impression that you are either anxious about time or have something more important to do.

Hair requires the same approach of simplicity and unobtrusiveness. Hair should be neatly trimmed around the ears and never extend below the collar in the back. If your hair musses easily, try holding it in place with a light spray, never with grease, pomade, or a lacquer-type spray. You should also avoid curly permanents, unless you want to look like a rock musician. Many men do not mind if their hair is all or partly gray, feeling that it enhances their image. Those who wish to trade a distinguished look for a youthful one, however, will find many preparations that will "cover" the gray, restoring the natural color.

Loss of hair calls for different steps. If your hairline is receding at the temples, part it at the point of greatest recession for the neatest look. Never try to grow hair to cover bald spots and receding hairlines—invariably you will not succeed, and your attempt will look obvious and vain. Many good-quality toupees are on the market, and a surprising number of men are choosing to wear them. Shop carefully, however, because even good hairpieces are fairly easy to spot, and bad ones look ridiculous. A bad toupee may curl strangely at the nape of the neck or stick out from the neck; it may not match the natural hair; it may have an unnatural, synthetic sheen; or it may have a part that looks artificial, or no part at all (everyone's hair parts in some fashion).

For the face, a clean-shaven look is still the most widely acceptable choice. Eschew cologne; it is distracting and inappropriate in a business environment. Mustaches have become more commonplace, especially among younger men. If you wear a mustache, keep it neatly trimmed above your lip, and do not extend it beyond the corners of your mouth. Waxed mustaches, as well as handlebars that extend up to sideburns, are not advisable for managers. Sideburns are best when they are short and trimmed. You need not look like a fresh army recruit, but do avoid muttonchops and cuts that extend far out onto the cheek or are slanted in a diagonal. Beards and goatees have more variable acceptance, being sported widely in some industries and rarely in others. Managers considering a hirsute look will want to carefully assess their business environments before growing a beard, and they should begin to cultivate it only on a long vacation, to have time to pass beyond the scruffy stage and judge its effect privately, before putting it on public view. On some faces and in some settings, a beard can enhance a person's authority and intelligence; but sometimes a beard can make others uneasy, since it hides the face and can make it harder for a person to gain the confidence of others.

For all managers, the key to dressing for success is using the same type of discipline they apply in their daily business affairs: knowing their objectives and putting together a program designed to accomplish them in the most efficient, effective way. You should approach building your business wardrobe with the same diligence you might apply to preparing a budget or marketing forecast. Your business wardrobe can be your enemy, or it can be a most helpful ally for you in achieving your career goals. The right clothes and the right accessories, in the right combinations, can help you create and maintain a positive image, one that can influence others to respect you, listen to you, trust you, and follow you.

CHAPTER 8

WOMEN AND MINORITIES IN MANAGEMENT

Despite all the movements for affirmative action, equal opportunities, and equal pay, America's business world still belongs to the white male. The corporate system was designed by and for these men, and others who aspire to climb the corporate ladder are to some extent seen as intruders. While minorities—and in management women are still very much a minority, even though they are a majority in the general population—have made significant strides in gaining acceptance and real power in management, they still face tremendous obstacles and prejudice that will probably take decades more to erase. Meanwhile, it is still true that the business world is one of double standards, and that women and minority managers must generally work harder and be more skilled and competent than their white male counterparts in order to succeed. Similarly successful male managers often have a much wider range of action; they can often "get away with" behavior that would be devastating to the career of a woman or minority manager. With all the changes of recent decades, women and minorities must still work doubly hard and overprepare to meet and overcome social obstacles to a successful career in management. For white male managers, this state of affairs implies the need for extra attention, not to provide special support for any one group, but to see that an operation is run in a fully professional manner, unaffected by sexual or racial questions. This chapter is primarily directed at those minorities, women included, who are still working to gain that fully neutral, professional acceptance in the management community, and secondarily to all managers who wish to run organizations free of discrimination.

ESTABLISHING AUTHORITY

Perhaps the most basic question for any manager is the need to establish authority. Women and minority managers seem to have gained considerable ground in recent decades; traditional stereotypes and prejudices have begun to diminish among top executives in major corporations. However, much prejudicial behavior is not overt, but very subtle; often it is unnoticed and unrecognized even by those who feel they are relatively "enlightened" managers. That very subtlety poses real problems for women and minority managers in establishing effective authority. And the problems extend both above and below, including subordinates who are unhappy taking orders from them, and superiors who find it difficult to promote them to higher-level managerial positions. Women and minority managers still have a lot of work cut out for them in destroying these negative attitudes.

Even up until the beginning of the 1980s, a good percentage of women and minorities hired or promoted to managerial slots discovered, belatedly and ruefully, that the posts were mere tokens in order to meet federal affirmative action requirements. The titles may have sounded important, the pay and even the perks may have been good, but no real authority or power went along with them. Some "tokens"

spent their days reading newspapers. Fortunately, tokenism
has declined sharply. But even though positions may carry
some real authority, women and minorities still have to work
to hang on to them and establish themselves as legitimate
power figures to be respected.

How do women or minority managers establish authority? First of all, they must look and act the part of professional managers at all times and in all aspects of their work.
They must realize that many employees in any company will
not take them seriously; they will have to earn the respect
that some others may be accorded almost automatically. Self-
confidence is crucial, because when people are self-confi-
dent, they naturally will be more assertive and seem more in
control. They must be aware of and control their manner-
isms, for any fidgeting or nervousness will work against
them.

Appearance also is crucial in establishing an image as a
professional manager. People form quick first impressions
based on appearance, and managers whose dress is not
conservative and professional may be automatically discounted.

Whatever else they do, women and minority managers
must maintain their composure, even when faced with criticism from a superior or when forced to discipline an employee. This is especially important for women, who are
often expected to be emotional and flighty. A male colleague
may fly off the handle at the slightest provocation and his
staff will lift their eyebrows and shake their heads at having
to work for such a temperamental boss; but a woman who
displays similar behavior risks losing authority.

Profanity, likewise, should be used cautiously. Some
women managers claim that an occasional well-placed exple-
tive gets them the proper attention and helps reinforce their
authority. However, while long-established managers may
swear like troopers in the office, they are likely to be shocked
and disapproving to hear the same language from a new
arrival, especially a woman. Swearing can also backfire,

drawing attention to itself and away from the point you are trying to make.

Managers reinforce their authority by making firm decisions and showing that they are not afraid to make them. Some women and minority managers stay on the defensive; out of fear of making a wrong decision, they would rather not act at all, but that is a more grievous mistake than making a bad decision. While managers should not rush to be railroaded into hasty or reckless decisions, they should not be afraid of failure or mistakes. Every successful manager has some failures, and decision making is crucial to the practice of management.

Hand-in-hand with risk taking go voicing opinions and making contributions in meetings. As a manager, you probably have to attend many meetings; do not take them lightly. Employees are constantly being sized up at meetings for those managerial qualities that will help them get the next promotion. Those who do not speak up do not move up. It is especially important for women and minority managers to take time to prepare for each meeting and to contribute something of value. Merely agreeing with someone else or offering thoughts that do not add to the matter under discussion will not do, however; to be meaningful, the contributions must be substantive, or they may be seen as time-wasters or time-servers.

HANDLING HOSTILE SUBORDINATES

Women and minorities are often more accepted generally than specifically. For example, many people feel that it is all right to promote women to managerial positions just as long as they themselves never have to report to one. Such a lack of acceptance in the workplace is the corporate version of ". . . but not next door." This attitude is more prevalent among men, but a surprising number of women feel this way, too, in spite of the fact that it is self-defeating to their own ambitions. Few women or minority managers are viewed as fast-track managers or real power brokers who have the clout to help others in their careers, so subordinates often see working for such a manager as a career setback, or at least as a situation of diminished visibility. "She's probably not going anywhere, so how am I going to move up?" thinks such a person. Even secretaries may consider assignment to a woman or minority manager to be a cut in status. Most difficult of all are the people who still cannot reconcile themselves to working for a woman or minority manager because of deep-seated chauvinism or prejudice; such people may often feel that women belong at home raising families rather than competing in a "man's world." If you encounter any of these attitudes among your own subordinates, and women or minority managers almost certainly will at least once in their careers, do not take them personally; they have nothing to do with you, but have instead to do with hard-dying perceptions about the place of women and minorities in the office. If you sense such resentment among your staff members, you must take steps to eliminate it. If you try to ignore it, it probably will not go away, but will fester and worsen, causing the overall performance of your unit—and you—to suffer. What is more, your peers and superiors may be quick to notice that you lack control over your staff and conclude you are not management material after all.

Working to establish your authority immediately is crucial; you must dress, look, and act the part of the professional manager. No one expects you to be a pal or a mother figure. Get to know your staff individually, on a one-to-one basis, and find out about their responsibilities and their own career goals. Emphasize that you expect a team effort and need their cooperation and support. If one or more of your staff members had hoped to be promoted into your position but instead must now report to you, be frank. Tell them you know they are disappointed they did not get the job, but that there undoubtedly will be other opportunities; stress that, meanwhile, you are depending on them to continue to make their best effort.

Your behavior should be cool and low-key. Flaunting your authority or power and issuing autocratic orders will only turn people off. Do not gossip, encourage gossip, or attempt to be too chummy.

Sometimes hostile behavior on the part of subordinates can be very subtle, so subtle that is almost impossible to confront anyone with anything. These situations can be tricky and should be handled with the utmost care. A deviously hostile employee can be very supportive to your face and work to undercut you behind your back, by doing such things as failing to pass along important information, or letting you know at the last minute that a report won't be ready for a meeting. You can discipline such employees by telling them that carelessness is unacceptable, but trying to make an issue out of your gender or race may land you in quicksand. It is easy for them to deny, and makes for more destructive gossip. If the bad attitude persists, despite warnings, you have no recourse but to let the person go. Once you have reached the last resort of firing, do not procrastinate; get it over with. You do no one a favor by allowing one person with a negative attitude to drag down everyone else's morale, including yours. And the longer you delay the action, the worse it reflects on you as a manager.

Much the same can be said if a superior is unalterably opposed to having a woman or minority manager on staff. If he or she cannot be won over by demonstrated ability, the unfortunate subordinate can do little about that but make the best of it while seeking a transfer or looking for another job.

HIRING AND FIRING

Naturally, women and minority managers have significant advantages whenever they can do their own hiring, as opposed to stepping in to run an already existing staff. They can screen candidates for the particular background, skills, and personalities with which they feel most confident and comfortable. They can weed out those candidates who seem to have reservations about working for them before they ever have a chance to cause trouble. Women managers should generally inquire whether or not the candidate—male or female—has any objections to working for a woman. If they sense any hesitation or uncertainty, they will probably be better off going on to another candidate. They certainly do not need a potential troublemaker on their staff, and they should not naively think that "things will iron themselves out later." If there is hesitancy in the beginning, it may solidify into something more serious later.

Once they have determined that a candidate possesses the right skills, they should look for compatibility and personality fit. Some questions to explore are: "How well will the two of you work together?" "Do you share some common attitudes and goals?" "How do you think you will handle conflict?" "Will the conflict be constructive?" "Is the chemistry right?" First impressions will tell a lot about a person, but no manager should hire someone just on the basis of one meeting. They should have at least two, perhaps even three, sessions. Some people are too self-conscious and nervous on their initial interview, and begin to loosen up on the next round. Others, who make a sparkling show on first impression, may reveal that their sparkle is only on the surface.

If, however, they choose wrong or inherit a staff not of their own choosing, women and minority managers may have some difficult personnel problems to deal with. Few managers enjoy disciplining employees, but the task has special pitfalls for women and minority managers. The impulse to be sympathetic, understanding, and easy-going may boomerang, for nothing cuts authority faster than failing to nip in the bud bad behavior or performance. If they have an employee whose work has been slipping, or who is chronically late, they must move deliberately but expeditiously to correct the situation. If such problems go uncorrected, subordinates may lose respect for their manager. Such problems usually escalate until the difficulty becomes apparent to their own supervisors and they appear to be unable to manage well. Some male managers rely on intimidation to keep subordinates in line, but this is not an appropriate choice for any professional manager. When criticizing employees, mix praise with criticism and end on a positive note.

If all else fails, you may finally have to fire someone whose unprofessional response to you as a manager under-cuts the effectiveness of your unit as a whole. Firing should always be handled with great tact and consideration, regard-less of who is doing the firing. But being fired by a woman may be difficult for some employees, particularly men, to handle; while being fired is humiliating and demoralizing, getting the ax from a woman is an extra blow to the ego. As in any firing situation, the best approach is a direct one, consid-erate but firm. Do not beat around the bush, but come directly to the point and tell employees why they are being let go, even if it is for disciplinary reasons. Inform them of what the company will do for them, such as amount of severance pay, outplacement counseling, resume updating, references, secretarial help, and so on. Make it clear that the decision is final.

Sometimes women and minority managers are seen as a soft touch, so some fired employees may plead for recon-sideration, citing financial or family difficulties, or promising to reform. It is important not to waver, nor to promise to intercede for someone, if the decision to lay off has come from higher up. It only makes you look weak as a manager. Indeed, if the firing is for cause, the employee has probably gone through a long period of warnings, probations and attempts at re-education. It is also true that most people get fired at least once in their careers and manage to go on without irreparable damage. Firing is never a pleasant task, even if you are genuinely glad to get rid of a bad employee, but it is one of the necessary evils that go along with being a manager.

ENTERTAINING AND TRAVELING

The double standard pervasive on the job also applies to the social side of business life. Behavior that is tolerated, some-times even admired in most managers, such as the ability to drink at the bar for hours, is scorned in women and minority managers. They must always be aware that, whether it is apparent or not, their behavior is being observed and noted, and negative impressions are formed easily.

Women have a particular problem in business entertaining; it has to do with who pays. It does not matter who does the asking, what their status is, or how big their expense account is; many men still do not like women to pick up the check. It makes them feel very uncomfortable and embarrassed. Increasingly, though, men are coming to accept equality in check-paying, especially when the woman puts the whole situation on a firmly professional basis. Occasionally, however, a man appears to be truly distressed at the idea of having his lunch paid for by a woman. In that case, after a gentle protest, the best course is to smile graciously and thank him. A fight over the check will only increase his discomfort and undo any good will established with him in the business relationship.

Many women managers avoid such scenes by making arrangements with the waiter or waitress in advance to have the check placed on their side of the table, so the check will not automatically be given to the man. In that situation, it is a good idea for her to have a credit card ready in advance, in a handy pocket or right on top in a purse, so she can immediately place the card on the table when the check comes. It is far better to pay with plastic than with cash, for riffling through bills seems to make men even more uncomfortable. The guest may still protest, and if he insists, the businesswoman will have to judge whether the price of lunch is worth his distress. Many businesswomen have learned to avoid the check scene altogether by arranging to pay in advance, so that a check never reaches the table. They search out one or two restaurants to patronize, go there regularly, and get to know the staff. Generally they present their credit cards in advance of a lunch date, specify the tip percentage (a generous one, so there are no slip-ups), and sign the check. If they patronize an establishment and tip well, the staff will be only too happy to accommodate them. The same procedure holds for entertaining while traveling out of town. It is wise to check out in advance restaurants where you will be likely to eat, introduce yourself to the maitre d'hotel or headwaiter, and explain how you want things handled when you bring your guest in.

Women managers also have a special problem with dinner dates, because they too often can lead to something else: people tend to be a little more relaxed and looser over dinner, and after a few drinks or a bottle of wine, it is all too easy to retire to the bar or a nightclub for a nightcap—and perhaps a proposition. If a male business associate suggests dinner, the wise woman manager will decline and suggest lunch or drinks instead. If she meets someone in a bar for drinks at the end of a working day, she can always excuse herself after one or two drinks, citing other plans or an appointment. In a place where there is music and dancing, she should decline invitations to dance, for then she would become a sexual object, not a businesswoman.

The area of social drinking poses hazards for all managers, but especially for women and minority managers. The practice of meeting associates for drinks after work should inspire caution. As a manager, you should not try to be "one of the boys." If members of your staff meet regularly for cocktails and you are invited to join, go once in a while, but not often. Remember that the invitations may be extended out of courtesy. More to the point, managers should not socialize too much with their staff, for they risk losing the needed distance from them.

Whether you are drinking with your peers, subordinates, or superiors, never try to keep up with others, and never allow yourself to get intoxicated. If you match them drink for drink, they may cheer you on at the table, but remember you as a hard boozer the next day at the office. The last thing you want is a reputation as a barfly. That caution applies especially to women. It does not matter that Charlie downed six doubles without looking any worse for it—the standards that apply to him and his male associates do not apply to women. If you feel yourself getting intoxicated, excuse yourself immediately and leave. It is far better to leave early than to risk slurred speech and sloppy coordination.

What you drink is as important as how much you drink. More and more managers are steering clear of hard liquor; it's a good idea—let others drink scotch and bourbon if they wish. One alternative is sherry, a drink you can sip and nurse for a long time. Beware, however; sherry's alcoholic content is greater than that of wine, and it will affect you more quickly. Beer is another alternative. Wine is probably the safest alcoholic drink, and it can also be sipped very slowly. A wine spritzer, which is wine mixed with soda or seltzer and served with ice, is even better, though you should be careful not to drink it quickly because it is diluted. Of course, you need not drink alcohol at all, either at lunch or after work, and many managers today do not. Mineral water with a slice of lemon or lime is perfectly acceptable and health-conscious. Not only will you keep your mental alertness, but you will be doing your figure and your health a favor.

As a manager, you may be expected to attend evening functions or to entertain at your own home. If you are entertaining at home, at a dinner party or cocktail party, do it in style, with hired help and a caterer. Nothing reduces your professional status faster than to run around fixing and serving food and drinks. Besides, you cannot really entertain your guests if you are preoccupied with kitchen and bar details. Hiring help will enhance your image and is well worth the cost. A single woman manager should never invite a lone male associate home for dinner, because it implies seduction.

The single businesswoman always has the dilemma of whether or not to bring an escort to business-social engagements. Wives tend to resent single women managers anyway, and if she is alone, she may appear to be even more of a predator who will snatch their husbands away. Yet an escort may be a handicap, requiring introduction, entertaining, and inclusion in business-oriented conversations. For these reasons, many businesswomen have decided it is best to forego the escort. However, it is a good idea for single business-women to go out of their way to meet the wives of their co-workers, superiors, and subordinates, and to try to put them at ease. They will seem less of a threat that way.

Although wives have the freedom to dress up for eve-ning functions, and some of them will go out of their way to look sexy, conservatism should be the rule of thumb for women managers. That does not mean wearing a navy blue business suit, but it does mean wearing modest, high-necked, and nonclinging clothes. Anything remotely sexy will counteract a professional image—and increase resent-ment from co-workers' wives.

Traveling also requires special attention for women and minority managers. If they are traveling alone, they may well encounter some discriminatory treatment in service estab-lishments, which are used to catering to the white male business traveler. Hotel clerks may slight them, reservation clerks may put them in rooms they would never dream of giving their preferred customers, and restaurant help may treat them like pariahs. It may be infuriating, but getting angry will accomplish little. If you are placed in such a situation, be polite and firm; do not accept second-class treatment. Refuse the table by the kitchen door, speak up when the service is slow, and do not hesitate to insist on another room if you do not like the one you were given. It will help if you always dress like a professional and tip well.

Traveling with males, whether they are superiors, equals, or subordinates, is often a touchy situation for women managers. Men often feel ill at ease, and some are downright resentful that they cannot really "cut loose" while they are away from wife and family. Because some men will naturally feel obliged to look after women companions while traveling, women managers must make it clear, politely, that they can shift for themselves. They should not drag along too much baggage, but pack the minimum and make sure they can handle it easily themselves. If they are fearful flyers, they should not admit it, no matter how terrified they are and no matter how much their traveling companions may rattle on about their own flying jitters. Women's behavior must be impeccably businesslike the entire time.

The woman who does not wish to dine with her male associates should decline with a simple but vague, "I've already made plans for the evening," even if it's only eating alone in the hotel room. If dining with one or more associates is unavoidable, she should do so but excuse herself at the end of dinner and not be enticed into going out for a night on the town, which is asking for trouble. At some point in her career, almost every woman manager will take a trip with someone who assumes that an out-of-town trip is reason for a one-night stand, someone who would never think of propositioning her back at the home office, but does it quite matter-of-factly on the road. (If you are a male manager, such behavior should be considered strictly off limits.) If you are a woman manager in that situation, do not puff yourself up indignantly and make a big deal of it, for you may have to travel with this person again. Decline politely and firmly in a nonpersonal way. You might add either that you are happily married or, if you are single, that you are involved with someone else—even if you are not at the moment.

THE OFFICE ROMANCE

That raises the question of the office romance. No matter how you look at it, managers who engage in an office romance, no matter what their professional level, stand to lose more than they gain. The risks are enormous. News of office romances has a way of getting around, no matter how careful or secretive people think they are being. It is gossip that spreads easily and quickly, especially because people are still all too willing to believe that professional women try to advance their careers through the bedroom.

At the very least, an office romance is distracting and disruptive, not only to you and your partner, but also to those you work with. Corporate policy may severely discourage sexual entanglements in the office; both the man and the woman—although sometimes only the woman—may be disciplined, let go, or transferred. Even without such action, the affair may run out of steam and leave both parties feeling extremely uncomfortable at having to continue working together. Many people argue in defense of office romances, saying they are inevitable as long as men and women are thrown together every day. Attraction and sexual tension naturally result. While it is true that some people manage to successfully carry off an office romance, affairs still backfire far more than they succeed. In general, you are better off leaving sexual tension unacknowledged, for acknowledgment requires some sort of action, either acceptance or refusal.

While affairs between peers are difficult, affairs between superiors and subordinates are even more perilous, for both parties. The superior risks at least loss of professional image, which can be disastrous for a woman or minority manager. The subordinate in such an affair is in an even more precarious position. Some think this will benefit their careers, and sometimes it does temporarily, although the benefits may be undone in the end. Co-workers will resent them for having an unfair advantage over others. If the lover departs, for another division or company, the new superior may swiftly throw out the remaining party. Or, if the affair dwindles, a superior may get rid of an ex-lover, who is an embarrassing reminder of a former dalliance. By far the worst kind of office romance involves partners who are married to others. The gossip can be far more malicious, and the consequences worse.

But, say some single managers, how is it possible to have a social life without dating people from the office? What if you do not like to go to bars, and your job keeps you too busy for involvement in clubs or organizations? It is a dilemma, and a tough one, without a pat answer. Still, the risks of office romances must be carefully weighed before you become involved in one. If you do become romantically involved with a co-worker, you are better off with someone from another department or division, not someone with whom you must work closely every day.

If you work for a company in a highly competitive industry, you also must be careful about seeing people who work for competitors. You may never breathe a word about business when you are together, but if your company finds out about your relationship, you may be out on the street before you know it—at best your position may be compromised. And women and minorities in management are particularly vulnerable to such actions.

No matter how attracted you are to someone at work, do not react impulsively or rashly. Keep a cool head and carefully assess your situation lest you undo a lot of hard work and years of effort to advance your career.

HANDLING PREJUDICE AND CHAUVINISM

Women and minorities may have come a long way, but chauvinism is still pervasive in the business world. Some of it is obvious and overt, and some of it is very subtle and difficult to counter. Some of it is even disguised as chivalry, as with the strongly prejudiced man who believes a woman cannot handle responsibility as well as a man, that she must be closely supervised, that she is just "biding time" in the job until she quits to have children or to spend more time with her family, and that she is really just a sex object. Other men may not have such extreme sentiments, but may still treat women differently due to upbringing and years of cultural conditioning that have taught them that women are not equal to men. These attitudes may be irritating, even enraging, but taking an aggressive posture against them will get you little more than an "angry feminist" label. That does not mean that women should have to put up with any demeaning behavior—just be cool in their counterattacks.

One of the most common sexist behaviors is the use of endearments, such as *honey, sweetheart,* and *doll.* It may seem harmless enough, but every time a woman lets someone get away with it, she has allowed herself to be reduced to a sex object. She should stop it immediately and firmly with a reply such as, "My name isn't honey, so please don't call me that," or, "My name isn't doll, it's Susan," repeated—always coolly—as often as necessary. Some men are chivalrously chauvinistic. They constantly remind a woman that she is not their equal through little courtesies such as helping her on with her coat, holding open doors, and making comments in meetings such as, "Well, Roberta's here now, so clean up your language," or, "Here comes Denise, now we can't tell any more dirty jokes." The woman involved should simply smile pleasantly and tell them it is not necessary to alter their behavior for her. If someone holds her coat or opens a door, she should accept the courtesy graciously but say, "Thanks, Tom, but that isn't necessary." She should never make a big deal out of it, especially in front of others. Men who have these habits are not even aware of what they are doing; they are not deliberately attempting to demean women. Some even think they are being casual and friendly, which is why it is inadvisable to leap down their throats. Attitudes do not change overnight; that takes a long, slow process of re-education. It is up to women—and really to all enlightened professional managers—to see that re-education takes place. Laws alone will not do it.

Fortunately, laws have gone a long way toward reducing sexual harassment in the workplace. Once it was quite pervasive, and women who complained about it were usually fired, while the offending men got off scot-free. Today, demanding sexual favors—regardless of whether a man or a woman is doing the demanding—is against federal law, and many companies are swift to react to it and stop it, punishing or firing the guilty. Alert managers should be sensitive to any such harassment in their organizations, and should take steps to stop it, rather than leaving a victim to handle the situation alone.

Sexual harassment usually occurs at the lower levels in a corporation, and most often is directed against the lowest level of female employees, such as secretaries and clerks.

Middle- or upper-level women managers will probably experience propositions, but little overt and persistent harassment. If, despite a professional attitude and dress, a female
manager receives a proposition, she should try to deflect it
without striking out at someone's ego or personality, no
matter how much she would like to. She can always plead
that she is married or involved with someone already and
then change the subject. Even if the situation turns more
difficult, the harassed party should always try to handle it on
a one-to-one basis. He or she should remind the offender that
asking for sexual favors is against the law; if that still does not
work, the situation should be referred to the offender's
superior. Court should be the last resort in seeking redress
for sexual harassment. Court suits take a long time to settle
and create bad feelings on both sides. The parties involved
should ask themselves if they can continue to work in an
organization together, as the proceedings get messier.

In recent decades, minority managers have become less
subject to overt kinds of harassment. But both women and
minority managers are subject to a wide range of covert
actions stemming from prejudice or chauvinism.

What if, as a woman or minority manager, you are in a
meeting or a group and someone deliberately tries to embarrass you with an insulting joke or remark, for example? You
are in a tough spot, because you can lose either way,
whether you speak up and challenge the offender or meekly
let it go by. One response will make you look like a militant
with no sense of humor, and the other will make you look like
a spineless jellyfish. If you are lucky and smart, you will have
cultivated some allies who will speak up for you. It is far
better for an offender to be censured by others, who make it
clear that that sort of behavior is unprofessional and unbe-
coming. If you have no such ally present, the best thing you
can do is ignore it. You may be being baited, and your refusal
to take the bait may make others uncomfortable enough to
discourage such remarks in the future.

But what if someone persists in trying to discredit or
embarrass you with rude remarks? You would be best ad-

vised to visit that person privately in his office and say something such as, "I'd like to establish a good, cooperative working relationship with you, but I'm a bit put off by the remarks you make about _____ [you fill in the blank] whenever I'm around." This approach is risky, because it can make the person very defensive. If the person is nasty enough, he or she may keep trying to undercut you in that or some other way. But a direct approach may jolt the person out of that behavior.

Another form of chauvinistic treatment that can be quite frustrating is to be discounted or even ignored. It usually happens in meetings. A woman or minority manager speaks up with a suggestion or idea, and no one seems to pay much attention; perhaps no one even responds directly to those remarks. Then, a few minutes later, someone else pipes up with almost the same idea, and everyone applauds the suggestion. That person takes the credit, and the originator has been discounted. If that happens to you, there is not much you can do about it but keep silent. If you try to point out it was your idea originally, you will only antagonize people and look like a whining poor sport. Instead, try to prevent it from happening in the future. That means making sure that others notice you when you speak. Women, especially, are often easy to overlook or ignore because they speak softly, sometimes even timidly. Practice projecting your voice so that it commands more attention. Be careful not to raise the pitch because your voice will begin to sound unattractive or screechy, and others will tune you out in self-defense. Keep the pitch low, but your voice strong. Get right to the point. If you are sitting in an audience, stand up when you begin to speak so that others can see you and focus their attention to you. And on days when you know you will be attending important meetings, wear a dark-colored, conservative suit; it will lend seriousness to your image.

The position of women or minority managers may be undercut in other ways, too. For example, they may be assigned secretarial duties at a business meeting. If asked in advance to take notes during the meeting to be written up as minutes, the best course is to demur, citing lack of shorthand knowledge and suggesting a secretary might be more appropriate. If that is met with the insistence that they "just jot down a few notes," managers may agree to do so, if the duty is shared by others at future meetings. If asked at the start of the meeting, in front of others, they should agree pleasantly, but should tell their superior in private that they do not wish to be exclusively delegated the task. Similarly, the woman or minority manager should not accept a "fetch-and-carry" role. If asked to see to the coffee before a meeting begins, the manager should turn that job over to a secretary or assistant. But whatever they do, managers never bring in coffee themselves, and should never clean up the empty cups and dirty ashtrays after a meeting.

Sometimes women and minority managers seem to get the dullest assignments. It is difficult to prove yourself ready for a promotion and more responsibility if you never get a chance to stretch your ability. Sometimes a department head is unconsciously favoring the white males on the staff; perhaps he or she distrusts women or minority managers or feels they need too much supervision to be able to handle more difficult assignments. In that situation, the slighted managers must deal with the question squarely. While noting that they appreciate the assignments they have received, they should explain that they are ready to tackle something more demanding, stressing their successes on previous projects. Mentors and sponsors, who will press the interests of their friends and protégés, are especially important to cultivate for aid in this area.

MOVING UP

All managers must actively pursue their own career interests. Women and minority managers must do so even more assiduously than most. It not only is acceptable to actively seek raises and promotions, it is expected. No manager should for a minute sit back and think that his or her good deeds and strong performance will be noticed and rewarded automatically. Even if noticed without their being pointed out, they may not be rewarded financially. Companies try to hold personnel costs down as much as possible, and if people are willing to work for less than their true market value, so much the better for the company. That is the employer's gain and the manager's loss. Do not be shy about tooting your horn, because no one else is going to do it for you. The longer people work for less than they should, the more it hurts them. It does not take long for percentage raises and bonuses to widen the gap between what you earn and what you *should* earn.

In order to make the most out of opportunities for advancement in pay and position, you must have a clear idea of your own career plans. What are your goals with your company? Will you need to broaden your base of experience or switch departments in order to realize them? Once you know exactly where you are headed, tell your superior and remind him or her periodically of your aspirations. Do it in a low-key fashion at the right moment, of course, such as when you sign up for a training course. If your advancement hinges squarely on your superior's advancement, you must be especially sensitive about making your plans known. No one likes to think that someone is out to get their job—especially while they are still in it and perhaps uncertain of promotion prospects.

If a slot opens up that you want, and you qualify, do not hesitate to speak up for it; otherwise no one may think of you as a candidate. Women and minorities are far more likely to be overlooked for advancement than are white men, who more or less take upward movement for granted. Many male supervisors still have a hard time thinking of women as ambitious. Be able to explain, with concrete examples, why you deserve the job and what you have to offer. Saying you have been in your present job long enough or that it is time to move on will not suffice. Cite your past performance and accomplishments, and the contributions you have made to the company's operations. If you work in a service area such as personnel or communications, where you do not have any hard cost or profit figures to show, you can still cite examples of how you improved or streamlined your function.

Even so, you may find yourself held back for no apparent reason. If you are routinely skipped over, and your superior seems to turn a deaf ear to your pitch to move up and on, give notice that you are going to take the matter up with the next level of management or personnel. That may get some action without your having to follow through; few managers like to see an issue in their department escalated, because it makes them look as though they cannot handle it themselves. If you do take your case to the next level and still get no results, prepare yourself to look for another job. You may be working for the wrong company.

If it is a raise in your current position you are after, be aware that there are good times and bad times to ask for more money. The best time is right on the heels of a major accomplishment that has earned you favorable recognition or attention. Do not wait for the glory to grow cold, hoping that you will be rewarded; step up and ask for it. Make your request at an appropriate moment, when conditions are favorable and time is available to consider the matter, not right before a major meeting or near an important deadline.

No matter how much you may deserve a raise, your chances of winning one will be sorely diminished if you choose to ask just when the company's earnings are down. Better to wait a few weeks. Never, however, let more than a year go by without asking for a performance review and raise. Most companies have regular schedules for such matters, but some smaller ones do not; as long as you let it slide, an employer is likely to let it slide, too.

On the other hand, mistrust excuses that put you off until another time, or justifications for small raises. Arguments that company profits are down or that a ceiling has been placed on raise amounts are often not completely true. Management somehow always finds a way to reward the good performers. Chances are, the gullible employees will buy the argument and settle for less or nothing, while the funds available for raises go to those who make a strong case for them. Be persistent and firm. Do not, however, be hasty in delivering an ultimatum ("If I don't get a raise, I'll quit!") because an ultimatum may backfire and work to an employer's advantage. Do not deliver one unless you are prepared to follow through on it. As with promotions, be sure you can back up your argument for more money by citing examples of performance. Never plead financial difficulty or give the lame reason that you just "deserve" more money.

When discussing salary for a new position, do not be afraid to negotiate. Many women and minority managers fear that if they try to negotiate, they will lose out altogether, but negotiation is a natural and expected part of the process for setting salaries. Know what your market worth is. You can keep current on this in a number of ways: through classified job ads in the Sunday newspaper, professional organizations, and executive recruiters. Also, know your own salary requirements. Have your business expenses increased, or are they expected to increase? Will your expanded job responsibilities require more travel, entertaining, or socializing? Would a new job or promotion mean additional wardrobe expenses to fit your new image?

Decide on a minimum figure you want to accept, and then ask for a figure higher than that. Give ample room for negotiation—remember, both sides will want to feel they have won something—but do not name an astronomically high figure. As always, be prepared to show why you should be earning the amount you are seeking.

If you are interviewing for a new position and your interviewer asks what you expect to earn in that job, never reply, "What does it pay?" Such an answer starts you off in a weak bargaining position. State firmly what you expect to make. Do not be surprised if the other person protests that your sum is too much; that is a common negotiation practice. Once the other person has named a figure, you can work out a compromise in between. Women and minority managers often get caught in a low-pay trap in salary negotiations. Most of them are underpaid for what they do; some are severely underpaid. An interviewer who asks what you are currently earning as a basis for calculating an offer will keep you in a low earnings trap, claiming the size of increase you are looking for cannot possibly be justified. Make it clear that your compensation must at least equal the compensation of others doing comparable jobs in your own company and throughout your industry.

If a salary ceiling on a job is firmly lower than desired, it is always possible to try to negotiate extra perks or a salary review within three to six months. Whatever arrangement is made should be confirmed in writing; otherwise a promised review can easily fall by the wayside because of a personnel change or for any number of other reasons or excuses.

Remember that the more money a manager commands, the more that manager is valued by a company. People who work cheap do not get the same respect as those whose price is high. If an employer has to pay well to get a manager, everyone will feel that he or she must be good at the job. It is automatic for the men who still do most of the hiring in the nation's corporations to expect women and minority managers to be happy working for less than other managers. A prospective employer should know right from the start that competent, serious professionals expect to be paid fair market value for their worth.

CHAPTER 9

JOB-SEEKING

Changing jobs well requires a good deal of preparation and the development of vitally important personal selling skills, whether the change sought is voluntary or involuntary, part of upward career mobility or a defensive move away from a troubled situation, inside your current company or to another company.

Professionalism, balance, integrity, personal warmth, a wealth of relevant skills and experience—all this and more we try to project to others during the course of our careers, as we move up and around in the world of American business. In one way or another, we project those images every day, as we pursue our careers. When we are involved in formal presentation situations, we do so more carefully. When we are in such selling situations as internal interviews for new assignments or periodic personal internal evaluations, we are very careful to do so indeed. And when we are seeking employment elsewhere, finding and meeting people who may or may not know something of us and our work, and who have not really worked with us before, we do everything we can to sell our prospective new employers on the immense benefits that will result from hiring us. Putting it a little differently, in all these kinds of situations we engage in persuasion, with the attention, time, and effort we put into them depending largely on how important they are to us and how difficult it may be to persuade others in the situation.

JOB-SEEKING AS SELLING

The essence of job-seeking—whether within or outside your present company—is that you are involved in a selling process, with you as seller. That description in no way vulgarizes or oversimplifies the process. It is a precise description of the main content of the transaction between you and whomever you are trying to convince. Nor is the process analogous to selling; it *is* selling, ultimately face-to-face selling. The successful job-seeker uses precisely the same procedures and techniques as does the successful face-to-face sales professional.

Job-seeking involves several kinds of preselling activities, many of them alternatives that depend on where you are starting from. It also involves a set of selling processes, again often alternatives, aimed at selling someone or a group on the desirability of seeing you face to face. And it involves a second set of selling processes, this one rather straightforwardly applying equally to almost all face-to-face selling situations, in which you and a prospective employer come together to sell and be sold on the desirability of hiring you above all others. In-house personal evaluations differ, in that you are not always seeking to make a sale, but many of the persuasive techniques used face to face are indistinguishable from those used in the job-seeking selling process. In-house job-seeking often involves some preselling activities, normally takes little interview selling, and involves essentially the same face-to-face skills and understandings that outside job-seeking requires. Two significant features make in-house job-seeking special: you are likely to know a good deal about company, division, and operation; and you may know those who make the hiring decisions—a real advantage because empathy in that case is often a good deal easier to achieve than with strangers or near-strangers.

Throughout these job-seeking processes, you should bear in mind some basic approaches. One is that what you are selling are the *benefits* that hiring you will bring. No, you are not selling *you;* it is both self-denigrating and inaccurate to think of job seeking as a process by which you sell yourself. You are not for sale; further, nobody should have any reason to buy you. Some, in their eagerness to sell themselves, lose both the image and the substance of personal integrity, and that is a personal and business disaster. What is for sale is not your time, loyalty, skill, or talent, either; those things have to do with you, not with the benefits that come from hiring you. That you have long and relevant experience is a *feature* of the product that is you; that your experience as part of a constellation of skills and qualities will bring new stability and ultimately profits to a floundering division is a *benefit* that you bring with you. That you have a wide range of government contacts is a *feature* of the product that is you; how you will use your contacts to develop lucrative government contracts for your new company is a *benefit* that hiring you brings. In short, as in all selling, it is a matter of putting yourself into the other guy's shoes and responding empathetically and specifically to that other guy's wants and needs. Those who want to hire will say: "This is what I think she [or he] can do for us." In contrast, "This is her [or his] background and experience" is the language used by those who have not been sold on the benefits that hiring you will bring. *Will* bring, not *can* bring. People hire the professional manager they believe will do the job. If there is an element of doubt in their minds, they will probably keep on interviewing. That is especially true in hard times, when competition is keener and hiring standards stiffen.

This question of selling the benefits that hiring you will bring is central, as it is in all selling, whatever is being sold. It is an understanding that should permeate every aspect of the job-seeking process, providing a proper basis for first approaches with potential job contacts, recruiters, personnel people, and those who hire, whether those contacts are face to face or in writing. And it should provide a takeoff point for all self-description, as in resumes and covering letters. People tend to take you at your own self-evaluation; they see the image you habitually project, so they will more easily see the truth of high self-evaluation if there is truth in it. But they need help in seeing how to apply your virtues to their business wants and needs. That is why selling benefits is so important.

These questions of understanding and personal attitude lead to another central matter in job-seeking. Put simply, you have to be "up and ready" for every relevant job-seeking personal contact. The old song has it that "nobody wants you when you're down and out." Quite right; nobody does. Nor when you're tired, ragged, affected in the slightest degree by alcohol, defeated, or "down" in any discernible way.

In one very significant way, job seeking is not like professional selling. In professional selling, you have to be able to close sales, day after day, year after year, never losing the sparkle that professionalism brings. In job-seeking, you need only make a single sale; you may not have to make another such sale for a decade or perhaps even for the rest of your life.

On the other hand, the sales professional knows how to stay "up"; it is a basic career need. The job-seeker is all too often in a series of unfamiliar situations, in a hurry, sometimes in urgent need of a job change, or unemployed, and he or she easily becomes disoriented by repeated seeming personal rejection. It is very easy when seeking a job to lose your "edge," to become perceptibly negative, and to thrust yourself upon potential employers as supplicant rather than as large potential asset. All of this results in more negative responses, more self-doubt, and a downwardly spiraling attitude from which it can be very difficult to recover. It is not so simple as "pumping yourself up" for every interview or contact; real attitudes show, whether we want them to or not.

The essential understanding is that you need only make one sale, and that each situation is new. Excellent sales professionals know that, and take great care to treat each

new prospect as a brand new ball game; so is each employment interview or personal contact. In job-seeking, the last
interview is just as important as the first. In each, you need to
be calm and cool, warm and eager, professionally distanced
and capable of being deeply involved with whomever you
are dealing with. You need to have researched well enough
and to emphathize enough so you can put yourself into the
other guy's shoes and apply your prepared benefits story to
your prospective employer's wants and needs. That is the
language of selling; it is also the language of successful job-
seeking.

A third basic is your physical appearance. Appearances
convey first what you are and the attitudes you carry to
others. The person who arrives at an office or restaurant on
a hot day somewhat wilted and sweaty, and who does nothing to freshen up before the meeting, will probably unfavor-
ably impress an executive recruiter or prospective employer,
stacking the deck in the direction of failure. It is far better to
be a few minutes late, those few minutes having been spent
in freshening up, than to move into a situation looking and
feeling less than your best. It is better yet to arrive early, cool
off, and freshen up, providing yourself with a chance to
review your research and your benefits story.

Clothing matters are also important in job-seeking. In
this context, we should stress only that flamboyance is out;
conservatism in dress and demeanor is in. In short, the old
rules still apply here, and especially for professional managers, who must be assessed in terms of their abilities to deal
with all kinds of people in many different situations.

Do not, under any circumstances, arrive with even one
modest drink under your belt. For some hirers, the slightest
hint of alcohol having been taken before arriving at a job
interview is a complete disqualifier, the kind of red flag that
cannot be disregarded. It is good to remember that, from the
prospective employer's point of view, there are all too few
personal keys to be perceived in an interview, and many
have learned to treat alcohol as the key negative.

At a luncheon or after-hours interview, it is wise not to
drink anything alcoholic, if possible; stress may cause even

one drink to have an unusually strong impact upon your
system, and especially on an empty stomach. Sometimes
abstention turns out to be impractical, as when a prospective
employer really presses you to take a drink as an "icebreaker," and you assess that it is he or she who really wants
the drink and would probably feel uncomfortable drinking
alone. Then the lightest drink possible is indicated—a glass
of wine, or perhaps a tall scotch and soda, to be sipped,
rather than gulped. A second drink can and almost always
should be refused. Even if it soon becomes apparent that it is
not you, but your interviewer, who may have a drinking
problem, it is entirely inappropriate to have more than one
drink. That may sound a little rigid, but interviews are easily
spoiled by drink, and it takes too much time, trouble, and
expense to get before a qualified prospective employer to let
a couple of drinks ruin a job opportunity. Even when drink
seems to be helping the situation a great deal, as you and
your interviewer seem to get on extraordinarily well in an
alcohol-induced haze, you are probably ruining your
chances; many a job offered the night before has been
withdrawn the morning after.

Smoking is not advised, either, unless your interviewer
makes it perfectly clear by smoking that it really is all right.
The nonsmoker who gamely invites you to smoke is highly
likely to remember only that you did smoke, and that it was
bothersome. That is especially true of the virtuous, recently
converted nonsmoker, who may be particularly bothered
when you smoke. And if you generally smoke cigars, do not
do it during an interview; the smell lingers and sours, and all
too often so does your prospective employer's recollection of
you.

PRESELLING MOVES

A great many things can happen before you even try to sell a
prospective employer on having you in for an interview.
Depending on such matters as positioning and career status,

it can be as easy as showing up at a recruiting session or responding affirmatively to an executive recruiter's or friend's call, or as hard as instituting a full-scale approach to hundreds of strangers via letter and resume, while answering as many advertisements, some seemingly appropriate, as can be found.

The best way by far to look for any kind of job is from a position of employed strength. That is something everybody knows. On the other hand, it is not something everybody, or even most of us, take as a guide to action. Again and again, in these times, we see managers "hanging in there" in situations that they know very well are fragile, to put it gently. We see companies that have been doing badly for years finally going under in generally worsened economic circumstances, their assets sold off, their employees, including their managers, given rather brief notice, and thrown out on the street to make their way as best they can. Our comment is often some equivalent of "Ain't it awful!" Yes, it is.

For professional managers, who have the training and current knowledge to see the near future of their operations, staying on is one of the avoidable disasters of modern life. Some will, of course, but you need not. It is far better to seek new employment from the strength of current employment. And so, too, for those who are facing, not companies going under, but adverse circumstances that may block advancement or lead to firings. And so too for those who want to make a move as part of career building rather than as defensive strategy. The key idea is to move from a position of strength.

Under such conditions, preselling moves include activation of previously made contacts outside the current company, and in some instances cultivation of new contacts, as when a manager very carefully arranges to attend industry and professional meetings and shows, becomes active in local industry and trade chapters, writes articles for professional and trade publications, and attends professional development courses—*after* making the decision, or tentative

decision, to seek new employment. Those are all things that
should be done routinely in all seasons and in all years; but,
being human, many of us tend to do them less than we
should, so swift catching up is indicated. It can be done that
way and work well; but it is hazardous, given the pace of
business change in these times. The danger is that you will
be caught unprepared by recognition of adverse business
circumstances and, when you should be activating a host of
contacts to move swiftly out of a bad situation while still
employed, events will overtake you while you are still trying
to catch up. Then, as so many have found to their painful
surprise, the contact who would gladly have recommended
you yesterday as a prime acquisition will suddenly find that
no openings exist, and will warmly urge you to "keep in
touch." The old saw has it that "success builds success." In
terms of job recommendations and referrals, that is certainly
true. People like to hire and recommend success, or at least
seeming success, and all too often have doubts today about
unemployed managers whom yesterday they would have
loved to steal.

Preselling moves from an employed position often include talking to executive recruiters. It is best here to be
talking to executive recruiters who have called you, rather
than approaching those who have not, although most executive recruiters will assure you that it makes no difference at
all who approaches whom first. The fact that previous conversations did not lead to a job is not a bar here; for most
recruiters, it only means that the valuable time and effort
expended to get to know and sell you can now be made to
pay off. And if you have previously turned down job offers
obtained through executive recruiters who have approached
you, so much the better. You are often viewed as a commod-
ity of greater value under those circumstances—as long as
you are still employed.

All this places a considerable premium upon talking to
executive recruiters who approach you, even though you
have no current inclination seriously to consider a job
change. You never know what career-building offers may be

out there; and in these times, you never know when you will have to change your mind about the desirability of making a move. An approach to an executive recruiter is as easy as a phone call, whether to someone you know or to a stranger. So is a broadcast letter approach to executive recruiting firms, although that is usually unnecessarily time-consuming for people currently employed.

Some of your closest business and personal friends outside your current organization can also be approached directly, as they would expect to be able to approach you. But job-seeking contacts with less close business and personal friends and acquaintances require considerably more care. They are not casual matters, for a bad first impression, a bad introduction, or bad timing may destroy an otherwise promising job contact. Most people know very well that these are difficult times for many, and know that although the basic thrust of your job approach may either be career building or defensive, it is quite likely in this period to have strong defensive aspects. Even so, and even with most business and personal friends, it is wise to remember that people feel most comfortable selling and hiring strength. When one of your friends recommends you somewhere, it feels far better to be able to say something like, "I have someone really great for us—hope I can convince him [or her] to move," than, "One of my friends is in real trouble over at AYZ Corp—think we might have anything open?"

If your friend is willing to say anything at all, that is. Or if that treasured job contact you've been associating with week after week at chapter meetings of your professional organization is really eager to hire you. You will seem more desirable to both if they see you as an asset ready to make a move up rather than someone about to be fired. A caution here: even your best friend may have second thoughts about hiring or recommending you if your approach comes over a couple of drinks at the end of a long, dispiriting day, week, or month, and takes the form of a desperate plea for help. The job-selling situation starts at the moment you raise the question of a new job face to face with a friend, recruiter, or

prospective employer. Therefore, it has to start when you
are entirely "up" for a new situation, have thought through
your benefits story, look your best, and are in all respects
ready to make this sale the one—and remember, you only
have to sell one.

As a practical matter, that often means making a very
difficult decision in private, often in considerable anguish
and in a state of mind quite closely approaching despair, or, if
it is basically a career-building move, in a state of considerable excitement. It is not every day you decide to make a
major job move; the day that you do so is not usually a good
time to try to do anything about it. Wait, at least until the next
morning, before you tell anyone, except perhaps those so
close to you that they have helped you make the decision,
such as spouse and closest personal friends. Then think it
over again, in the cold light of day. If it still looks like a good
decision, it then becomes time to update your resume, develop a benefits story adapted to each of your current best
job prospects, assess your wardrobe and the rest of your
personal appearance, and begin to make your moves. Although you only need to sell one, your first few moves are
likely to be toward your best prospects, and any one you lose
early because of inadequate preparation may have been
your best opportunity. In some ways, then, the first few job
contacts may be more important than most of the others you
may have to try further on down the line.

But it does sometimes happen that we are unemployed
when we go out seeking jobs. That is, of course, true of
beginners; there, positioning makes a great deal of difference. And it is all too true, especially in these times, that
seasoned managers can find themselves in the same position.
Then several preselling approaches become not only possible, but necessary.

First, when you are unemployed, it is best to see yourself
as engaged full-time in the business of finding—that is, selling yourself into—a job. You then become a full-time seller;
not always a sales professional, but a full-time seller nonetheless. Then it becomes something quite different from leaving

no stone unturned in your search for a new job. Sales professionals do not do that; instead, they identify the most likely prospective purchasers—called prospects—for what they have to sell, and move to sell them in the most persuasive and efficient ways they can devise. Good sales professionals do not go out "smokestacking," that is, calling on every business in sight, regardless of whether or not a properly qualified prospect has been located in that business, or whether that business can really use a specific line of products. They research, identify, dig up leads, sell a qualified prospect on the desirability of an interview, and then go to that interview ready to sell, which means with a benefits story fit for the specific prospect, with supporting sales materials as necessary, and quite convinced that a sale is about to be made, or "closed."

RESUMES

Another preselling requirement—really part of the nuts and bolts of job seeking—is a good basic resume, which will properly include work and personal history cast in a selling form attractive enough to help you secure an interview. Rather too much is made of resumes, really. They do not ever get you a job; at best they help you, with appropriate covering letter and other approaches, to get in the door and face to face with a prospective employer.

Resumes have a basic role to play, however. A good resume does not merely tell an amorphous group of potential employers something about you, so that they will be able to see whether or not they want to interview you. A resume that does only that—and that includes by far the overwhelming majority of resumes—does you an enormous disservice. Such a resume performs approximately the same function as an operating manual or a similar piece of background or how-to-use material; you do not sell very well from that kind of material.

A good resume *sells*. It is not general, for all possible

industries or functions, but directed at specific industries or functions, and sometimes both. It aims to put you, your previous training, and your career to date in the most favorable possible light for the kind of job you are seeking. It tries to provide specifics, which can be alluded to in your covering letter, that will cause a prospective employer to want to see you in relation to a specific job. But both should sell. The resume and your covering letter are a single selling package, rather than your resume being a straight broadcast document, leaving your covering letter to do all the selling.

That is why the general broadcast resume, with or without broadcast covering letter, is generally ineffective. By its very nature, it is very hard to develop as a selling tool, being general. Its frequent rejection by prospective employers tends to make you think that you have used up possible employers, when in fact you usually have not even begun to approach them. And it can make you think that something must be wrong with you, when in fact what is wrong is that you have not begun to sell. To send broadcast resumes to hundreds of potential employers can be a waste of time and effort; to cover them with letters that in no way specifically reach for the employer's wants and needs may merely waste good prospects. The broadcast resume should only be considered in two types of situations. If you are rather well known in a field or industry, the broadcast letter and resume serve to alert your contacts quickly to your availability; even so, the technique is to be used very cautiously. However, an unemployed manager who has used up many of his or her best prospects might lose very little by using it.

Rather than a broadcast resume, you should develop a series of resumes tailored to the different industries and functions that interest you. There is everything right about developing more than one resume, whether you are looking for your first job or have years of experience as a professional manager. As a practical matter, it will in most elements be a single basic resume, with adaptation to different kinds of employers—in some instances, to a single employer, when time and situation allow. A basic resume will be used for certain purposes; for example, it may be sent in response to advertisements asking that applicants include resumes or to prospective employers turned up through research on whom insufficient data have been developed to "customize" the resume. But whenever possible, and however much work it entails, that basic resume should be adapted for a particular purpose. And the resume should always be topped by a personal letter to a prospective employer, unless your resume has moved through an executive recruiter or some other employment organization, in which case they will supply the covering letter.

Figure 4 is an example of an illustrative resume, one that does its best to sell, rather than merely to list. This resume is not done in the only form we think workable for managers; there are several available resume forms and approaches, and some works focused solely on job hunting suggest as many as ten or a dozen. It is illustrative only; Robin Jones, who might be a man or a woman, is a composite, and is not a real person.

This is the resume of a middle manager who has had considerable practical experience in several different areas. It starts with name, address, and telephone numbers; moves immediately to a summary statement of objectives cast as benefits resulting from the hiring of Robin Jones; moves into a chronological account of work history, which continues to stress achievements and imply benefits; and then outlines education, nonwork accomplishments, and relevant personal data, ending with a promise to furnish references and supporting information as necessary on request.

It is as long as it happens to be. The many who counsel short resumes and the few who counsel relatively long resumes are reminiscent of those advertising people who argue interminably about whether ad copy should be short or long for maximum effectiveness. The truth is that excellent copy sells, whatever its length, and that bad copy does not sell, whatever its length. If a resume is intrinsically interesting—if it sells well—then it will be read, no matter how long or short

(Text continues on page 261.)

FIGURE 4

RESUME

Robin Jones
2222 Jones Boulevard
Chicago, Illinois, 11111
(987) 555-1212 (home)
(987) 444-3131 (office)

Objective

The opportunity to profitably grow a substantial business organization into an even more substantial one, using the proven management skills and resources developed during the course of a very successful career as a broad-gauged professional manager who has been engaged in doing precisely that for company after company. Major qualifications and experience include development of a medium-sized regional computer peripherals company into a highly profitable national company, which became six times larger over a five-year period, and turnaround of two companies, one a failing manufacturer of farm equipment and the other a national distributor of industrial products. Fully equipped to apply the tools and techniques of modern management to the widest possible range of problems and opportunities.

Experience

November, 1979   KLZ Corporation, Chicago,
to present   Illinois

Executive Vice President of this $40 million-per-year manufacturer and national distributor of vending machines and related equipment, reporting to company President. Member of Executive Committee and of corporate finance committee, and as such functioning at corporate level regarding all phases of company planning, control, and financing. Directly responsible for all marketing and distribution functions.

Fully responsible for marketing turnaround, adding 50% to net before taxes and 40% to gross in two-year period. Reorganized company distribution function, contributing to turnaround by cutting warehouse costs per unit by 22% in first year and 10% more in second year, while greatly improving on-time delivery performance.

1973 to 1979   WXA Corporation, Denver,
                                Colorado

Vice President and General Manager of this fast-growing and highly profitable manufacturer and distributor of microcomputer equipment, which was profitably grown from $1 million-per-year annual gross level in 1973 to $10 million per year by 1979. Reported to President and functioned as member of all corporate-level committees, including Board of Directors. Directly responsible for all administrative functions.

At center of small and fast-growing company, hired and trained all key administrative personnel and instituted cost-conscious, computerized internal control and management information systems essential to the orderly and profitable development of a small company growing larger very quickly in a volatile industry. As chairman of Marketing Committee, guided growth of entire marketing function, which grew national dealership and direct-selling organizations from small group selling mainly by mail and only regionally in early years.

1968 to 1973   BSB Corporation, Atlanta,
                                Georgia

Marketing Director of this $50 million-yearly farm equipment manufacturing and distributing division of a large, diversified international company from 1971 through 1973. Reported to Vice President Marketing, and member of Marketing Committee. Directly responsible for sales force, development of distributorship network, and all marketing support functions.

Responsible for hiring, training, and supervising dealer sales force, doubling it in a two-year period, with sales and profits in that period increasing by 200% and 250%, respectively.

From 1968 through 1970, was successively internal consultant, dealer service manager, and sales manager, in each instance being promoted within a year to a position of greater growth and profit-and-loss responsibility.

Basic Education

M.B.A. University of Chicago, 1968, *cum laude,* with particular emphasis upon marketing and computer science.

B.A. Louisiana State University, 1965, *cum laude,* Phi Beta Kappa, majoring in business administration, and with special emphasis upon business modeling, marketing, computer science, and economics.

Continuing Professional Education

Seminars, Harvard Business School, Cambridge, Massachusetts, 1972, 1974, 1976, 1980, 1985
Seminars, American Management Association, New York, New York, 1975, 1979, 1982, 1987

Seminars attended covered a wide range of professional management matters, with emphasis upon new computer technology and management science applications, financial management, and the use of statistical tools and business models in marketing and other corporate applications.

Publications

New Profits From Old Products, Journal of Widget Marketing, Volume 22, #11, November, 1980.

Community Activities

Chairman, Corporate Fund Appeal, United Fund, Denver, Colorado, 1975, 1977, 1978.
Vice Chairman, Corporate Fund Appeal, United Fund, Atlanta, Georgia, 1972.

Hobbies

Tennis, golf, personal computer programming.

Personal

Married, two children, excellent health.

References and personal data on request.

---

it is, or how busy its reader. A too short resume may not take the time to sell as well as it should; a long, badly written resume may not be read at all. What does matter is that a resume be written clearly, tell its benefits story, and serve as a basis for an interview. You are wisest to adopt that selling style that works best for you, however short or long the resume turns out to be.

This example is a basic resume, describing a varied array of accomplishments, which can be turned in whatever the desired direction by executive recruiter, by business friend, by Robin Jones's own covering letter, or during the face-to-face interview. It stresses achievements common to all profit- and growth-oriented managers and companies, rather than functional and industry achievements. That is a matter of language and leaning; the same accomplishment can be put in one way or another. In your basic resume, the best rule is to put them in such fashion as to imply benefits recognizable in any industry or function.

It does not state age, although age is implied by length of work and related history. "They're either too young or too old" is a response you need not court. The resume helps sell the interview; a prospective employer's preconception about age—which might be a "knockout" factor if age is stated in the resume—can often be easily dealt with face to face. It states nothing about sex, race, religion, or ethnic origin, recognizing that those matters are irrelevant to the central selling questions involved in the hiring situation. Nor does it include earnings history; the question of price is here entirely premature, as the sale has not even started. If absolutely necessary, you can include some earnings history data in your covering letter. It does, however, include data indicating a high level of energy and community involvement, matters of considerable importance to many who make interviewing and then hiring decisions.

It strongly indicates activities directed at lifelong professional development, especially in the area of the development of new computer-based and computer-assisted management tools, mastery of which is so increasingly important for modern managers. Similarly, it indicates professional publications—here only a single article in a professional journal—which gain added importance when linked with professional self-development activities. This is the resume of a professional manager, able to move into any management situation and make a very substantial contribution, rather than someone bound by work history and narrowness of view to function or industry.

The letter covering this resume will be able to take any of the varied and successful experiences described in the resume and turn them toward a specific job opportunity. Where experience may be somewhat light, basic management education, continuing professional education, and above all the attitudes displayed and sold throughout the resume will tend to sell a prospective employer on the desirability of interviewing Robin Jones. For this is the resume of a management generalist, a professional manager who has taken great care to accrete wide experience, build success on success, and keep up with the fast-changing world of modern management. This is a manager who very clearly and from the first has been profit- and growth-oriented, unafraid to move into new areas and take up new challenges, and who can be relied upon to make a substantial contribution to any company, whether that company is experiencing the problems created by explosive growth or those created by business difficulties during hard times. In those hard times, Robin Jones may have made a mistake in moving from a smallish but highly successful computer company in a growth industry to a much bigger job in a company badly positioned to take the impact of plant closings and reduced work weeks. Small matter; this professional manager will land on his or her feet. Indeed, if the vending equipment company is in trouble, this move may be precisely the kind of timely move we have previously discussed, for this is someone moving from one top job to what will probably be another, rather than someone who stayed on too long fighting the good fight in a failing situation.

Note that although Robin Jones has had more to do with selling and marketing than anything else, every attempt is made in the resume to build a picture that includes substantial financial management skill and experience, with particular attention to early and continuing professional education. As short-term profit needs continue to dominate management thinking, financial management skills become a more and more important factor in hiring even nonfinancial managers.

Along the same lines, note the continuing emphasis on profit-consciousness and accomplishments. But also note that profits and growth are continually linked; in the long run, they are inextricably linked, and that traditional linkage continues to dominate the thinking of many top American corporate managers, however they must bow to the needs of the moment. The manager who promises to turn a short-term profit is valued, and very highly so in times like these; but the manager who promises to turn that profit and grow besides is one you want with you for the long haul, for that is the prototype of the successful American corporate manager.

These are important matters, underlying all the mechanics of resume, covering letter, contacts, and appearances. The promises you make and the attitudes you bring with you are central hiring matters. Your success in job-seeking depends in large measure upon how well you convey those promises to others, first while selling the interview, and later face to face in the direct job-selling situation.

PREPARING FOR THE INTERVIEW

However the process of selling the interview starts, whether through your mailed letter and resume, as in response to an advertisement, through the referral of a business friend, or through the initiative of an executive searcher in your employ or a recruiter engaged by a prospective employer, there will be some interviews.

Before you have those interviews, however, two other things are likely to happen. The first is a phone call, which may either set an interview or serve as a screening device—and you cannot know which it is when you pick up the phone. The second is your own research on the company and, when possible, on the individual with whom you will be meeting.

The screening call is easy enough to handle—if you bear firmly in mind throughout the conversation not to go off the deep end and try to sell yourself into the job while on the phone. That hardly ever works, and very often it sets up barriers between you and your prospective employer that either cause cancellation of the projected interview or make the interview far more difficult than it should have been. On the telephone, all you are doing is continuing to sell the interview, and, after that has been done, trying to leave the most favorable possible personal impression, as preparation for the actual face-to-face interview. Be as brief as you reasonably can, answer whatever questions are asked as best you can, make it clear that you look forward to the interview and the possibility of working with the company and individual enormously, but never take that one step beyond and try to sell yourself into the job on the phone.

With the interview sold, it is time to do some research. Where the firm involved is one you have been interested in, you may already know a good deal about company, key personnel, strengths, weaknesses, future prospects, and where you would like to fit in. Otherwise, all that must be accomplished between the time an interview is set and the time it takes place. Try to leave yourself enough time for that kind of research. Clearly, if someone you want to see is eager to see you immediately, you will make the appointment, skimp on the research, and hope that your prospective employer's eagerness to see you can be used far more effectively than the selling tools any research would have yielded; but if some research time can be arranged, take it.

Some of your most valuable insights may result from a series of calls to your business friends, inquiring about the company, its situation, and its people. It is not at all unlikely that one or more people in your web of contacts will know a good deal about your prospective employer. You may also get a good deal of hard and detailed information relating to what your prospect may be seeking, information that can help you turn your background and skills into a solidly effective benefits story that you can use to sell yourself into the job. Indeed, you may find yourself talking to a good friend who is capable of paving the way for you with a glowing recommendation to a friend of long standing who is about to interview you for that job.

On the other hand, your friends may be able to make it clear that you would be unwise to touch that prospective job and employer with a ten-foot pole. That, too, is an extraordinarily valuable insight, although you are likely to want to make up your mind for yourself by going through with the interview. You cannot know what you will get from your business and personal friends until you ask, and you should never be shy about asking for information. That is what friends are for, and a lot of what networking is all about. And if you ask them now, they will be encouraged to ask you later, which only solidifies friendships.

There are formal sources of information, too. One of the best of such sources is really not a single source, but a vehicle more and more in evidence upon the desks of American managers. It is the computer terminal, hooked into one or more massive distributed data networks, such as Lockheed's Dialog, which taps hundreds of massive databases. Through such a terminal, it is possible to secure corporate disclosure statements filed with the federal government pursuant to the securities laws; yearly and quarterly financial statements, such as profit and loss statements, cash flow statements, and balance sheets; lists of directors and officers; business press articles relating to the company and its people; and a wide miscellany of other quite relevant materials capable of helping you build a job-getting benefits story.

There is another such vehicle, too, and a time-honored one. It is the nearest specialized business library or large public library, which will have many similar information sources in its print-on-paper forms, and sometimes on computer terminals as well. These will also have trained business and general reference librarians, who can be invaluable in helping you frame the right questions to ask about your prospective employer and in finding the answers to those questions. Here, as with your friends, do not be shy about asking. Librarians will help a great deal, if you let them.

These on-line and print sources can yield a great deal of basic information, and even sometimes yield—as through an astutely researched and written article on the company—a lot of what you need to know about the company, as to both selling yourself into the job and whether or not you want the job. A series of financial statements and accompanying materials can tell you how the company is doing and is likely to be doing in the near term. Company people are likely to paint a rosier picture than is justified by the hard facts; you need to try to learn something about those hard facts before you go into that interview.

CHAPTER 10

GETTING THE JOB

And now to the face-to-face interview, where it all comes together, and where you and your prospective employer are involved in the process of deciding whether or not you want to work with each other.

We have so far cast this discussion in selling terms. That is proper; when a manager seeks a job, the essential transaction that continues to take place throughout the process and until a job offer has actually been made is a selling process, with manager as seller and prospective employer as buyer. The fact that seller is sizing up buyer quite as actively as the other way around is not relevant to the central transaction. Be aware that if you spend too much time and attention probing and sizing up a prospective employer, it may indicate less than the active interest in the job you may otherwise be expressing, possibly harming your ability to "close the sale." There are questions to raise, many of them, but they should be seriously raised only after a job offer has been made, so as not to interrupt the flow of the selling process before and during the face-to-face interview.

That face-to-face interview may be one of many. You may meet with the person to whom you will report only once, and get a job offer. Or you may meet with someone from a company personnel department, then several members of top management one at a time, and finally with a president or board chairman, who can make or break a decision tentatively made by others—and all before you have a firm job offer. Aside from the personnel department screening interview, it matters little how many times you are interviewed, and by whom; the basic situation changes little from interview to interview. You still need to "put yourself in the other guy's shoes" in order to empathize successfully and thereby become able to adapt and focus your benefits story so that it properly speaks to the wants and needs of your prospective employer. Achieving empathy is really the key to the face-to-face job interview with someone who will be your superior or peer in a new company, just as it is the key to all selling success.

Empathy-building skills and attitudes come rather easily to many professional managers, who, as problem-solvers, are accustomed to factoring people's wants and needs into the solution of business problems. Those managers who do not have good people-handling habits are less effective managers for the lack; likewise those managers who have poor empathy-building skills are less effective job-seekers. Empathy building is, more than anything else, listening in a relaxed and responsive way and signaling to others by every nonverbal and verbal means at our command that we care a good deal about what they have to say, and want to hear it. It requires knowing what you plan to say, at least in its general outlines, extremely well, so that you can focus hard on what "the other guy" is communicating to you verbally and nonverbally. Then it is relatively easy to find the specific insights you need to fit yourself so well into the situation that you are clearly the person for the job. And underneath, empathy requires genuine human sympathy for those with whom you are meeting, for sham almost always is apparent, and especially to people who are just as experienced as you. Real empathy requires real human sympathy.

Operationally, it starts with as simple a move as a calm, warm, friendly handshake, and an icebreaking comment about the restaurant you are meeting in, a trophy on the office wall or outside in the reception area, and a straightforward query about what the company and interviewer have in mind for the job in question. After all, the interviewer has your resume and may know a good deal more about you besides. Many will respond to that kind of approach. People do like to talk about their work, their companies, and their own careers, and it is always a good idea to encourage them to do so. For then you stand a very good chance of learning what you need to know to secure the job offer later. You are also likely to pick up painlessly much of the basic insight you need to make your own decision as to whether or not to take the job if offered. All this depends, of course, on whether you listen responsively enough so that the flow of talk will continue.

Then, and usually fairly soon, it will be time to tell your story. The opportunity then lies in casting your personal and work history as a series of potential benefits that will derive from hiring you, each facet of your background meeting employer needs and desires as squarely as possible. The hazard lies in forgetting about benefits, and merely telling your story as a series of incidents in which you are the prime figure, thereby ensuring that you seem narrowly self-centered. It can be compounded by focusing on negatives, such as how unfairly treated you were on this job or that, but few of us are so naive as to do that. The main danger is self-absorption in the telling, rather than careful focus on what hiring you will do for your interview's company and, if possible, for the interviewer as well.

You are best advised to "assume sale" throughout, as do the best sales professionals. When you walk through a prospective employer's door, you expect to get the job. You really do; it sticks out all over you. You are relaxed, but ready to go, eager to get started on what promises to be the job of a lifetime. You want to hear all about it, are ready to tell your interviewer all about yourself, but regard all that as a mere formality, because once the company understands what you can do for it, you will be offered the job. No, you should not be as rawly ebullient as that, but almost. A quiet but firm assumption that you are going to get the job will very often during the course of an interview build precisely that view in the mind of your interviewer.

You will be ready for such standard questions as, "Why are you leaving your present company?" or, "Why do you want to come and work with us?" or, "Where do you see yourself in five or ten years?" or, "What do you see as your key strengths and weaknesses?" Those kinds of questions are easily handled, if prepared for; their answers should be as much part of your planned presentation as your basic resume and covering letter story, as adapted during the interview. If you were a sales professional, you would sell with a completely thought-through presentation complete with the basic answers to the standard questions, stalls, and objections raised by prospects. That is the way it should be when you function as a seller in a job situation, too. By all means, write the answers to what you feel will be the basic questions you will be asked; memorize those answers, if you feel that will help. At the very least, memorize the key words and phrases you will need in dealing with such standard questions.

It will help to learn how to "take the prospect's temperature," in selling called the *trial close*. It is not really an attempt to get a firm decision; in an interview, that is rarely appropriate. Rather, it is a query such as, "Does that make sense to you?" or, "Does that square with your view of the matter?" It is an attempt to find agreement between you and prospective employer on matters key to the hiring decision; to the extent that you successfully find common ground, you have moved closer to a favorable decision.

From a selling point of view, the interview generally consists of an early introductory and empathy-building period; a presentation period in which you tell your benefits-laden story; a wide-ranging discussion period, in which you handle questions and possible reservations about hiring you, while continuing to build empathy and find areas of agreement; and a near-close, in which you come as close as you can to receiving a firm job offer. As to the last, this situation differs somewhat from that encountered in most selling situations. In selling, you usually try very hard to close the sale during the interview, knowing that a sale deferred is usually a sale that has to be made all over again later. In the job interview situation, it is quite likely that no decision will be made on the spot, unless you are at the end of a whole selection process, in which instance you will be best advised to fight hard to "close" the job then and there.

We are not here describing a fixed sequence of events. You may find yourself engaged in a wide-ranging discussion of business events from the moment you move into a company president's office, never sequentially present your benefits story, and find yourself with a firm job offer half an hour after you meet for the first time. You may meet a compulsive talker and self-aggrandizer, who hardly lets you get a word in edgewise, talks uninterruptedly about his or her own family matters for two hours, ultimately regrets that you did not have more time together, and does not hire you because you somehow "failed to impress." Or you may find yourself in the middle of a well-oiled, multi-meeting hiring process, in which you never really get to first base with whoever counts, although you meet with a whole series of managers and personnel people over a period of months.

When you are talking to someone who will make a hiring decision, it is quite often the first few minutes that count the most. These are those utterly crucial moments in which you make a first impression, begin to develop empathy with your prospective employer, and begin to show an experienced eye who and what you are. After all, that is what the experienced eye looks for first: who and what you are, not where you have been, what you have done, how you have been educated, and what you know. All those things can be put on paper, weighed, and analyzed, but they are not why you hire such key people as professional managers. From the viewpoint of the experienced manager who is deciding whether or not to bring you on board, all the paper is background—essential background, but only that. It is the face-to-face interview or series of interviews that tells the experienced manager who and what you are, and determines whether or not you are the one for the job.

For most of us, those first few minutes work well or ill almost accidentally. We do indeed try to put our best foot forward, but too often we have so little skill at listening hard and responsively, and are so full of ourselves, that we have not the slightest notion as to proper direction, tone, and tempo; we thereby let all real initiative go over to the interviewer, losing much of our ability to develop information and empathy, and hurting ourselves irretrievably as regards the job offer. Most job offers are in fact lost in the first few minutes, and most real contenders for jobs are born during the first few minutes of the face-to-face interview. Yet whether or not those first few minutes go well or badly is not a matter of chemistry (often used as a synonym for *accident*), as so many think. The kind of chemistry that occurs between seller and buyer has little to do with accident, and much to do with the seller's art. Those first few minutes together provide—or fail to provide—an excellent first impression and the beginning of empathy, and that is the formula that gets job offers.

You should bring to the interview copies of your resume, letters of reference, and key supporting documents, and be prepared to use the resume as the basis for a connected life history. Very often, you will not present that life history, or any large part of it, during the interview. On the other hand, you may find yourself being interviewed by someone who wants you to do just that; when that happens, you must have the best-prepared presentation you can muster. There are those who will want to hear you talk about yourself for a while, while they orient themselves and size you up. Others will come to the interview unprepared and need to hear your story to even begin to assess your possibilities.

The interviewer who says, "Why don't you tell me a little about yourself?" should not then be treated to an off-the-cuff, undirected discussion of family, childhood dreams, and miscellaneous unconnected professional accomplishments.

That question should never be treated casually in an interview; it should be seen as opening up an opportunity to tell your carefully prepared benefits story, in which personal and business histories together point to a series of substantial benefits flowing from your hire for the job in question. An experienced interviewer will normally expect you to be able to do that, and failure to at least start to make a highly professional presentation can weigh heavily against you.

That presentation should clearly show a career-building line of previous jobs, with you going to more and more pay and responsibility. Where there are breaks in that line, clear, sharp, and positive explanations should be ready. For example, trying to go it on your own and failing can be seen as a negative, but if cast properly it can be seen as proof that you are entrepreneurially minded and are therefore better able to make a contribution than many who have played it safe and never ventured out by themselves. A caution here, though—those who hire are usually at least as experienced as those who come to be hired. If you have had a bad career break and it shows, say so, indicate how much the experience helped you to learn proper career directions, and move on. It will seldom then be seen as a negative in the hiring situation.

Your presentation should include the reasons you made each move, and focus strongly on your reason for leaving your current or last employment, if at all possible casting that move as a positive career-builder. Here is where the desirability of moving from currently employed status to a new job becomes particularly apparent.

It is enormously important not to be seen as a restless job-hopper, one who moves around from job to job not for good career-building reasons, but rather out of impatience, boredom, and perhaps incompetence, never stopping long enough to build anything anywhere. Nobody really wants one of those around, no matter how good the formal educational and work records look on the surface. Even if you have made a fair number of moves—as many as four or five in 10 to 15 years—you may have been pursuing a firm career-building line rather than job-hopping. Here it is the explanation that makes all the difference. The prospective employer who is convinced that you are basically stable and capable of moving ahead strongly will usually have no difficulty with several previous job moves, if they make good career sense. On the other hand, if those moves convincingly indicate a pattern of instability, and you are unable to dispel that impression face to face, your cause is probably lost.

Throughout your presentation, you should find opportunities to link up what you have learned during the first portion of the interview with your past history and current job objectives—that is, if you have properly developed information and started building empathy in those crucial first few minutes. Bear in mind that the job presentation that goes most smoothly and with the fewest interruptions is the one that is probably going worst. Without interruptions and the ability to build areas of agreement, you are probably not making any significant contact and are getting nowhere. Contrary to how it is normal to feel while presenting your story, interruptions are good for you and passive and seeming acceptance is bad. If you have done your early work well, and started to build empathy early, you will be interrupted, be unable to finish your story, find yourself building agreement, be able to assume success easily throughout the interview, and stand a good chance of getting the job.

The same is true with questions, especially during and after you have told something of your story. The engaged prospective employer will very often ask searching questions, demand clear answers, and go back again and again to matters of particular interest, hearing you on the same subjects from different vantage points. When that happens, what you are getting is enormously important insight that can help you get the job, for then what you are seeing is exposure of the employer's own concerns and interests, which makes it possible for you to sharply adapt your selling story to perceived employer needs.

GETTING THE OFFER

Although most job interview situations will not result in an opportunity to try to make an on-the-spot close, some will. There are times when you may find yourself meeting with someone who can make the hiring decision and is ready to do so, then and there. On rare occasions, it will be at a first interview; but the manager who hires that way will seldom hire well. But it can come on a callback interview, when most applicants have been weeded out, and it is down to you and very few others; or at a time when there are still many applicants under consideration, but you strike someone who has a hiring decision to make as particularly right for the job and perhaps personally very compatible.

Sometimes it is quite clear that the person you are meeting with cannot make a hiring decision, as when you are applying for a key job and are meeting with someone from a personnel department rather than a divisional or company officer. Often, though, you do meet with someone who can hire, and the question is whether or not he or she is willing to make a hiring decision now. Often, the question seems to be, "When do I ask?" Well, if you have done your selling job well, and built real empathy between you and your interviewer, it never hurts to ask, and it never hurts to ask again and again. On the other hand, if it has not gone well, and your first asking runs into a stone wall, you will know it. Then it hurts a good deal to ask again and again, for then you are likely to be regarded as pushy. There is no magic about closing, no foolproof technique that works better than any other technique, no way to force or trick anyone into hiring you, and no optimum number of times to ask for a job during an interview. Closing techniques in this context consist only of a few ways of asking for the job, some of which will be more appropriate in one situation, or with one person, than another.

Sometimes it is most appropriate simply to ask. If you have built empathy, told as much of your story as seems desirable to both of you, discussed whatever needed to be discussed, agreed a good deal on important matters, and have been together doing all this for a good while, it may be perfectly natural to say something like, "It all sounds wonderful to me, and it's beginning to sound to me as if you feel the same way. Do I get the job?" Or it may seem better to put it a little less baldy, given the situation and the people involved. Then you may simply assume sale, and ultimately say something like, "Great! When do I start?" Alternatively, you may want to put it in terms of a post-decision choice, assume that a favorable decision has been made, and say something like, "Fine. I can start on the first of next month, if that suits you. Or, if you like, I can give a little less notice, and start two weeks from today. Which would you prefer?" A caution here: this "choice close" works well in selling goods and services, but should be used cautiously in the hiring situation only if you are quite sure you are dealing with someone very close to a favorable decision and yet so indecisive as to need a bit of a push in a direction he or she really wants to go. For the really undecided, this kind of push may be counterproductive, causing an almost committed interviewer to back up and want to think about it all over again.

Sometimes, you will not say anything at all, using the weight of silence—and silence has a great weight—to work for you. For example, far down the line at the end of a hiring interview, you might say something like, "It looks good to me. How does it look to you?" . . . and wait. Then, as silence grows between you, so does a certain kind of confrontation, and with it considerable pressure to make a decision. A caution here, too: these are pressure tactics, and they can rebound to your disadvantage.

On balance, it is usually better to play this kind of close rather conservatively, with "Do I get the job?" or "When do I start?" or "Which would you prefer?" These are better closing choices—when you do have a chance to try to close.

And close you will, whether during or after the ultimate hiring interview, for if you learn how to move from job strength to strength, build your network of contacts well, research and prospect effectively, develop sound written materials and prepared presentations, and above all sell face to face empathetically and therefore extremely well, you will be far better equipped than most managers to build your career through a series of increasingly satisfying jobs.

NEGOTIATION AND DECISION

As a prospective employee, you will have many questions about job, company, and related matters. Many of these will be answered during the course of the interview or series of interviews, often as part of the interviewer's discussion of the job in question. Some will not, and will need to be answered before you can decide on acceptance or rejection of the offer. It is often tempting to raise some of those questions during the course of hiring interviews, but it is wiser to wait until you have a specific offer, even if it means going through the process and spending time that might ultimately prove to have been unprofitably spent. It is very difficult to put questions so well that none of them will be seen as objections or premature negotiations, and the last thing you want to do during the job selection process is to shift focus from the enormous benefits to be derived from hiring you to your own possible objections, or begin to negotiate terms before receiving a firm offer. If there are really major objections, such as a mandatory relocation when you will not relocate, or a salary range that at its top is far too low for you even to consider, then you should stop the job selection process as soon as that is known, which will usually be very early. But if the job is worth considering, then let the focus continue to be on the hiring decision, and that means going through to the end of the hiring process and receiving a firm offer.

Once you do have a firm job offer, then negotiations are very much in order. For then all has reversed; you are wanted, rather than wanting. The seller has sold and, with firm offer in hand, has become the buyer. Prospective employer is now desirous employer, engaged in selling you on the wisdom of taking the proffered job, and therefore almost always willing to make some concessions on top of the firm job offer in hand. Now the company has time and money invested in you, and a decision has been made that no one is likely to want to remake. And whoever has made the hiring decision has ego and hopes invested in you, too. It is very much like dealing with someone who has spent a good deal of time agonizing over which of several boats to buy, who then waits with ill-concealed impatience for delivery. Your bargaining position is small before the hiring decision has been made, but it is never better than just after, and before you have accepted, the job offer.

Note that this is a time when you may have new bargaining power in your current job, as well. Some current employers will not negotiate against a new job offer, as a matter of policy; but many will. A good manager is hard to find, and just as hard to keep; when someone else has recognized your worth, the new offer may remove blinders and unlock previously locked doors in your current company. No, we do not suggest soliciting an offer from another company to use as a lever in negotiations with your current company. That is a very dangerous game indeed, and can rebound to your very great disadvantage. But when you do have a firm offer and are quite ready to take it, then by all means consider giving your company a chance to make a better counter-offer. The way to do it is to be very simple and straightforward. With satisfactory new offer firmly in hand, tell your current company that you have an offer and that, although you hate to leave, you are very seriously considering taking it, and plan to respond affirmatively tomorrow or the next day. Say no more; your attitude will indicate clearly enough that you might respond favorably to a counter-offer. Then wait. If no counter-offer is forthcoming, take the new job, for you have very likely burned your bridges by informing your current company of your readiness to make the move. On the other hand, you may get a counter-offer; if so, it must be specific and immediate, rather than a general promise to somehow take care of you later on. Of course, if you cannot wait to get out of an uncongenial situation, then you should simply go when the going is good.

Negotiating ability varies, of course, as does available flexibility on the part of a prospective employer. A president hiring a seasoned professional to head a division or subsidiary has a great deal more flexibility as to salary and other terms than a personnel manager hiring scores of young managers right off business school campuses. For most experienced managers, though, it is possible to do a good deal of negotiating between the time you say, "That's wonderful! When can we talk about the details?" and when you say, "Okay, that's it; I'm satisfied if you are. I'm giving notice Monday morning."

A prospective employer will usually go to considerable trouble and expense to see to it that you have the kind of information and incentives you need to be able to make a favorable decision on the job offer. Some of that information is precisely the kind of insight you may have been able to discover through business friends and published sources before going into the interview. Whether before or after the interview, though, you will certainly want to know as much as possible about prospective employer and company prospects before accepting a job offer. That may involve trips to home offices and sometimes other locations at company expense, to see facilities and talk with company people. It may, in the instance of international relocation, mean a trip abroad, again at company expense. It is very difficult, however, to size up a job offer from a distance; the possibility of making a major mistake becomes very large if you are interviewed, negotiate, and accept a job offer far from your eventual operations base. And even when your job move is within your present geographical area, or to an area you know well, it is wise to size up company and people on-site, rather than taking anything at all for granted. That is particularly true in difficult times, for yesterday's affluent, growing company may be today's company in deep trouble, and yesterday's plum of a job may be today's personal and business disaster.

RELOCATION

Relocation questions can deeply affect both your basic decision as to the desirability of a proffered job and your negotiating stance on several elements of the total compensation package. You may be delighted by the prospect of a move to San Francisco or Phoenix from New York or Detroit, or dismayed at the thought of trying to cope with New York's extraordinarily difficult living conditions and cost factors. You may be aware that one area is far more expensive than another, in terms of your quality-of-life requirements, whatever the Consumer Price Index indicates as to relative price levels, generating the need to negotiate a higher salary offer before an otherwise desirable job can be accepted. Sometimes the factor creating difficulty is the quality or kind of schools available, or cultural life, or recreation, or professional opportunities for a spouse. All require careful examination before effective negotiation and decision making can eventuate. No, you will hardly ever have as much insight as you would like in accepting or rejecting a job offer involving relocation, but you can try very hard to get as much insight as possible before making a decision.

Happily, the corporate job-moving styles of the 1950s and 1960s are less and less prevalent. Few corporations today attempt to routinely move their managers from installation to installation every few years. Some do; whenever possible, those should be avoided, for they provide only a fragmented, corporate-dependent life, with little opportunity for real professional growth and no opportunity to put down satisfying personal and economic community roots. That corporate transfer style causes enormous personal difficulties; rootless families are, far more than most, disoriented and deeply problemmed families. So are rootless managers, for that matter.

One large reason for the demise of the corporate transfer style is the emergence of the movement for women's liberation and sexual equality. Many women today reject the role of nonworking wife and mother, much preferring to pursue satisfying and lucrative careers. Many transfers that formerly would have been accepted are now refused, because the career dislocation and loss of income resulting to a working spouse are often an unacceptable price to pay for a corporate transfer, even when that transfer involves a substantial promotion and raise in pay.

It makes very little sense to trade two careers for one by accepting a corporate transfer that effectively puts one spouse out of work or sets back that spouse's career development by many years. A psychologist or lawyer who has spent many years developing a practice cannot redevelop that practice at will and quickly in another location, perhaps even in another state with different certification requirements, and should not be asked to do so just because her husband has been transferred or promoted. That goes either way, of course; women in management today find themselves facing the same transfer and promotion questions as do men.

In terms of family and professional security, two careers are far better than one. Two professionals in one family can together build some savings and investments, and thereby develop a cushion against such adversities as the loss of a job or serious illness. Two professionals with such a cushion can afford to make job moves that involve a certain degree of risk, or venture into their own businesses; the result is a flexibility rarely available to one worried manager with a mountain of bills, children to educate, and a nonworking spouse. With fewer transfers, companies may have somewhat more difficulty meeting changing staff requirements, but for individual managers it is usually far better to stay in place, develop two lucrative careers rather than one, and reap the benefits of setting roots into a community, as well.

Sometimes, though, a relocation seems right, as for a promotion within your own organization, a step up to a better job in another organization, or a move from unemployment to employment. When that occurs, you will want to explore personally several related cost and quality-of-life factors, if at all possible on the spot and, if you are married, with your spouse. For even your best friends—sometimes especially your best friends—will shade the truth when they are trying to convince you to make a move. Before deciding to accept a job offer, you will want to see several things for yourself.

You will want to check out where you will work, with whom you will work, and the general working atmosphere of the place. All too often, that lovely installation in a parklike setting that looks so wonderful in the photograph turns out to be windowless, with air conditioning that works erratically, when it works, and to contain several hundred—or several thousand—harried, exhausted people who are trapped in an inimical environment and a troubled company. You cannot see that very easily from afar; it may be perfectly obvious close up. To fail to go and look for yourself is an elementary error, but one that far too many managers continue to make.

You will want to investigate where you and your family, if you have one, would like to live, within reasonable distance of your workplace. Within reasonable distance, that is; the community that is "only" an hour away in the suburbs of a big city may turn out to be an hour and a half away in rush hours and two hours away in rush hours in midwinter. There may be several such communities; there may be only one; there may be none. There is often a balance to be struck between quality-of-life and cost factors, and there may be negotiations that must be undertaken before a job offer becomes acceptable. It can also happen that careful examination of an area makes it clear that you want no part of it— and then it will not matter how good the job offer is in other ways; you will either reject it, or spend some very, very unhappy months or years before you decide to give up on what turns out to have been a bad job-changing decision.

Within compatible communities, you will have some further, quite standard, quite indispensable explorations to pursue, including the following.

Nature and Cost of the Housing Available. That means consulting with local real estate agents on home and mortgage prices and availability. By all means, visit some homes for sale, so that you can see what is really available at indicated prices. The same for rentals—if you plan to rent rather than buy, include visits to available rentals. And since real estate agents are in the business of selling homes, it is wise to double-check their information on mortgage rates and terms at some local banks. Some of this information becomes important when finally negotiating the job offer, if you indeed decide to take the job. You may need to negotiate sale of your current home guaranteed by your transferring company or new employer, with purchase of your old home at a guaranteed base price a condition of employment. You may need mortgage assistance in your new location to get any mortgage credit at all, with company payment guarantees if mortgage rates and "points" are over guaranteed maximums. You will be very wise, for example, to try to get the company to pick up mortgage interest payments over a guaranteed maximum interest rate, if you take a flexible-rate mortgage, which can rise over the years and ultimately become far more expensive than you had anticipated.

Schools. If you have children, you must be sure to take a personal look, which can usually be arranged without any trouble with local school officials, who are quite used to such requests. The schools may indeed look fine to you; on the other hand, you may decide that expensive private schools will be necessary or desirable for your children, with the very large additional costs then involved. Such costs, measured in aftertax rather than pretax income dollars, can make a big difference as to salary needs, and may have to be figured into negotiations. You may also find that no available schools are acceptable, and that may be a knockout factor, making the job offer unacceptable. That is especially important if you have a child who needs special education that may be available in your current location, but is unavailable in the area into which you may be relocating.

Cultural and Social Amenities. Concerts, theatres, sports facilities, local libraries, churches, and synagogues— such facilities can have profound impact upon the quality of life as perceived by you and your loved ones, and therefore upon your job decision.

Commuting Conditions. A long, difficult commute from the nearest suitable community in an area can be daunting. Perhaps it should be daunting more often than it actually is, for in the long run, it can disastrously affect the quality of your own life. Once again, there is no substitute for actually doing it; take the drive or the bus or train, more than once if possible, and carefully consider it as a major job-decision element.

Educational Opportunities Available. You may want to pursue additional formal professional education, for example. The existence of a major business school nearby can have significant impact upon your job decision. Or your spouse may want to pursue additional education or get some basic education; what is available can become very important in career development terms. And one state may offer your children fine state colleges, at small cost, while another has a rather poor state college system, necessitating large college costs at private colleges. The difference to them and you can be tens of thousands of dollars.

Professional and Other Career Opportunities for Your Spouse. That lovely installation in a parklike setting may be just as lovely as it looks in the picture, if it is located 50 miles from the nearest fair-size city, but your tax accountant or psychologist spouse may have an impossibly difficult time making professional connections, making the move unacceptable. On the other hand, you and your spouse may long have dreamed of doing some farming, and a move into a country setting may be an opportunity to make that dream come true—and perhaps offer an alternate career for one or both of you as well. A major job move requires considerable self-analysis on the part of all those moving.

Relocation is a particularly difficult problem when it involves an international move, and especially for those with families. For then a spouse's career can be in very serious jeopardy, and the related quality-of-life and cost-of-living questions must be examined with extraordinary care. There are tax and foreign exchange factors to consider as well. Before you accept a posting abroad, by all means take at least one trip to the proposed location, as an indispensable part of the decision-making process. Accept with thanks the advice and materials furnished by your prospective employer or current company, and then read and discuss the proposed place and situation with everyone you know and respect, including your accountant and lawyer, before and after you make that trip abroad and before you make the job decision. Then, if your decision is affirmative, seriously consider going on ahead by yourself for a considerable period, to pave the way.

Many managers do decide to hedge their relocation bets, whether they are going abroad or staying in their home countries. Some commute long distances to their new jobs for a period. Sometimes people commute daily or several times a a week, as when a transferred manager commutes by air for some months to a city 200 miles away. Others return home only for weekends for a period of as much as a year or more. Others come home less frequently, as in the instance of an international move. That is often a quite necessary set of arrangements, as when it is important for children to finish a school term or year in place, rather than suffering the dislocation of a mid-term move; or when the process of selecting, closing, and readying a home for occupancy takes months, and begins only after the job has actually started. It is also often a very prudent approach, for no matter how carefully a job move is considered before it is actually made, many a move goes sour soon after. Unanticipated internal moves, business difficulties beyond your control, even allergies surfacing in new climates—a score of things can turn a job move bad, even if the original decision was a correct one. Sometimes the move is simply recognized too late as a mistake, for whatever the reason. When a job move does turn out badly early in the game, the ability to return to your previous community and business environment can make a relatively

painless correction out of what might have been a family
disaster, if you had picked up stakes and moved entirely to
the new job and community.

THE SINGLE MANAGER

For those who travel alone, relocation questions are often
just as difficult as for those with family ties. Even those just
starting out, having been hired for their first management
jobs right off college campuses, can face difficult and potentially very expensive career decisions—and before they have
any experience to fall back on.

Some of the potential problems faced by beginners are
economic. A 25-year-old new MBA may be single, but is
rarely unencumbered, in these times of huge college costs
and shrinking family abilities to pay. The new graduate is
quite likely to have large debts; have little or no capital with
which to acquire such goods as automobiles, clothes, and
furniture; and command a not-very-large aftertax salary. It
may be difficult, under those circumstances, to make ends
meet anywhere, and particularly difficult in such expensive
headquarters cities as New York and Houston. Yet housing
must very often be obtained in the most expensive portions
of center cities, as working hours for beginners may be
extraordinarily long during the years of apprenticeship, and
commuting costs and the automobiles necessary to live in
suburbs in themselves add large expense items to modest
budgets. And beyond the pure economics of the matter, it
can be terribly lonely, and therefore demoralizing, to be
young and virtually friendless in a new town, and stuck out
in the suburbs. Most young people need to be where other
young people are to be found, and where the "action"—such
as it is—functions as icebreaker and group maker for people
like themselves. It is not at all unusual, therefore, to find
young managers living beyond their means in center cities,
while commanding seemingly large salaries that should guarantee immediate solvency. The young manager who can't

save anything is not to be censured; that is merely normal in our time.

But lack of solvency can cause career problems, for this is a time when mobility is a must, and early solvency therefore is far more than a prudent approach to savings and investment. Young managers need money to be able to move from job to job and from industry to industry, as apprenticeship needs and desires on the one hand, and defensive needs on the other, demand. A young manager who has been fired because of company cutbacks or failure, and who has neither a strong track record nor financial reserves, can be in deep personal trouble, for he or she is probably also carrying a sizable education debt and may need to relocate to find a new job. A young manager who clearly sees that a move should be made, and wants to gamble, for example, on a move to a small, untried company in a growing new industry, must have some savings to fall back on if the gamble does not work out, or in all probability should not and will not make what might otherwise be an excellent career move.

Given the economic conditions of this very difficult period, it may be unwise for most prospective managers to go heavily into debt to finance graduate business education, though some may profitably continue to do so. An MBA from a top business school, such as Harvard or Stanford, may lead to a fast and very lucrative career track, but many may be better off to take their MBAs after moving into the business world. Many companies will pay all or part of tuition for employees, and will cooperate in other significant ways to help their people through graduate school.

Similarly, economic factors may cause young managers just starting out to reach for jobs in major metropolitan areas, where many potential employers exist, and where job moves may not require relocation. For it is all very well to get relocation help when taking a job, but when leaving a job you may have to bear the costs of relocation yourself, and those costs may prove prohibitive. A young manager who has taken a job in a single-industry town, lost that job, and has had to relocate to a big city, broke and jobless, has little bargaining power. Without realistic severance arrangements—and that means more than a return airplane ticket to the campus from which you were recruited—the enticing job in a fine but isolated physical location may be a career and personal mistake.

For any single person, and for a good many married people as well, relocation can bring loneliness. The easiest and most attractive country or small-city life style may be a personal disaster for someone who is a confirmed city dweller used to the cultural and social amenities available in a major metropolitan area. The church-centered social life so attractive to some may be anathema to the agnostic or atheist. For the devoted small-town churchgoer, on the other hand, life in a big center city may be wholly unacceptable. For all of us, a long, searching look at the social and physical environment within which we are going to work in a proffered new job is just as important as our assessment of the job itself. We are whole people, and we must try to view business and personal needs and desires as an intertwined whole.

In sum, then, it is wise to regard most aspects of an offered job as negotiable, including salary, moving expenses, house-selling and mortgage assistance, stock options and the several other aspects of deferred compensation, insurance plans, club memberships, and vacation arrangements. Negotiable, that is, after the offer and before acceptance—and all cast in terms of helping you to best do the job you are now setting out to do. You should not have to be worried about a less-than-adequate salary in inflationary times; or about being unable to sell an old house or properly finance a new one; or about inadequate incentives or tax-advantaged deferred compensation arrangements—not when you are setting out to do the job of your life in the opportunity of a lifetime.

INDEX